# The Duke
# of Wellington
# 1769-1852
## A Bibliography

# Meckler's Bibliographies of British Statesmen

*Series Editor: Gregory Palmer*

## Series ISBN 0-88736-518-3

1.  William Pitt the Younger 1759 - 1806:
    A Bibliography
    A.D. Harvey
    ISBN 0-88736-314-8  CIP 1989

2.  Lord Grenville 1759 - 1834:
    A Bibliography
    A.D. Harvey
    ISBN 0-88736-313-X CIP 1989

3.  George Grenville: A Bibliography
    Rory T. Cornish
    ISBN 0-88736-306-7  CIP *forthcoming*

4.  Charles James Fox: A Bibliography
    David Schweitzer
    ISBN 0-88736-292-6  CIP *forthcoming*

5.  Lord Curzon: A Bibliography
    James G. Parker
    ISBN 0-88736-308-8  CIP *forthcoming*

6.  Neville Chamberlain: A Bibliography
    Stephen Stacey
    ISBN 0-88736-294-X CIP *forthcoming*

7.  Lord Nelson 1758 - 1805:
    A Bibliography
    Leonard W. Cowie
    ISBN 0-88736-295-8  CIP 1990

8.  Robert Harley: A Bibliography
    Alan Downie
    ISBN 0-88736-286-9  CIP *forthcoming*

9.  William Ewart Gladstone:
    A Bibliography
    Nicholas Adams
    ISBN 0-88736-361-X CIP *forthcoming*

10. The Duke of Wellington:
    A Bibliography
    Michael Partridge
    ISBN 0-88736-297-4  CIP 1990

11. Lord North: A Bibliography
    Rory T. Cornish
    ISBN 0-88736-292-3  CIP *forthcoming*

12. Sir Robert Walpole: A Bibliography
    Alan Downie
    ISBN 0-88736-284-2  CIP *forthcoming*

13. Joseph Chamberlain:
    A Bibliography
    Scott Newton and Dilwyn Porter
    ISBN 0-88736-684-8  CIP *forthcoming*

14. Lord Chatham: A Bibliography
    Karl Schweizer
    ISBN 0-88736-293-1  CIP *forthcoming*

15. Charles Stuart Parnell: A Bibliography
    Alan O'Day
    ISBN 0-88736-556-6  CIP *forthcoming*

16. Lord Palmerston: A Bibliography
    Michael Partridge
    ISBN 0-88736-690-2  CIP *forthcoming*

# THE DUKE
# OF WELLINGTON
# 1769-1852

## A Bibliography

Michael S. Partridge

**Bibliographies of
British Statesmen
no. 10**

Meckler

Westport • London

**Library of Congress Cataloging-in-Publication Data**

Partridge, Michael S.
    The Duke of Wellington, 1769-1852 : a bibliography / Michael S.
Partridge.
        p. cm. -- (Meckler's bibliographies of British statesmen ;
10)
    Includes index.
    ISBN 0-88736-297-4 (alk. paper) : $
    1. Wellington, Arthur Wellesley, Duke of, 1769 - 1852--Bibliography.
I. Title. II. Series.
Z8963.8.P37  1990
[DA68.12]
016.94107'092--dc20                                     90-6574
                                                           CIP


**British Library Cataloguing in Publication Data**

Partridge, Michael S.
    The Duke of Wellington, 1769-1852 : a bibliography. -
(Meckler's bibliographies of British statesmen, no. 10)
    1. Great Britain. Wellington, Arthur Wellesley, Duke of,
1767-1852. Bibliographies
    I. Title
016.94107092

    ISBN 0-88736-297-4

Meckler Corporation, 11 Ferry Lane West, Westport, CT 06880.
Meckler Ltd., Grosvenor Gardens House, Grosvenor Gardens,
    London SW1W 0BS, U.K.

Printed on acid free paper.
Printed and bound in the United States of America.

# Contents

# Preface

The bibliography of the Duke of Wellington is, inevitably, a long one. The Duke's own papers are a significant collection of some 100,000 pieces. He figures in the unpublished correspondence of both government offices and of private individuals. In his lifetime, he was pursued by writers and artists, and there have been numerous biographies and essays written about him since his death. The continued interest in the Peninsular war and Waterloo has resulted in numerous publications, while the Duke's political career continues to attract scholars and his personal life has not been allowed to remain completely private.

Accordingly, in compiling this bibliography, certain constraints have been applied. Only those unpublished collections which contain a significant number of letters from and to the Duke have been included. A complete list of all collections of papers in which the Duke features is provided in an annual print out by The Royal Commission on Historical Manuscripts, Quality House, Quality Court, Chancery Lane, London, WC2A 1HP. Printed books and articles have been included only if they contain significant mention of the Duke, or cover little known aspects of his career. Almost every memoir written during and just after Wellington's lifetime includes several stories about him: some degree of selection has, therefore, been inevitable.

In the preparation of all published work, many debts are incurred. In this case, my thanks are due to Greg Palmer, who set me to work on the Duke; to those librarians and archivists who provided information and help with collections in their custody; and to my wife, Karen, who not only assisted in the preparation of this work, but prepared this typescript for publication.

*An oil painting by Sir Thomas Lawrence (1769-1830), completed in 1814.*
*It shows the Duke in full dress uniform and hangs in Apsley House, London.*

# Biographical Essay

Arthur Wesley was born in Dublin on 1 May 1769, the third surviving son of Garrett, first Earl of Mornington and Anne, nee Hill. In 1781, he was sent to Eton. He left Eton in 1784 and two years later was sent to Angers Military Academy, in preparation for his eventual destination, the army.

Arthur Wesley was gazetted an ensign in the 73rd Foot in March 1787, but he saw no service with the regiment and he quickly transferred to other units, being promoted each time. In November 1787 he was appointed an aide-de-camp to the Lord Lieutenant of Ireland. He was also elected to a seat in the Irish House of Commons. Arthur Wesley saw his first active service with the Duke of York's ill-fated expedition to the Low Countries in June 1794. At Boxtel, Colonel Wesley's 33rd Foot repulsed an attacking French column by forming line and discharging an accurate volley at close range: the lesson was not lost on the Colonel.

Colonel Wesley sailed for India in April 1796. The active policy of his brother Richard, appointed Governor General of India in 1798, and Richard's patronage, gave Arthur the opportunity to distinguish himself. In 1799 he took a leading role in the defeat of Tipu Sultan of Mysore, and, much to the dismay of his senior officers, he was then appointed Governor of Seringapatam, which he used as a base for operations against the robber chief, Dhoondiah Waugh. His greatest Indian success came in the third Mahratta war. On 23 September 1803 he launched a headlong attack on the Mahrattas at Assaye: he was successful, but at great cost. The war ended after another engagement at Ahmednagar, with the capture of Gwalior.

When he resigned his posts in India, in February 1805, Major General Sir Arthur Wellesley returned to England, a successful general, but not yet a widely-known one. During the next two years, his main duty was political: he served as Chief Secretary for Ireland, interrupting this with service on expeditions to Bremen (1805-6) and Copenhagen

(1807).

Sir Arthur's next destination was Spain, but, following a French invasion of Portugal, his force was diverted and he landed near Lisbon in July 1808. He then fought and won two battles against the French, at Rolica and Vimeiro. The latter encouraged the French to seek terms for an evacuation of Portugal and Sir Arthur and his newly-arrived superior officers agreed to, and signed, the Convention of Cintra, to this effect. The Convention was bitterly attacked in Britain, but Sir Arthur had friends in the government, which fully recognised the value of his services, and he was exonerated by the subsequent enquiry into the circumstances surrounding the signature of the Convention.

In April 1809 Sir Arthur Wellesley resigned as Chief Secretary for Ireland and left once more for Portugal. He was not to see Britain again for five years. The story of the Peninsular War is well-known: in every campaigning season between 1809 and 1814, Sir Arthur Wellesley, successively Viscount, Earl, Marquess and Duke of Wellington engaged and defeated French forces arrayed against him.

Between 1809 and 1812, Wellesley's campaigns took the form of an advance from Portugal into Spain, followed by a retreat to winter quarters in Portugal. In these years he won battles at Talavera (1809), Busaco (1810) Fuentes d'Onoro (1811) and Salamanca (1812). In 1813 he advanced through Spain to the frontiers of France, winning a major battle at Vitoria.

Initially, Wellington's operations were not viewed favourably in some political circles in Britain, but Wellington, despite his complaints, received as much support from the home government as could be spared - although the amount that could be spared certainly increased as time went on. The final battle of the war was fought at Toulouse on 10 April 1814, after Napoleon's abdication.

By the time the Peninsular War ended, Field Marshal the Duke of Wellington was Britain's most famous soldier. He served briefly as Ambassador to France in 1814, but his sternest test was yet to come. When Napoleon returned to France, Wellington accepted command of the allied army in the Low Countries. This was an army numbering some 70,000 men - larger than any he had commanded in the Peninsula - and it included contingents from several countries. Operating in conjunction with it was a Prussian army of 80,000 men, commanded by Marshal Blucher. The co-operation of these two men was crucial to the outcome of the campaign.

Wellington was convinced Napoleon meant to attack his forces first, and was taken aback when the Emperor struck first at the Prussians. The Duke's attendance at the

Duchess of Richmond's ball in Brussels hid the seriousness of the situation as hasty redeployments were made. The decisive battle of the war was fought at Waterloo on Sunday, 18 June 1815. Repeated French attacks on the British and Allied lines were beaten off, while the Prussians engaged the right flank of the French army, causing them to divert valuable troops away from the assault on Wellington's men. The result was the decisive defeat of the French.

The battle of Waterloo set the seal on Wellington's greatness: but it was a "greatness" his subsequent career did much, at times, to diminish.

After three years' service as Commander-in-Chief of the Allied armies of occupation in France, Wellington returned to Britain, and politics, in December 1818. He was appointed Master General of the Ordnance, with a seat in Lord Liverpool's Cabinet. His friend, Lord Castlereagh, was Foreign Secretary, but Wellington thoroughly disliked Castlereagh's successor, Canning. The consequence of this was that when Liverpool retired and Canning became Prime Minister, in April 1827, Wellington resigned all of his offices (he had been Commander-in-Chief in January that year).

His resignation seemed to prove that Wellington was an Ultra Tory. He certainly carried the hopes of the Ultra Tories with him when, in January 1828, on the resignation of the ineffective Goderich, he became Prime Minister. Once again - although he never understood why it was necessary - Wellington resigned as Commander-in-Chief (he had been re-appointed to the post in August 1827). But Wellington's government was a bitter disappointment to the Ultra Tories, and they never forgave him. First, between March and May 1828, he removed legal disabilities against dissenters, and then, in April 1829, he did the same for Roman Catholics - this latter action led to his duel with Lord Winchilsea in March 1829. But the Duke was no liberal. In November 1830 he declared, in the face of rising popular discontent, that the British Constitution was perfect, and Parliamentary reform was not needed, or wanted. He was almost immediately voted out of office by a Whig-Ultra Tory coalition.

Wellington's response to the Reform Bill crisis typifies his political outlook. He declared outright opposition to reform at first, but being persuaded that reform <u>was</u> necessary, he attempted to form a government to pass a reforming measure, failed, and then refrained from opposing the final version of the Whigs' Bill. Wellington believed that "the King's government must be carried on": accordingly, when William IV dismissed his Whig Ministers in November 1834, Wellington took office on behalf of Sir Robert Peel. Until Peel could be summoned from Italy, the Duke became "caretaker" Prime Minister - an office he combined with those of Foreign, Home and Colonial Secretary. He served as Foreign Secretary in Peel's brief administration.

The final stages of the Duke's political career were
dominated by Peel. Wellington was Leader of the Conservative Party in the House of Lords. He supported Peel when
he tried to form a Ministry in May 1839 and became a
Cabinet Minister without office in Peel's 1841 administration. He also became Commander-in-Chief, for the third
time, on the death of Lord Hill in August 1842. As
Commander-in-Chief, the Duke's main concern was with
national defences, and, if this concern was not so
irrational as some critics have argued, his tenure of
office was not altogether happy. He had little sympathy
with those who looked for "improvements" in the manpower of
the army, and fought against the issue of medals to
veterans of the Peninsular War.

In Cabinet, the Duke loyally supported Peel during the
Corn Law crisis of 1845-6. He did not believe repeal was
necessary but argued that the House of Lords should not
oppose the expressed will of the House of Commons on a
question of this sort. When Peel resigned in June 1846,
the Duke's career as an active party politician was more or
less over. But he remained loyal to Peel, and was very
upset by his accidental death in July 1850.

Wellington had become Lord Warden of the Cinque Ports
in January 1828, and it was at the Lord Warden's official
residence, Walmer Castle, that, on the morning of 14
September 1852, he was taken suddenly ill. He died later
the same day. His burial, in St. Paul's Cathedral, on 18
November 1852 was a day of national mourning.

The Duke's private life was not altogether happy. In
1806 he married Catherine Pakenham, a young lady he had
first met in Ireland before he left for India. They had
two sons, Arthur Richard, afterwards second Duke of
Wellington, and Charles, father of the third Duke. Kitty
Pakenham, unfortunately, grew rather afraid of Sir Arthur
and appeared to him, at least, not to fit into the
increasingly exalted circles in which he moved.
Consequently, the Duke's name became linked with high
society ladies, while his wife lived mainly in semi-retire-
ment at Stratfield Saye, the country estate in Hampshire
purchased for him in 1817. The Duchess of Wellington died
in the Duke's London residence, Apsley House, on 24 April
1831. The Duke was at her bedside.

Wellington did not get on exceptionally well with his
children, although his younger son was staying with his
family at Walmer Castle when his father died. He was,
however, fond of his daughters-in-law and his grandchildren.
In his later years the Duke became increasingly isolated by
deafness, and some of his relationships grew rather strange:
in particular, those with the religious enthusiast, Miss
Jenkins, and with Miss Burdett-Coutts, who in February 1847,

when he was aged 77 and she only 32, even offered to marry
him.  The closest friends of his later years were the
second Marquess of Salisbury and his wife, Mary, and the
Marquess of Anglesey, who had lost a leg while second-in-
command at the battle of Waterloo.  It is said that when
these two veterans visited the Great Exhibition in 1851,
each believed he was helping the other to get around.
Wellington was fascinated by the exhibition: it seems not
to have troubled him that many people looked on him as one
of the exhibits!

The Duke of Wellington's career spanned eighty-three
troubled years.  His rise to eminence was due to his great
abilities as a military commander, at a time when such
abilities were sorely needed.  The Duke was both a shrewd
strategist and a first-rate tactician: he must be
considered one of Britain's greatest soldiers.  His
subsequent career as a politician was not untroubled.  An
Ultra-Tory by inclination, he seems to have emerged as he
got older as a liberal conservative, capable of acts of
liberality and of acts of some pettiness.  By the time of
his death he was a national institution, superior to mere
party politics.  Perhaps a comment, taken from a letter
he wrote to John Wilson Croker in 1846 best sums up the
Duke's attitude to his whole career: "I am", he declared,
"the retained servant of the Sovereign of this Empire".

# Chronology

| | |
|---|---|
| 1 May 1769 | Born in Dublin |
| September 1781 | Sent to school at Eton |
| 1786 | Sent to Angers Military Academy |
| 7 March 1787 | Gazetted as Ensign, 73rd Foot |
| November 1787 - March 1793 | A.D.C. to the Lord Lieutenant of Ireland |
| April 1790 - June 1795 | M.P. for Trim in the Irish House of Commons |
| June 1794 - March 1795 | Service with the Duke of York's expedition to the Netherlands |
| 14 December 1794 | Skirmish at Boxtel: Arthur Wellesley's first engagement |
| April 1796 | Left for India |
| 17 February 1797 | Landed in Calcutta |
| February 1799 | War against Tipu Sultan |
| May 1799 | Capture of Seringapatam |
| 6 May 1799 | Appointed Governor of Seringapatam |
| August 1799 - September 1800 | Operations against Dhoondiah Waugh |
| 10 September 1800 | Defeat of Dhoondiah Waugh |
| 29 April 1802 | Promoted to Major-General |

| | |
|---|---|
| August - December 1803 | Third Mahratta War |
| 23 September 1803 | Battle of Assaye |
| 29 November 1803 | Battle of Ahmednagur |
| 15 December 1803 | Capture of Gwalior |
| 24 February 1805 | Resigned posts in India |
| March 1805 | Left India |
| September 1805 | Arrived in England |
| December 1805 - February 1806 | Service on expedition to Bremen |
| 25 February 1806 | Appointed to command a Brigade at Hastings |
| 1 April 1806 | Elected M.P. for Rye |
| 8 April 1806 | Appointed Chief Secretary for Ireland |
| 10 April 1806 | Married Catherine Sarah Dorothea Pakenham |
| 3 February 1807 | Birth of Arthur Richard Wellesley (afterwards second Duke of Wellington) |
| September - October 1807 | Service on Copenhagen expedition. |
| 16 January 1808 | Birth of Charles Wellesley |
| 2 April 1808 | Appointed to command British troops in Iberia |
| 12 July 1808 | Left for Portugal |
| 15 August 1808 | Battle of Rolica |
| 21 August 1808 | Battle of Vimeiro |
| 22 August 1808 | Signed armistice |
| August 1808 | Convention of Cintra |
| 6 October 1808 | Return to England |
| 17 November - 22 December 1808 | Board of Enquiry into the Convention of Cintra |

| | |
|---|---|
| 4 April 1809 | Resigned as Chief Secretary for Ireland |
| 16 - 22 April 1809 | Return to Portugal |
| 12 May 1809 | Crossed the Douro |
| 6 July 1809 | Appointed to command the Portuguese army |
| 28 July 1809 | Battle of Talavera |
| 4 September 1809 | Created Viscount Wellington |
| 27 September 1810 | Battle of Busaco |
| October - November 1810 | Lines of Torres Vedras |
| 5 May 1811 | Battle of Fuentes d'Onoro |
| 8 May - 10 June 1811 | Unsuccessful seige of Badajoz |
| 5 August 1811 | Promoted to General |
| September 1811 | Retreat to Portugal |
| 19 January 1812 | Capture of Ciudad Rodrigo |
| 18 February 1812 | Created Earl Wellington |
| 16 March - 6 April 1812 | Seige and capture of Badajoz |
| 22 July 1812 | Battle of Salamanca |
| 12 August 1812 | Entered Madrid |
| 18 August 1812 | Created Marquess Wellington |
| September - October 1812 | Unsuccessful seige of Burgos |
| 22 September 1812 | Created Generalissimo of Spanish army |
| November 1812 | Retreat into Portugal |
| 28 November 1812 | Frenada General Order, very critical of the troops' conduct during the retreat |
| 4 March 1813 | Created a Knight of the Garter |
| 21 June 1813 | Battle of Vitoria |
| 3 July 1813 | Promoted to Field Marshal |

| | |
|---|---|
| 31 August - 9 September 1813 | Seige and capture of San Sebastian |
| November 1813 - February 1814 | Battles in the Pyrenees |
| 27 February 1814 | Battle of Orthez |
| 10 April 1814 | Battle of Toulouse |
| 3 May 1814 | Created Duke of Wellington |
| 5 July 1814 | Appointed British Ambassador to France |
| 15 February 1815 | Appointed British Minister at the Congress of Vienna |
| 4 April 1815 | Accepted command of the Allied army in the Low Countries |
| 15 June 1815 | Duchess of Richmond's Ball in Brussels |
| 16 June 1815 | Battle of Quatre Bras |
| 18 June 1815 | Battle of Waterloo |
| 22 October 1815 - 21 November 1818 | Commander of the Allied Armies of Occupation in France |
| 9 November 1817 | House at Stratfield Saye purchased |
| November - December 1818 | Attended Congress at Aix-la-Chapelle |
| 26 December 1818 | Appointed Master General of the Ordnance, with a seat in the Cabinet |
| 19 December 1820 | Appointed Lord Lieutenant of Hampshire |
| October - November 1822 | British observer at the Congress of Verona |
| February - April 1826 | Special Envoy to Tsar Nicholas I of Russia |
| 22 January 1827 | Appointed Commander-in-Chief |
| 12 April 1827 | Resigned from the Cabinet and as Commander-in-Chief and |

|  | Master General of the Ordnance |
|---|---|
| 8 August 1827 | Reappointed Commander-in-Chief |
| 9 January 1828 | Became Prime Minister |
| 11 January 1828 | Resigned as Commander-in-Chief |
| March - May 1828 | Repeal of Test and Corporation Acts |
| 20 May 1828 | Resignation of Huskissonites |
| 20 January 1829 | Appointed Lord Warden of the Cinque Ports |
| 21 March 1829 | Duel with Lord Winchilsea |
| 13 April 1829 | Catholic Emancipation Bill passed House of Lords |
| 28 December 1829 | Appointed Constable of the Tower of London |
| 2 November 1830 | Declaration against the reform of Parliament |
| 15-16 November 1830 | Resignation as Prime Minister |
| 24 April 1831 | Death of the Duchess of Wellington |
| 27 April 1831 | Windows at Apsley House broken by a mob |
| 9-15 May 1832 | Unsuccessful attempt to form a Government |
| 7 June 1832 | Reform Bill passed |
| 29 January 1834 | Elected Chancellor of Oxford University |
| 15 November - 9 December 1834 | Caretaker Prime Minister, Foreign Secretary, Home Secretary and Secretary for War and the Colonies |
| 9 December 1834 | Became Foreign Secretary in Peel's first administration |
| 7 April 1835 | Resignation of Peel Ministry |

| | |
|---|---|
| 22 May 1837 | Became Master of Trinity House |
| 8-10 May 1839 | "Bedchamber Crisis" |
| 1 September 1841 | Cabinet Minister without office in Peel's second administration |
| 15 August 1842 | Appointed Commander-in-Chief for life |
| 6 December 1845 | Resignation of Peel's Ministry |
| 20 December 1845 | Peel returns to office |
| 26 June 1846 | Corn Law repeal passed: fall of Peel's Ministry |
| Autumn 1846 | Erection of Wyatt's equestrian statue at Hyde Park Corner |
| 9 January 1847 | Letter to Sir John Burgoyne on national defence written |
| 4 January 1848 | "Burgoyne letter" published |
| 10 April 1848 | Chartist demonstration in London |
| 31 August 1850 | Appointed Ranger of Hyde Park and St. James Park |
| 22 June 1852 | Last speech in House of Lords |
| 14 September 1852 | Death at Walmer Castle |
| 18 November 1852 | Funeral in St. Paul's Cathedral |

# Part One
# Manuscript and Archival
# Sources
## Section A
## Wellington Papers: Unpublished

British Library, Department of Manuscripts,
Great Russell Street, London, WC1B 3DG.

1.        Additional Manuscripts.
        29238      Letter Book of Colonel Arthur
                      Wellesley. May 1800.
        29239      Letters of Colonel Arthur
                      Wellesley to Sir Thomas Munro,
                      1800; 1803-4.
Two letter books relating to affairs in India, mostly
unpublished. The former contains copies of eighty-eight
letters, the latter, twenty original letters.

British Library, India Office Library and
Records, 197 Blackfriars Road, London, SE1 8NG.

2.        Mss Eur. E. 216    Letter Book of Colonel
                              Wellesley, 1803-4.

Letters, mostly to Sir Barry Close, relating to the
Third Mahratta war.

Duke University, William Perkins Library,
Durham, North Carolina, 22706, U.S.A.

3.        Wellington Papers

Seventy-three individual letters and one volume of
correspondence, covering a wide range of subjects ranging
from politics to patronage and promotion in the army,
dating from the 1820s and 1830s.

Hertfordshire Record Office, County Hall,
Hertford, SG13 8DE.

4.        D/EWI, T10-T24.    Wellington Estate Papers,
                              1742-1852.

A miscellaneous collection of deeds relating to

property owned by the Duke in Hertfordshire.

> Southampton University Library, Southampton,
> SO9 5NH.

5.         Wellington Papers.

A good brief summary of the contents of this very
large collection is given by R.J. Olney, "The Wellington
Papers, 1790-1978", Archives, XVI (1987): 1-11.

Much more information is provided by the Manuscripts
Librarian at Southampton University: C.M. Woolgar, A
Summary Catalogue of the Wellington Papers (Southampton
University. Occasional Paper No. 8, 1984). This should be
used in conjunction with the "Report on political, military
and official correspondence and papers of Arthur Wellesley,
First Duke of Wellington, mainly 1833-1852 in Southampton
University Library", prepared by the Royal Commission on
Historical Manuscripts in 1983.

1.     General Correspondence and memoranda, 1790-1832.

| | |
|---|---|
| 1/1-3 | Early letters and papers, 26 March 1790 - 13 December 1797. |
| 1/4 | Colonel Wellesley's Bills and miscellaneous papers, 1795-1802. |
| 1/5 | Miscellaneous papers, 1796-98. |
| 1/6-8 | Letters from and to the Duke, 1797-98. |
| 1/9-11, 13, 16-18, 21, 22, 24, 25, 27, 29, 31, 32. | Letters from and to the Duke, 1799. |
| 1/12, 33. | Miscellaneous papers. 1799-February 1800. |
| 1/14 | Letters from the Duke, May 1799-March 1800. |
| 1/15, 20, 23, 26, 28, 30. | Miscellaneous papers. 1799. |
| 1/19 | Letters from the Duke, July 1799 - March 1800. |
| 1/34 | Letters to the Duke, January 1800; January 1801. |
| 1/35, 37, 39, 42, 44, 45, 47, 48, 50, 51, 53, 54, 56-61, 63. | Letters from and to the Duke, 1800. |
| 1/36, 38, 41, 43, 46, 49, 52, 55, 62, 65. | Miscellaneous papers, 1800. |
| 1/40 | "Malabar papers regarding Goorkal's Insurrection". 18 April 1800. |
| 1/64 | Copies [c. 1875] of letters from the Duke. 1800. |

| | |
|---|---|
| 1/67 | Marquess Wellesley's correspondence with Vice Admiral Rainier and others respecting expeditions to Egypt, Mauritius and Batavia.  1800. |
| 1/68, 69, 71, 73, 75, 76, 78-80, 82-84, 86-88, 90, 91, 93, 94, 96-101, 103-105. | Letters from and to the Duke, 1801. |
| 1/70, 72, 74 77, 81, 85, 92, 95, 102, 106, 107. | Miscellaneous papers, 1801. |
| 1/108-133 | Letters from and to the Duke, 1802. |
| 1/134 | Miscellaneous papers, 1802. |
| 1/135-137, 140-148. | Letters from and to the Duke, 1803. |
| 1/138, 139, 149, 150. | Miscellaneous papers, 1803. |
| 1/151-152 | Letters from and to the Duke, 1804. |
| 1/153, 156, 157. | Miscellaneous papers, 1804. |
| 1/154 | Correspondence from the Governor General of India. 22 March 1804. |
| 1/155 | Inclosures in Lord Castlereagh's correspondence. 22 May 1804. |
| 1/158-160 | Letters from and to the Duke, 1805. |
| 1/161-163 | Miscellaneous papers, 1805. |
| 1/164 | Miscellaneous papers, 1806 |
| 1/165 | Three letter books and miscellaneous papers, 1806-7. |
| 1/166-181 | Letters from and to the Duke, 1807. |
| 1/182-186 | Miscellaneous papers, 1807. |
| 1/187-211, 213-220. | Letters from and to the Duke, 1808. |
| 1/212, 222-226. | Miscellaneous papers, 1808. |
| 1/221 | Miscellaneous papers.  Irish affairs, 1808. |
| 1/227, 229 231, 233, 235, 238, 240, 242, 244, 246, 248, 250, 252, 254, 257, 259-290. | Letters from and to the Duke, 1809 |
| 1/228, 230, 232, 234, 236, 237, 239, 241, 243, 245, 247, 249, 251, 253, 256, 258. | Letters from and to the Duke.  Irish affairs, 1809. |
| 1/291-294. | Miscellaneous papers, 1809. |
| 1/295. | Miscellaneous papers. Portugal and Spain. 1809. |

| | |
|---|---|
| 1/296 | Miscellaneous papers. Ireland. 1809. |
| 1/297, 298 | Miscellaneous papers. Military. 1809. |
| 1/299-320 | Letters from and to the Duke, 1810. |
| 1/321-323, 325-343. | Letters from and to the Duke, 1811. |
| 1/324 | Correspondence and other papers, 1811. |
| 1/344 | Miscellaneous papers, 1811. |
| 1/345-56 | Letters from and to the Duke. 1812. |
| 1/357 | Papers. The Military School at Belem. 1812. |
| 1/358-363 | Miscellaneous papers. 1812. |
| 1/364-383 | Letters from and to the Duke. 1813. |
| 1/384 | Correspondence respecting the Command of the Blues. 1813. |
| 1/385 | Intercepted letters. 1813. |
| 1/386 | Claims for medals. 1813. |
| 1/387-389 | Miscellaneous papers. 1813. |
| 1/390 | Miscellaneous papers. 1813-19. |
| 1/391-429, 431-438. | Letters from and to the Duke. 1814. |
| 1/430 | Two maps of the Low Countries. 2 October 1814. |
| 1/439-443, 445. | Miscellaneous papers, 1814. |
| 1/444 | Miscellaneous papers. French, Spanish and Portuguese affairs. 1814. |
| 1/446 | Vouchers for extraordinary expenses, August-November 1814. |
| 1/448-471, 473, 474, 476-486. | Letters from and to the Duke. 1815. |
| 1/472 | Letters to the Duke. Military affairs. 1-3 July 1815. |
| 1/475 | Letters from the Duke. Military affairs. 1-4 July 1815. |
| 1/487, 488 492-495. | Miscellaneous papers. 1815. |
| 1/489 | Miscellaneous returns for medals. 1815. |
| 1/490 | Miscellaneous Paymasters' memorials. 1815. |
| 1/491 | Miscellaneous papers. Waterloo recommendations. 1815. |
| 1/496-501, 503, 504, 506-510, 513, 514, 516, 517, 519-526. | Letters from and to the Duke. 1816. |
| 1/502, 512, 527-531. | Miscellaneous papers. 1816. |
| 1/505 | Miscellaneous papers (Sir Charles Stuart to Lord Castlereagh). April 1816. |
| 1/511, 515, 518. | Miscellaneous papers. Claims. June-July 1816. |
| 1/532-565 | Letters from and to the Duke. 1817. |
| 1/566, 567 | Miscellaneous papers. 1817. |
| 1/568-599 | Letters from and to the Duke. 1818. |

| | |
|---|---|
| 1/600 | Miscellaneous papers. Letters from Sir John Malcolm and Sir Thomas Munro respecting military operations in India 1818. |
| 1/602-604 | Miscellaneous papers. Congress at Aix-la-Chapelle. 1818. |
| 1/605-607 | Congress at Aix-la-Chapelle. Protocols. 1818. |
| 1/608 | Miscellaneous papers. Waterloo prize claims. 1818. |
| 1/609 | Miscellaneous papers. Memoranda respecting Russia. 1818. |
| 1/610 | Miscellaneous papers respecting a fire at Eupen Castle. 1818. |
| 1/613-636 | Letters from and to the Duke. 1819. |
| 1/637-658 | Letters from and to the Duke. 1820. |
| 1/659 | Miscellaneous papers. 1820. |
| 1/660 | Miscellaneous papers. Cato Street Conspiracy. 1820. |
| 1/661-666, 668-673, 676, 677, 679, 680, 682, 683, 685, 686, 688, 689. | Letters from and to the Duke.   1821. |
| 1/667 | Miscellaneous papers.  Despatches on Italy, Turkey and Greece. April-June 1821. |
| 1/674, 675, 678, 681, 684, 687. | Miscellaneous papers.  Turkish affairs. July-October 1821. |
| 1/690 | Miscellaneous papers.  Insurrection in the Sardinian army. 1821. |
| 1/691 | Miscellaneous papers. Austrian loan. 1821. |
| 1/692 | Miscellaneous papers. Slave Trade. 1821. |
| 1/693 | Papers from Lord Londonderry respecting the re-establishment of Roman Catholicism in the states of Southern Germany. 1821. |
| 1/694 | Miscellaneous papers.  Biography of Jean de l'Or. 1821. |
| 1/695 | Miscellaneous papers. 1821. |
| 1/696, 697 699, 700, 702, 703, 705, 706, 709, 710, 712, 713, 715, 716, 718-720, 722-724, 725-732, 736-739, 744-746. | Letters from and to the Duke. 1822. |
| 1/698, 701. | Miscellaneous papers.  Turkish and Russian affairs.  1822. |
| 1/704 | Miscellaneous papers.  Turkish affairs; Austrian loan.  1823. |
| 1/707, 708 711, 714, | Miscellaneous papers.  Foreign affairs. 1822. |

717, 721,
725-727,
733-735,
740-743,
747.

| | |
|---|---|
| 1/748-753 | Miscellaneous papers. 1822. |
| 1/754-780 | Letters from and to the Duke. 1823. |
| 1/781-808 | Letters from and to the Duke. 1824. |
| 1/809 | Miscellaneous papers. 1824. |
| 1/810-834 | Letters from and to the Duke. 1825. |
| 1/835, 838 | Miscellaneous papers. 1825. |
| 1/836 | Miscellaneous papers. Imports and exports. 1825. |
| 1/837 | Miscellaneous papers. Returns of strength of Rifle Brigade and Royal Horse Guards. 1825. |
| 1/839 | Miscellaneous papers. Roman Catholic question. 1825. |
| 1/840 | Miscellaneous papers. Defence of Canada. 1825. |
| 1/841-843, 845. | Miscellaneous papers. Foreign affairs. 1825. |
| 1/844 | Miscellaneous papers. Affairs at Constantinople. 1825. |
| 1/846-868 | Letters from and to the Duke. 1826. |
| 1/869, 871, 872, 877 | Miscellaneous papers. 1826. |
| 1/870 | Miscellaneous papers. Extracts from Sir John Malcolm's work on India. 1826. |
| 1/873 | Miscellaneous papers. Memorandum on the war in Russia, 1812. 1826. |
| 1/874-876 | Miscellaneous papers. Foreign affairs. 1826. |
| 1/878 | Miscellaneous papers. St. Petersburg brouillons. 1826. |
| 1/879-904 | Letters from and to the Duke. 1827. |
| 1/905-912 | Miscellaneous papers. 1827. |
| 1/913-975 | Letters from and to the Duke. 1828. |
| 1/976-986 | Miscellaneous papers. 1828. |
| 1/987-1065 | Letters from and to the Duke. 1829. |
| 1/1066-1070, 1078-1082. | Miscellaneous papers. 1829. |
| 1/1071 | Miscellaneous papers. Trade, shipping. 1829. |
| 1/1072 | Miscellaneous papers. East Indies trade. 1829. |
| 1/1073 | Miscellaneous papers. Coal trade (H. Goulburn). 1829. |
| 1/1074 | Miscellaneous papers. London coal trade. 1829. |
| 1/1075 | Miscellaneous papers. Baden and Bavarian disputes. 1829. |
| 1/1076 | Miscellaneous papers. Sir Robert Wilson's case. 1829. |
| 1/1077 | Miscellaneous papers. Public works in Ireland. 1829. |

| | |
|---|---|
| 1/1083-1158 | Letters from and to the Duke. 1830. |
| 1/1159 | Miscellaneous papers. Warnings of assassination. 1830. |
| 1/1160-1164, 1166. | Miscellaneous papers. 1830. |
| 1/1165 | Miscellaneous papers. The King's health. 1830. |
| 1/1167 | Miscellaneous papers. London Bridge Bill 1830. |
| 1/1168 | Miscellaneous papers. Civil List. 1830. |
| 1/1169 | Miscellaneous papers. Royal Parks Farm case. 1830. |
| 1/1170 | Miscellaneous memoranda by the Duke. 1830. |
| 1/1171 | Miscellaneous papers. Corn Laws and the import of corn. 1830. |
| 1/1172 | Letters from Joseph Mould. 1830-32. |
| 1/1173-1206 | Letters from and to the Duke. 1831. |
| 1/1207 | Miscellaneous memoranda by the Duke. 1831. |
| 1/1208, 1209 | Miscellaneous papers. 1831. |
| 1/1210 | Miscellaneous papers. Oxford University and proposed Charter for London University. 1831. |
| 1/1211 | Miscellaneous papers. London University Charter. 1831. |
| 1/1212 | Miscellaneous papers. Trinity House, the Charterhouse and Christ's Hospital affairs, 1831. |
| 1/1213-1241 | Letters from and to the Duke. 1832. |
| 1/1242 | Miscellaneous papers. Foreign affairs. 1832. |
| 1/1243 | Miscellaneous papers. Proposed Reform Bill. 1832. |
| 1/1244 | Miscellaneous papers. 1832. |

Letters and papers from and to the Duke covering all aspects of his career down to 1832. Arranged chronologically, by date of writing.

2.  General correspondence and memoranda, 1833-1852.

| | |
|---|---|
| 2/1-6 | Letters and papers. 1833. |
| 2/7 | Letters and papers. December 1833 - January 1834. |
| 2/8-23 | Letters and papers. 1834. |
| 2/24-36 | Letters and papers. 1835. |
| 2/37 | Letters and papers. December 1835- January 1836. |
| 2/38-43 | Letters and papers. 1836. |
| 2/44-47 | Letters and papers. 1837. |
| 2/48 | Letters and papers. November 1837- January 1838. |
| 2/49-55 | Letters and papers. 1838. |
| 2/56-63 | Letters and papers. 1839. |

| | |
|---|---|
| 2/64 | Letters and papers. December 1839-January 1840. |
| 2/65-72 | Letters and papers. 1840. |
| 2/73 | Letters and papers. December 1840-January 1841. |
| 2/74-82 | Letters and papers. 1841. |
| 2/83 | Miscellaneous papers. 1841. Letters and papers. January 1842. |
| 2/84-95 | Letters and papers. 1842. |
| 2/96-115 | Letters and papers. 1843. |
| 2/116-125 | Letters and papers. 1844. |
| 2/126 | Letters and papers. December 1844-January 1845. |
| 2/127-135 | Letters and papers. 1845. |
| 2/136 | Letters and papers. December 1845-January 1846. |
| 2/137-150 | Letters and papers. 1846. |
| 2/151-156 | Letters and papers. 1847. |
| 2/157-160 | Letters and papers. 1848. |
| 2/161-163 | Letters and papers. 1849. |
| 2/164 | Letters and papers. November 1849-January 1850. |
| 2/165-167 | Letters and papers. 1850. |
| 2/168, 169 | Letters and papers. 1851. |
| 2/170 | Letters and papers. November 1851-February 1852. |
| 2/171, 172 | Letters and papers. March-September 1852 and undated. |
| 2/173 | Memoranda. 1833. |
| /1-27 | Abolition of Slavery Bill.  May-June 1833 |
| /28-66 | Irish Church. July 1833. |
| /67-71 | India Bill. June-July 1833. |
| 2/174 | Memoranda. 1833-34. |
| /1-9 | Indian affairs. 1833 and undated. |
| /10-23 | Army affairs. 1833. |
| /24-50 | Ireland. 1833-34. |
| /51-94 | Eastern question. August-December 1834. |
| 2/175 | Memoranda. 1834-35. |
| /1-21 | Switzerland. November-December 1834. |
| /22-35 | Irish tithes. February 1835. |
| /36-45 | Irish Church Bill. July 1835. |
| 2/176 | Memoranda. 1835. |
| /1-28 | British mission to Persia. January-March 1835. |
| /29-47 | St. Thomas, Danish West Indies. April-October 1835. |
| /48-71 | Spain. 1830-35. |
| 2/177 | Memoranda. 1834-38. |
| /1-17a | South Africa. Kaffir War. January 1835-December 1836. |
| /18-48 | Lieutenant Colonel Hill's case. February 1834-November 1837. |
| /49-68 | Afghanistan. November 1838. |
| 2/178 | Memoranda. 1838-39. |
| /1-18 | Lieutenant Colonel Gurwood's affairs. April 1838-January 1839. |

| | | |
|---|---|---|
| 2/179 | /19-31 | Defences of Gibraltar. December 1838. Memoranda. 1839-40. |
| | /1-16 | Parliamentary business. May-August 1839. |
| 2/180 | /17-74 | Afghanistan. 1839-40 and undated. Memoranda. 1841. |
| 2/181 | /1-38 | Afghanistan. September-December 1841. |
| | /39-51 | China. August-October 1841. Memoranda. 1841-42. |
| 2/182 | /1-39 | Corn Laws. 1841-42. |
| | /40-59 | National finances. 1842. Memoranda. 1842. |
| 2/183 | /1-52 | Afghanistan.  January 1842. |
| | /53-103 | Afghanistan.  January-March 1842. Memoranda.  1842. |
| 2/184 | /1-105 | Afghanistan.  January-July 1842. Memoranda 1842. |
| 2/185 | /1-75 | Afghanistan. May-September 1842. Memoranda. 1842. |
| | /1-43 | India. February-October 1842. |
| | /44-58 | China. March 1842. |
| 2/186 | | Memoranda. 1842-43. |
| | /1-56 | Afghanistan. November 1842-February 1843 |
| | /57-76 | Afghanistan. 1842-43. |
| | /77-82 | Canada. c. October 1843. |
| 2/187 | | Memoranda. 1843. |
| | /1-32a | Church Endowment Bill. March-July 1843 |
| | /33-75 | Proposed order against duelling. September 1843. |
| | /76-99 | National finances.  January-August 1843. |
| 2/188 | | Memoranda. 1843-44. |
| | /1-9 | Deccan Prize Fund. April 1843. |
| | /10-19 | Earl of Dundonald's case. March-September 1844. |
| | /20-36 | India. December 1843-March 1844. |
| | /37-45 | Health of Towns Commission. c. 1844. |
| 2/189 | | Memoranda. 1844. |
| | /1-67 | India. December 1844. |
| 2/190 | | Memoranda. 1844-47. |
| | /1-22 | Deccan Prize Fund. June 1844. |
| | /23-38 | Maynooth College Bill. c. May-June 1844. |
| | /39-45 | New Zealand.  November 1844. |
| | /46-85 | Army enlistment. December 1846-April 1847. |
| 2/191 | | Memoranda. 1846-52. |
| | /1-25 | India. 1846-47. |
| | /26-35 | Navigation Bill. 1849. |
| | /36-54 | Ireland. 1850. |
| | /55-65 | Army depot system. February 1852. |
| | /66-72 | Burmese war. May 1852. |
| 2/192 | | Memoranda. 1833-38. |
| | | 12 miscellaneous memoranda by the Duke. |
| 2/193 | | Memoranda. 1839-44. |
| | | 113 miscellaneous memoranda by the Duke. |
| 2/194 | | Memoranda. 1845-52. |
| | | 13 miscellaneous memoranda mostly by the |

Duke.

These papers, like the first series of correspondence are arranged chronologically, by date of writing, and cover all aspects of the Duke's later career. Papers addressed to the Duke, as well as by him.

2/195-211       Correspondence and papers of the Duke as Constable of the Tower of London and Lord Lieutenant of Tower Hamlets. January 1827-September 1852.

These papers deal with questions relating to the fabric and garrison of the Tower, the appointment of Yeomen Warders, the commission of the peace for the liberty of the Tower, the Tower Hamlets militia and other questions.

2/212-214       Correspondence and papers of the Duke as a Governor of The Charterhouse. January 1829 - November 1851.

Deal mainly with the nomination of scholars and Poor Brothers, appointments, Governors' meetings and accounts.

2/215-240       Correspondence and papers of the Duke as Lord Warden of the Cinque Ports. January 1829-May 1853.

/215-219        Correspondence and papers. Cinque Ports Pilots. July 1829-February 1851.

/220-238        Correspondence and papers. Cinque Ports. General. January 1829-February 1853.

/239, 240       Correspondence and papers. Cinque Ports Salvage depositions. October 1846-May 1853.

2/241-243       Correspondence and papers of the Duke as an Elder Brother (from 1829) and Master (from May 1837) of Trinity House. January 1829-September 1852.

Mostly concern routine patronage matters.

2/244-256       Correspondence and papers of the Duke as Chancellor of the University of Oxford (from January 1834). November 1833-July 1852.

Include papers dealing with the revision of University Statutes, examinations and prizes, appointment to Professorships, and the affairs of Pembroke College and the University Halls.

2/257           Correspondence and papers of the Duke as Chief Ranger and Keeper of Hyde Park and St. James' Park. August 1850-September 1851; July 1852.

Includes papers on the preparations for the Great Exhibition in Hyde Park in 1851.

2/258           Miscellaneous papers 1833-1852

3. Indian Letter Books.

| | |
|---|---|
| 3/1 | First Series |
| /1/1-3 | Out Letters. May 1798-May 1799. |
| 3/2 | Second Series |
| /2/1-18 | Out Letters. May 1799-June 1801. |

[The volume for 7-22 May 1800 is now British Library Add. Mss 29238 [1]].

| | |
|---|---|
| 3/3 | Third Series |
| /3/1-4 | Correspondence with the Governor General April 1803-March 1805. |
| /3/5-8 | Correspondence with Major Merick Shawe, private secretary to the Governor General. January 1803-February 1805. |
| /3/9-13 | Correspondence with the Secretaries to the Government, Fort William, Calcutta. November 1802-January 1805. |
| /3/14-15 | Correspondence with Lord William Bentinck, Governor in Council, Fort St. George, Madras. November 1803-February 1805. |
| /3/16-17 | Correspondence with the Secretaries to the Government, Fort St. George. January 1803-February 1805. |
| /3/18-20 | Correspondence with Hon. J. Duncan, President and Governor in Council, Bombay. February 1803-February 1805. |
| /3/21-25 | Correspondence with Secretaries to the Government, Bombay.  January 1803-February 1805. |
| /3/26-27 | Correspondence with the Commander-in-Chief, India. July 1803-April 1804. |
| /3/28-29 | Correspondence with the Secretary to the Commander-in-Chief, Fort St. George. February 1803-February 1805. |
| /3/30-31 | Correspondence with the Adjutant General of the Army, Fort St. George. February 1803-February 1805. |
| /3/32-33 | Correspondence with the Commander-in-Chief, Adjutant General and Government Storekeeper, Bombay.  May 1803-June 1804. |
| /3/34-38 | General correspondence.  1800-March 1805. |
| /3/39 | Copies of letters to Captain Baynes. March 1803. |
| /3/40 | Correspondence with Major (afterwards Lieutenant Colonel) Broughton. January 1804. |
| /3/41-42 | Correspondence with Major General D. Campbell. August 1803-January 1805. |
| /3/43-44 | Correspondence with Colonel Sir William Clarke, British envoy at Goa. June 1802 -February 1805. |
| /3/45-50 | Correspondence with Lieutenant Colonel Barry Close, Resident at Poona. February 1803-March 1805. |

/3/51-52     Correspondence with Lieutenant Colonel Edward Coleman, commanding officer at Poona. August 1803-February 1805.

/3/53-54     Correspondence with Colonel J. Collins, Resident at the Court of Dowlut Rao Scindiah. April-October 1803.

/3/55-56     Correspondence with the Hon. Mountstuart Elphinstone. April 1803-February 1805.

/3/57-59     Correspondence with Captain (afterwards General) J.G. Graham, Collector at Ahmednaggar, and his successor. August 1803-February 1805.

/3/60-63     Correspondence with Major (afterwards Lieutenant Colonel) J.A. Kirkpatrick, Resident at Hyderabad. April 1803-March 1805.

/3/64-65     Correspondence with Lieutenant Colonel J. Haliburton. July 1803-February 1805.

/3/66-67     Correspondence with Lieutenant Colonel G. Harcourt, Commissioner for the affairs of Cuttack, July 1803-March 1805

/3/68     Copies of letters to Lord Hobart, the Governor of Ceylon and others. May 1803-March 1804.

/3/69     Letters from Captain D. Mahony, Resident with the Rajah of Coorg. July 1804-February 1805.

/3/70-74     Correspondence with Major (afterwards Lieutenant Colonel) John Malcolm. June 1803-March 1805.

/3/75-76     Correspondence with Colonel Montressor, commanding the provinces of Malabar and Canara and others. January 1803-January 1805.

/3/77     Letters from Major Thomas Munro. January 1803-July 1804.

/3/78-79     Correspondence with Colonel J. Murray and others. January 1803-November 1804.

/3/80     Letters from Frederick North, Governor of Ceylon. September 1803-August 1804.

/3/81-82     Correspondence with Captain J.G. Scott. February 1803-February 1805.

/3/83-84     Correspondence with Colonel J. Stevenson. March 1803-January 1805.

/3/85-86     Correspondence with E. Strachey, on a mission to Southern Mahratta chiefs, June-December 1804.

/3/87-88     Correspondence with Lieutenant General Stuart, February 1803-February 1805.

/3/89-90     Correspondence with Major John Symons, Agent for the Public Cattle etc., Seringapatam. November 1803-February 1805.

/3/91-92     Correspondence with Lieutenant Colonel Wallace. February 1804-February 1805.

|          |                                                                                                            |
|----------|------------------------------------------------------------------------------------------------------------|
| /3/93-94 | Correspondence with Josiah Webbe, Resident with Dowlut Rao Scindiah. January 1803-January 1805.            |
| /3/95-96 | Correspondence with Captain (afterwards Major) M. Wilkes, Resident in Mysore. November 1803-January 1805.  |
| /3/97    | Letters from Lieutenant Colonel Henry Woodington and Major A. Walker, August 1803-April 1804.              |
| /3/98-99 | Correspondence with the Southern and Mahratta Chiefs. March 1803-March 1805.                               |
| /3/100   | Miscellaneous papers. Mysore. January 1803-July 1804.                                                      |

A series of letter books covering the whole of Wellington's career in India. The bound volumes comprise, in most cases, a mixture of original incoming letters, and drafts and copies of outgoing ones.

4.  Letters and papers of the Duke as Lord Lieutenant of Hampshire.  December 1828-September 1852.

|           |                                                        |
|-----------|--------------------------------------------------------|
| 4/1       | Letters and papers. First series.                      |
| /1/1      | General. December 1828-December 1829.                  |
| /1/2/1-2  | General. 1830.                                         |
| /1/3/1-4  | General. 1831.                                         |
| /1/4/1-3  | General. 1832.                                         |
| /1/5/1-3  | General. 1833.                                         |
| /1/6/1-3  | General. 1834.                                         |
| /1/7/1    | General. December 1835-July 1836.                      |
| /1/7/2    | General. August-December 1836.                         |
| /1/8      | General. December 1836-September 1837.                 |
| /1/9      | General. December 1837-December 1838.                  |
| /1/10     | General. 1839.                                         |
| /1/11     | General. 1840.                                         |
| /1/12     | General. 1841.                                         |
| /1/13     | General. 1842.                                         |
| /1/14     | General. 1845.                                         |
| /1/15     | General. 1846.                                         |
| /1/16     | General. 1847.                                         |
| /1/17     | General. 1848.                                         |
| /1/18     | General. 1849.                                         |
| /1/19     | General. 1851.                                         |
| /1/20     | General. 1852.                                         |
| 4/2       | Letters and papers. Second series.                     |
| /2/1      | General. 1829-1852.                                    |
| /2/2      | General. March-April 1829.                             |
| /2/3      | General. 1830.                                         |
| /2/4      | Papers relating to Havant Dispute. August-November 1830. |
| /2/5      | Correspondence. Arms of Hampshire Militia. November 1830. |
| /2/6      | Correspondence. Hampshire Yeomanry and Volunteers. November-December 1830. |

| | |
|---|---|
| /2/7 | General. May 1833-October 1837. |
| /2/8 | General. November 1837-December 1838. |
| /2/9 | General. April 1839-November 1843. |
| /2/10 | General. February-October 1843. |
| /2/11 | General. January 1844-March 1847. |
| /2/12 | General. April 1847-September 1852. |

Correspondence on all aspects of the Duke's duties as Lord Lieutenant of Hampshire. Correspondence for the period from 19 December 1820, when the Duke was first appointed, to 1828, is in the main series of general correspondence. The collection of Lieutenancy papers has only recently been re-united.

5. Bound Volumes of Papers.

| | |
|---|---|
| 5/1 | Papers referring to the Duke's tenure of particular offices. |
| 5/1/1 | Papers as Commander-in-Chief in the Peninsula, Low Countries and France. |
| /1/1/1 | Copies of letters to Earl Bathurst, November 1812-May 1813. |
| /1/1/2 | Claims against France for reparations. 1818. |
| 5/1/2 | Regulations for the conduct of the Ordnance Office, 1683-1810. Prepared for the Duke when he became Master General of the Ordnance. 1819. |
| 5/1/3 | Register of correspondence as Special Envoy to Russia. February-April 1826. |
| 5/1/4 | Documents relating to the Deccan Prize Fund. 1826. |
| 5/1/5 | Letter Books of the Duke as Foreign Secretary. |
| /1/5/1 | Copies of letters to Earl Granville, Ambassador to France, and to the Foreign Office, on French affairs. November 1834-January 1835. |
| /1/5/2 | Abstracts of letters received from George Villiers, Ambassador to Spain. November 1834-February 1835. |
| 5/2/1 | Patronage book. 1828-30. |
| 5/3/1 | Manuscript of a book, in Spanish, about English seafarers in the reign of Elizabeth I, dedicated by the author to the "noble lor Wellington, Duque de Ciudad Rodrigo" etc. |
| 5/4 | Parliamentary papers. |
| /4/1-5 | Printed parliamentary papers, dating from 1833 to 1840 on the administration of the army, and pilotage regulations. |

6. Indexes to the papers.

| | |
|---|---|
| 6/1/1-23 | Indexes of correspondence from and to the Duke, 1801-1818 [prepared c.1805-18] |

6/2/1-6        Index of correspondence from and to the
               Duke, 1819-30 [prepared c.1827-30]
6/3/1-23       Index of correspondence from and to the
               Duke, 1828-50 [prepared 1829-50]
6/4/1-43       Indexes of correspondence from and to
               the Duke, 1790-1843 [prepared 1858-64].
6/5/1-2        Index of the Duke's papers, 1769-99,
               1843 [prepared c.1858-64].
6/6/1          Notes on the index volumes by Charles
               Holman. 1902.
6/7/1          Lists of missing papers, 1809-12, and
               notes by Colonel Gurwood on attempts to
               locate copies.

## 7.   Printed copies and proofs of the Despatches

7/1/1-13       The Despatches of Field Marshal the
               Duke of Wellington, during his various
               campaigns from 1799 to 1818. ed. J.
               Gurwood, new edition, London, 1837-9.
7/2/1-31       Galley proofs to the Supplementary
               Despatches.
7/3/1-27       The second Duke's galley proofs to the
               Supplementary Despatches.
7/4/1-2        The second Duke's page proofs to the
               Supplementary Despatches.
7/5/1-17       Supplementary Despatches and Memoranda
               of Field Marshal Arthur Duke of
               Wellington, K.G. ed. second Duke of
               Wellington, London, 1858-72.
7/6/1-20       Galley proofs of the Civil Despatches.
7/7/1-8        The second Duke's galley proofs of the
               Civil Despatches.
7/8/1-2        Page proofs of the Civil Despatches.
7/9/1-8        Despatches, Correspondence and
               Memoranda of Field Marshal Arthur, Duke
               of Wellington. ed. second Duke of
               Wellington, London, 1867-80.
7/10/1-3       Proofs to an unpublished volume of civil
               despatches, relating to 1833-34.
7/11/1-2       Papers relating to the publication of
               the Despatches and Supplementary
               Despatches, c. 1859-72.

## 8.   Correspondence with Colonel Gurwood

8/1            Correspondence of the Duke with Colonel
               Gurwood, respecting publication of the
               Despatches.  1842-43.

## 9.   Military Archives.

9/1            Records of the Adjutant General's
               Department in the Peninsula and South
               of France.
/1/1/1-10      Letter Book. May 1809-September 1814.

| | |
|---|---|
| 1/2/1-8 | Register of General Orders issued. June 1809-July 1814. |
| 9/2 | Records of the Military Secretary in the Peninsula and South of France. |
| /2/1/1-2 | Letter book. November 1810-December 1812. |
| /2/2/1-50 | Correspondence and papers. February 1812-October 1814. [mostly letters to and from the Military Secretary]. |
| /2/3/1-3 | Papers. Board of Claims. 1812-16. |
| 9/3 | Records of the Paymaster in the Peninsula and South of France |
| /3/1-3 | Register of warrants issued for extra-ordinary expenses. April 1809-April 1814. |
| 9/4 | Other military papers. Peninsula. |
| /4/1/1-7 | Ciphers and codebooks. 1809-1812. c. 1814. |
| /4/2/1 | Statement of money received and dis-bursed by Sir Robert Kennedy, Commissary General. 1809-14 [May 1829]. |
| 9/5 | Records of the Adjutant General's Department. Germany, the Low Countries and France. |
| /5/1-2 | Letters books. December 1813-July 1816. |
| 9/6 | Records of the Military Secretary's Department. France. |
| /6/1 | Letter book. May-September 1818. |
| 9/7 | Other military records. Germany, the Low Countries, Waterloo campaign, France. |
| /7/1-3 | Miscellaneous records, mostly returns. July 1814-October 1818. |
| 9/8 | Applications for ensignships. |
| /8/1-3 | Registers of applications. 1807-8; 1810-18. |
| 10. | Letters from Henry, third Earl Bathurst to to the Duke. |
| 10/1/1-2 | Letter books. November 1813-April 1816. [copies of the letters are in the Bathurst papers, British Library Loan 57 [47]]. |
| 11. | Papers of Richard, Marquess Wellesley, as Governor General of India. |
| 11/1/1-3 | Letter books. Copies of letters to Henry Dundas, Viscount Melville, President of the Board of Control. February 1798-August 1802. |
| 11/2/1-3 | Summaries of letters to Dundas, November 1797-November 1800. |

| | |
|---|---|
| 11/3/1-9 | Miscellaneous correspondence of Marquess Wellesley, c. 1802-36. |
| 11/4/1 | Proceedings of the "Secret Department", Fort William. 23 June 1802. |
| 11/5/1 | Copies of books by and about Marquess Wellesley. 1838-40. |

12.   Correspondence of the Duke with Henry Wellesley, first Baron Cowley.

| | |
|---|---|
| 12/1 | Letters from the Duke. |
| /1/1-2 | March-December 1810. |
| /1/3-4 | 1811 |
| /1/5-6 | 1812 |
| /1/7-8 | 1813 |
| /1/9 | January 1814-June 1815 |
| 12/2 | Copies of letters to the Duke. |
| /2/1 | September 1810-January 1811. |
| /2/2 | January-August 1811 |
| /2/3 | August 1811-September 1813 |
| /2/4 | January 1813-March 1814 |
| 12/3 | Miscellaneous papers |
| /3/1 | Register of Despatches sent to the Duke and Viscount Castlereagh, March 1810-August 1815 |

These papers include returns on casualties etc. sustained during the war, and mostly relate to Henry Wellesley's period as envoy extraordinary and afterwards Ambassador to Spain, from November 1809 (to March 1822).

15. Maps, plans and drawings.

| | |
|---|---|
| 15/1-4 | France, c.1815-30 |
| 15/5-19 | India and Burma, c.1799-c.1860 |
| 15/20-26 | Ireland. 1800-44 |
| 15/27-30 | Jamaica. c.1808-44 |
| 15/31-50 | Peninsula, c. 1770-1836 |
| 15/51 | Russia c. 1820 |
| 15/52-53 | Scandinavia c.1800 |
| 15/54 | Unidentified stretch of coastline. Before 1868. |

Large maps and plans, extracted from the general correspondence. Other maps remain in those series.

16.   Papers of William Augustus, Duke of Cumberland

| | |
|---|---|
| 16/1 | Catalogue of letters and papers as Commander-in-Chief.   1760. |

It is not known when Wellington took possession of these papers.

# Section B
# Wellington Papers: Published

6.       <u>Biographical Memoranda of Arthur, Duke of Wellington, compiled from his Despatches, Unpublished Letters, Original Documents, Autographs, Transcripts, and Notes of Conversations which were repeated to the writer.</u> London, 1853.
Really a didactic survey of the Duke's life by a partisan observer, and a defender of Colonel Gurwood.

7.       Brett-Jones, Antony, ed., <u>Wellington at War, 1794-1815. A Selection of His Wartime Letters.</u> London, 1961.
The letters are arranged chronologically: each new phase of the Duke's career is prefaced by an introduction giving background to the events described. Other contemporary sources are sometimes used to illustrated the development of the Duke's character. The letters are taken from the printed <u>Despatches</u> and <u>Supplementary Despatches</u>.

8.       Brooke, John and Julia Gandy, <u>The Prime Minister's Papers: Wellington, Political Correspondence. I. 1833-November 1834.</u> London, 1975.
A lavish edition of small selections of the Duke's correspondence preserved at Southampton University. Like the manuscripts the letters are chronologically arranged, by date of writing, not receipt. A short introduction is provided, but there is no explanation in the text.

9.       Burghclere, Lady, ed., <u>A Great Man's Friendship. Letters of the Duke of Wellington to Mary, Marchioness of Salisbury, 1850-1852.</u> London, 1927.
Numerous letters covering a great variety of events of both public and personal interest, including, for example, Wellington's health, Lady Salisbury's children, Palmerston's foreign policy, the Great Exhibition.

10.       <u>My Dear Mrs. Jones. The Letters of the First Duke of Wellington to Mrs. Jones of Pantglas.</u> London, 1954.

Gossipy letters from the last two years of
Wellington's life, with some passing references to public
events. Nicely produced. Reprinted from the <u>Century</u>
<u>Magazine</u> of December 1899.

11.       <u>The Eastern Question. Extracted from the</u>
          <u>Correspondence of the late Duke of Wellington</u>.
          London, 1877.
Letters, despatches and memoranda, principally
addressed to Lord Aberdeen, presenting the Duke's views of
the Eastern crisis of 1828-9, commenting mainly on Russian
policy, England's position, and the Treaty of Adrianople.
Extracted from the New Series of Wellington Despatches.

12.       Francis, G.H., <u>Maxims and Opinions of Field-</u>
          <u>Marshal His Grace the Duke of Wellington, Selected</u>
          <u>from his Writings and Speeches During a Public Life</u>
          <u>of More than Half a Century. With a Biographical</u>
          <u>Memoir</u>. London, 1845.
Includes extracts from Peninsula Despatches but gives
more space to a collection of the Duke's pronouncements in
the House of Lords on all the leading questions of the day.

13.       Gurwood, Lieutenant Colonel John, ed., <u>The</u>
          <u>Despatches of Field Marshal The Duke of Wellington,</u>
          <u>K.G. during his various campaigns in India: From</u>
          <u>1799 to 1805.</u>  3 vols., Calcutta, 1840.
A full collection of Wellington's letters and papers
written while he was in India, with a brief introduction.
Chronologically arranged.  Volume one covers the period from
Wellington's arrival down to June 1803, including the attack
on Seringapatam and defeat of "Doondiah Waugh": volume two
from June 1803 to June 1804, and covers the Mahratta
campaign;  and volume three from June 1804 to January 1805,
including letters of thanks and his resignation.  Includes
a useful glossary, but no table of contents.

14.       Gurwood, Lieutenant Colonel John, ed., <u>The</u>
          <u>Despatches of Field Marshal the Duke of Wellington</u>
          <u>during his Various Campaigns from 1799 to 1818.</u>
          1st edition, 13 vols., London, 1834-9.
The original series of Wellington's despatches, and an
indispensable printed source for the Duke's campaigns.
Almost solely letters from the Duke.  Arranged chronologically, although supplementary volumes had to be added as
more material came to light from the Duke's early days in
India.  No index is provided.  Some individuals names have
been blanked out.

          <u>Volume 1</u> (1834).
Covers the period from 1799 down to the end of
December 1803.

          <u>Volume 2</u> (1835).
Covers the years from January 1804 to September 1807,

includes the end of Wellington's service in India and a
few letters on the Copenhagen expedition of 1807.

Volume 3 (1835).
Supplementary to volumes 1 and 2.  Prints letters
relating to Indian affairs from November 1802 to July 1804.
Includes a preface, showing where they should be placed in
the first two volumes.

Volume 4 (1835).
Returns to the chronological sequence of volume 2:
includes despatches and other papers covering the Duke's
departure to the Peninsula in June 1808, and operations
there until August 1809.

Volume 5 (1836).
Peninsula operations, August 1809 to March 1810.

Volume 6 (1836).
Peninsula operations, April 1810 to August 1810.

Volume 7 (1837).
Peninsula operations, November 1810 to June 1811.

Volume 8 (1837).
Peninsula operations, June 1811 to March 1812.

Volume 9 (1837).
Peninsula operations, March 1812 to December 1812.
(including three letters from January 1812 omitted from
volume 8).
Volume 10 (1838).
Peninsula operations, December 1812 to August 1813.

Volume 11 (1838).
Peninsula operations, August 1813 to April 1814.

Volume 12 (1838).
France and the Low Countries April 1814 to November
1815.  Includes a note from Colonel Gurwood explaining his
decision not to publish, as he had proposed, papers
relating to the Duke's command of the army of occupation in
France between 1815 and 1818.

[Volume 13]
A supplementary and originally unnumbered volume,
adding yet more papers to those relating to India, printed
in volumes 1 to 3 of this series.

15.        Gurwood, Lieutenant Colonel John, ed., The
           Despatches of Field Marshal the Duke of Wellington
           during his various campaigns from 1799 to 1818.
           1st edition, revised, 13 vols., London, 1837-9.

An amended version of Gurwood's original edition,
which incorporates material originally printed in the

supplementary volumes 3 and 13, into their correct place in the chronological sequence.  Volumes 9 to 12 of this and the original series are identical.

Volume 1 (1837).
1798 - June 1803.
Volume 2 (1837).
June 1803 - January 1804.
Volume 3 (1837).
January 1804 - March 1805.
Volume 4 (1837).
August 1807 - September 1809.
Volume 5 (1838).
August 1809 - March 1810.
Volume 6 (1838).
April 1810 - November 1810.
Volume 7 (1838).
November 1810 - June 1811.
Volume 8 (1838).
June 1811 - March 1812.
Volume 9 (1838).
March 1812 - December 1812.
Volume 10 (1838).
December 1812 - August 1813.
Volume 11 (1838).
August 1813 - April 1814.
Volume 12 (1838).
May 1814 - November 1815.
Volume 13 (1839).
Index.  Arranged alphabetically by person and subject.

16.          Gurwood, Lieutenant Colonel John, ed., The Despatches of Field Marshal the Duke of Wellington during his various campaigns ...  2nd edition, 8 vols., London, 1844-7.
A revised and enlarged version of the new, consol- idated first edition.  Includes more letters about and to Wellington, as well as those from him.
Volume 1 (1844).
Covers Wellington's campaigns in Holland and India down to 1803.  The first letter is dated 1794.  Includes brief notes as well as long formal despatches.
Volume 2 (1844)
India.  October 1803 to July 1805 - the end of Wellington's service there.  Includes, besides letters, drafts of letters and despatches on various subjects connected with Indian administration etc.
Volume 3 (1844).
Denmark 1807, and the Peninsula, 1808 to the end of March 1810.  Despatches and other letters by Wellington, with some official French reports on proceedings in the Peninsula.
Volume 4 (1844).
Peninsula, April 1810 to April 1811.  Peninsular operations.

Volume 5 (1844).
Peninsula, May 1811 to July 1812. Operations in
Portugal and Spain.
Volume 6 (1845).
Peninsula, August 1812 to September 1813. Operations
in Portugal and Spain.
Volume 7 (1845)
Peninsula and France, September 1813 to March 1815.
Operations in Spain, France and the Low Countries.
Volume 8 (1847).
Germany, the Low Countries and France, March 1815 to
May 1818. Papers relating to the Waterloo campaign. Also
includes some later papers by the Duke - on ranks of civil
and military officers (1827); selections from correspondence
on military discipline (1827); Wellington's evidence to the
Royal Commission on military punishments and a memorandum to
Hill on military governments (1833).

17.        Gurwood, Lieutenant Colonel John, ed., The
           General Orders of Field Marshal the Duke of
           Wellington, K.G., etc. etc. etc., in Portugal,
           Spain, and France, from 1809 to 1814; and in the
           Low Countries and France, in 1815; and in France,
           Army of Occupation, from 1816 to 1818. 2nd ed.,
           London, 1837.
Taken from the printed despatches, with some minor
textual corrections. This work was designed for the
military student; the orders are arranged under subject
headings, alphabetically, and are fully cross-referenced.
The first edition, published in 1832, omits the General
Orders issued in France in 1816 to 1818.

18.        Gurwood, Lieutenant Colonel John, ed.,
           Selections from the Despatches and General Orders
           of Field Marshal the Duke of Wellington. London,
           1841.
Selections from the original series of printed
despatches, covering in chronological order, Wellington's
career down to 1815. This volume also reproduces one or
two papers from the Duke's term as Commander-in-Chief in
1827-8, and extracts from his evidence to the Select
Committee on military punishments in 1829.

19.        Gurwood, Lieutenant Colonel John and W. Hazlitt,
           eds., The Speeches of the Duke of Wellington in
           Parliament. 2 vols., London, 1854.
A compilation of all of Wellington's significant
Parliamentary speeches, taken from official records.
Volume one begins in January 1792 and ends in 1834. Volume
two begins in 1835 and ends with the Duke's death.
Arranged chronologically, and includes letters written by
Wellington to the Speaker while in the Peninsula. Dedicated
to Lord Brougham and completed by Hazlitt after Gurwood's
death.

20.          Herrick, Christine Terhune, ed., <u>Letters of the</u>
             <u>Duke of Wellington to Miss J. ... with Extracts</u>
             <u>from Miss J.'s Diary</u>. London, 1889.
   A series of very personal letters from the Duke to the
rather unstable Miss Jenkins, dating from 1834 onwards.

21.          Olney, R.J. and Julia Melvin, <u>The Prime</u>
             <u>Minister's Papers Series: Wellington. II.</u>
             <u>Political Correspondence, November 1834 - April</u>
             <u>1835.</u> London, 1986.
   A further extract from the Wellington papers at
Southampton University covering the period of the Duke's
"caretaker" ministry, and Peel's "hundred days" in office.

22.          Owen, S.J., ed., <u>A selection from the</u>
             <u>despatches, memoranda and other papers relating to</u>
             <u>India of Field Marshal the Duke of Wellington.</u>
             Oxford, 1880.
   Selected extracts from Wellington's printed despatches
covering the years from 1798 to 1805, but arranged by
subject rather than chronologically.  Mostly letters from
Wellington.  Includes a long introductory essay on his
career in India and a useful map.

23.          de Pange, V., <u>The unpublished Correspondence of</u>
             <u>Madame de Stael and the Duke of Wellington.</u>
             Translated by H. Kurtz, London, 1965.
   Reproduces nineteen letters from both parties, written
between November 1814 and June 1817, mostly while Wellington
was Commander-in-Chief of the Allied armies in France,
linked together by a long commentary and editorial notes.
Madame de Stael is the heroine of this work, edited by a
descendant.  This is a slightly amended translation of a
French edition of 1962.

24.          <u>The Principles of War, exhibited in the</u>
             <u>practice of the Camp; and as developed in a series</u>
             <u>of General Orders of Field Marshal the Duke of</u>
             <u>Wellington, K.G., etc.,etc., etc., in the late</u>
             <u>Campaigns in the Peninsula; with parallel orders of</u>
             <u>George the Second, the Duke of Cumberland, the Duke</u>
             <u>of Marlborough, Earl of Albemarle, Lord Staire,</u>
             <u>General Wolfe, etc., etc.</u> London, 1815.
   A collection of the Duke's General Orders in the
Peninsula, arranged by subject but not confined to any
particular area.  Designed to educate officers of the army.
The contributions of the others are brief, but complement
Wellington's.

25.          Rathbone, Julian, ed., <u>Wellington's War.</u>
             London, 1984.
   Extracts from the Duke's despatches from the
Peninsula, with a commentary.

26.          Rousseau, I.J., "Unpublished Letters of

Wellington, July-August 1812." <u>Cambridge Historical
Journal</u>, 3 (1929): 96-101.
Several letters from Wellington to Sir Benjamin
D'Urban, respecting the pursuit of the French after the
battle of Salamanca.

27.      Stocqueler, J.H., comp,, <u>The Wellington Manual,
being a compilation from the Dispatches of His
Grace the Duke of Wellington, embracing his senti-
ments on various points relating to military
discipline and administration ...</u>   Calcutta, 1840.
A brief selection of extracts from Wellington's
printed despatches, arranged by subject, so as to be of use
to officers in the field on "parallel occasions".  Edited by
an ardent admirer.

28.      Walford, Edith, comp., <u>The Words of Wellington.
Collected from His Despatches, Letters, and
Speeches, with Anecdotes, etc.</u>  London, 1869.
Numerous quotations from letters and speeches by, and
other stories about, Wellington, covering the whole of his
career, military and political.

29.      Webster, Sir Charles, ed., Some Letters of the
Duke of Wellington to his brother, William
Wellesley-Pole." <u>Royal Historical Society, Camden
Miscellany, volume 18.</u>  London, 1948.
A collection of thirty-seven letters, mostly dated
between 1807 and 1809, and dealing mostly with the Duke's
conduct of military operations.  Also included are dis-
cussions of the conduct of the Marquess Wellesley and
Gerald Wellesley, and a brief note about the battle of
Waterloo.

30.      Wellington, Duke of, <u>General Orders.</u>  10 vols.,
London, 1811-18.
Ten volumes of the Duke's general orders, printed by
the War Office - following an order from Wellington of 14
November 1810.  Arranged in chronological order.  Some
editing of orders has been undertaken, to eliminate matters
of transient interest.  The purpose of these volumes is
didactic: they were to be issued to all regiments as they
joined the army in the Peninsula, to act as a guide to
conduct.  All kinds of subjects are covered, including
orders of march, billeting arrangements, courts martial
findings, and so on.  A chronological index, giving brief
notice of the subject of each order, is included in every
volume.  Most orders come from the Adjutant General's
Department in the Peninsula, but one or two from the Horse
Guards are included, as are some copies of correspondence
from the Horse Guards.
Volume I. General Orders. Spain and Portugal.
<u>April 27th to December 29th, 1809.</u>  (London, 1811).

Volume II.  General Orders.  Spain and Portugal.
<u>January 2nd to December 29th 1810.</u> (London, 1811).

Volume III. General Orders. Spain and Portugal.
January 1st to December 31st 1811. (London, 1812).

Volume IV. General Orders. Spain and Portugal.
January 1st to December 30th 1812. (London, 1813).

Volume V. General Orders. Spain and France.
January 7th to December 28th 1813. (London, 1814).
This volume is somewhat larger than the preceding
ones, and the index is arranged by alphabetical order of
the surname of the person or persons to whom they apply,
and not chronologically.

Volume VI. General Orders. France. 1814. To which
is added, a general alphabetical index for the
orders of 1809, 1810, 1811 and 1812. (London,
1817).
The index supplements those in the first four volumes,
and is arranged by subject, e.g. "rations", "quarters", etc.
or by title of office holders and other individuals.
Printing delayed, presumably by the preparation of this
index.

Volume VII. General Orders. Flanders and France.
April 11th to December 31st, 1815. (Paris, 1815).
Printed at the military press in Paris by "Sergeant
Buchan, 3rd Guards". A long volume, with alphabetical/
subject index.

Volume VIII. General Orders. France. 1816.
("Printed at the Headquarters of the Army"
[Cambrai], 1816).

Volume IX. General Orders. France. 1817.
([Cambrai], 1817).

Volume X. General Orders. France. 1818.
([Cambrai], 1818).

Colonel Gurwood's published edition of the General
Orders of 1837 was prepared from these volumes, which he
edited and issued in a more compact format.

31.        Wellington, Second Duke of, ed., Supplementary
           Despatches and Memoranda of Field Marshal Arthur
           Duke of Wellington, 1794-1818. 15 vols.,
           London, 1858-72.
Letters and papers, completed and in draft and from
and to the Duke, covering his whole military career.
Intended as a supplement to the first consolidated edition
of Gurwood's despatches, reproducing some letters about
the Duke, printed only in the rarer, second edition.
Arranged chronologically; includes more letters to the
Duke, and less from him in later volumes.

Volume 1 (1858).
India, 1797 to June 1800.

Volume 2 (1858).
India, June 1800 - December 1801.

Volume 3 (1859).
India, December 1801 to February 1803.

Volume 4 (1859).
India, February 1803 to March 1805, and a few later letters.

[All Indian volumes contain only letters from Wellington].

Volume 5 (1860).
Ireland: March 1807 to April 1809 (entitled "Civil Correspondence and Memoranda"). Mostly papers from the Duke relating to his civil duties as Chief Secretary for Ireland. A frank selection, although the names of individuals are sometimes excised.

Volume 6 (1860).
"Expedition to Denmark - Plans for Conquest of Mexico - Expeditions to Portugal in 1808 & 1809 - And the First Advance of the British Army into Spain, July 1807 - December 1810." Many letters and papers by Wellington, but increasing numbers of letters to him, as well as inter- cepted correspondence of Marshal Soult. Chronologically arranged, but this volume does not cover Ireland which is dealt with in Volume 5.

Volume 7 (1860).
Peninsula, December 1810 to June 1813. A good selection of despatches to, as well as from, the Duke, dealing with military affairs in the Peninsula.

Volume 8 (1861).
Peninsula and South of France, June 1813 to April 1814. Mostly letters and papers addressed to the Duke, rather than by him - but includes some general orders and other letters.

Volume 9 (1862).
South of France, Embassy to Paris and Congress of Vienna, April 1814 to March 1815. Similar to volume 8, but contains more papers by the Duke not published by Gurwood.

Volume 10 (1863).
"Waterloo, the Campaign in France and the Capitulation of Paris by a military convention with the allied British & Prussian Armies (March-July 1815)." Consists almost entirely of despatches and other papers sent to the Duke.

Volume 11 (1864).
"Occupation of France by the allied armies; surrender of Napoleon; & Restoration of the Bourbons. July 1815 -

July 1817.  As volume 10, but contains rather more papers
by the Duke, relating to his own position, and that of the
army of occupation.

Volume 12  (1865).
   "Settlement of Claims on France; Financial State of
France; Difference between Spain & Portugal; Negotiations
respecting the Colonies of Spain in America; Plot &
Attempt to Assassinate the Duke of Wellington; Evacuation of
France by the allied armies." June 1817 to the end of 1818.
Mostly papers sent to the Duke, but also includes quite a
number by him, on a wide variety of questions connected with
the army of occupation.

Volume 13 (1872).  "Appendix. 1794-1812."
   Supplementary to volumes 1 to 5.  Includes letters
from the Duke not previously published, but also increasing
numbers of papers by his juniors, general and other orders,
and so on.

Volume 14 (1872).  "Appendix: 1812 to the end of
the military series."
   Supplemental to volumes 5 to 12, dealing with military
affairs from January 1812 to May 1827, including papers
captured from the French in the Peninsula, and some further
papers on the Duke's diplomatic career.

Volume 15  (1872).
   "Index to the Wellington Supplementary despatches,
volumes I to XIV, with chronological list of letters,
memoranda etc. published in the First (A New) Edition of
Gurwood and in the Supplementary Despatches."  A compre-
hensive index and calendar which reveals that Gurwood's
(New 1st edition) and the supplementary despatches between
them print some 7,200 letters and papers attributable to
Wellington.

32.          Wellington, Second Duke of, ed., Despatches,
             Correspondence and Memoranda of Field Marshal
             Arthur, Duke of Wellington, K.G. (in continuation
             of the former series).  8 vols., London, 1867-80.
   Numerous letters from and to the Duke, covering his
career as a diplomatist and politician down to December
1832.  Chronologically arranged - each volume is prefaced by
an index of correspondents.  No overall index is provided.
This series is often referred to as the "Civil Despatches"
of the Duke of Wellington.

Volume 1 (1867).
   "Congress of Verona; insurrection in Spain; Question
of occupation of Spain by foreign troops; armed inter-
vention by France; Portugal and Brazil; Independence of
Spanish & Portuguese America; The Slave Trade; Russia &
Turkey; Commerce of the Black Sea; Russian claims on the
N.W. coast of America; Austrian debt to England.  January
1819 - December 1822."  Mostly letters and memoranda by the

Duke on these questions, with some letters to him.

Volume 2 (1867).
January 1823 to December 1825.  Includes papers on the
many subjects, both domestic and foreign, brought to the
Duke's attention.

Volume 3 (1868).
December 1825 to May 1827.  Takes the story up to the
Duke's becoming Commander-in-Chief and includes papers on
both domestic and foreign politics.

Volume 4 (1871).
May 1827 to August 1828.  Covers the Duke's relations
with Canning and Goderich's Ministries, his resignation as
Commander-in-Chief and his becoming Prime Minister.

Volume 5 (1873).
September 1828 to June 1829.  Deals with the first
nine months of Wellington's premiership, including the
passage of Catholic Emancipation.

Volume 6 (1877).
July 1829 to April 1830.  Further papers on the Duke's
ministry.

Volume 7 (1878).
April 1830 to October 1831.  Covers the downfall of
the Duke's ministry in November 1830 and the beginnings of
the reform bill crisis.

Volume 8 (1880).
November 1831 to December 1832.  Includes numerous
papers upon political events, the Duke's reflections on
the reform bill and the state of society.

This series has recently been continued by the Royal
Commission on Historical Manuscripts (see Brooke and Gandy
(8) and Olney and Melvin (21)).

33.        Wellington, Seventh Duke of, ed.,  A Selection
           from the Private Correspondence of the First Duke
           of Wellington.  Privately printed, London, 1952.
An interesting collection.  It is divided by subject
and includes letters from Colonel Wesley to Catherine
Pakenham; letters to and from, and about the Duke's sons;
letters and papers on George IV's will, the Duke of York's
estate and the Duchess of Kent; letters on "the Duke and
the artists" - his architect, and painters and sculptors;
miscellaneous letters in which the Duke figures, and letters
of condolence on his death.

34.        Wellington, Seventh Duke of, ed., Wellington
           and His Friends.  Letters of the First Duke of
           Wellington to the Rt. Hon. Charles and Mrs.

Arbuthnot, the Earl and Countess of Wilton, Princess Lieven, and Miss Burdett-Coutts. London, 1965.
An interesting collection of extracts from private letters, throwing much light on the Duke's character and opinions.

35.       The Wisdom of Wellington, or Maxims of the Iron Duke.  London, [1852].
Interesting collection, arranged mostly chronologically, of extracts from Wellington's despatches, linked by a thoughtful biographical sketch.  Primarily concerned with events in the Peninsular war.

36.       Wood, Walter, ed., The Despatches of Field Marshal the Duke of Wellington During his Campaigns in India, Denmark, Portugal, Spain, the Low Countries, and France, And Relating to America, from 1799 to 1815.  London & New York, 1902.
A condensed version of Gurwood's Despatches. Some "uninteresting" text has been omitted and some footnotes added.  Gurwood's chronological arrangement is followed - one quarter of the book is devoted to India - except for those few papers relating to America, which have been gathered together from several volumes of the original work.

37.       Wyatt, R.J., "Wellington's Published Despatches and Correspondence." Journal of the Society for Army Historical Research, 62 (1984): 244-6.
A brief description of the various editions of the Duke's despatches and other correspondence.

# Section C
# Other Unpublished Papers
## (i) Official Papers

All of the following papers are to be found at the Public
Record Office, Ruskin Avenue, Kew, Richmond, Surrey, TW9 4DU.

38.         Colonial Office Papers

CO323/199.     Correspondence with Ordnance Department
               1824.

CO323/202      Out letters. Public Offices. 1825.

        These two volumes are the only Colonial Office papers
with significant mention of Wellington. Piece 199 includes
many papers on the defence of the West Indies; piece 202
includes letters from Wellington and Lord Fitzroy Somerset
on the Duke's behalf, relating to the transfer of respons-
ibility for Colonial military installations from the
Colonial Office to the Ordnance Office.

39.         Foreign Office Papers.

    a)      Correspondence as Commander-in-Chief in the
            Peninsula.

    FO63/137      Correspondence. Portugal. 1812.
    FO72/133      Correspondence. Spain. 1812.
    FO72/164      Correspondence. Spain. 1814.

    b)      Correspondence as Ambassador to France, 1814 and
            Commander-in-Chief, Allied Army of Occupation in
            France, 1815-18.

    FO27/112      Correspondence. France. 1815.

    FO27/113      Correspondence. France (Lord Fitzroy
                  Somerset). 1815. January - June.

    FO27/114      Correspondence. France. (Lord Fitzroy
                  Somerset) 1816.

FO92/13        Despatches to the Duke of Wellington.
               1815.
FO92/14        Despatches from the Duke of Wellington.
               1815.
FO92/31        Correspondence with the Duke of
               Wellington. 1816.
FO92/32        Correspondence with the Duke of
               Wellington. 1817.
FO92/37        Correspondence with the Duke of
               Wellington. 1818.

c)    Congress of Troppau/Laibach

FO92/44        Memoranda by Wellington. 1820.

d)    Correspondence as British observer at the
      Congress of Verona, 1822.

FO92/48        Despatches to the Duke of Wellington.

FO92/49        Despatches from the Duke of Wellington.

FO92/50        Despatches from the Duke of Wellington.

FO92/51        Despatches from the Duke of Wellington.

FO92/52        Despatches from the Duke of Wellington.

e)    Correspondence as Special Envoy to Russia, 1826

FO65/153       Despatches to the Duke of Wellington,
               1826. February-April.

FO65/154       Despatches from the Duke of Wellington.
               1826. February-March.

FO65/155       Despatches from the Duke of Wellington.
               1826. April.

The Duke was sent by Canning to congratulate the new
Tsar, Nicholas I, on his accession, and to negotiate with
him on the Greek question.

f)    Correspondence as Foreign Secretary, November
      1834 - April 1835.

Despatches to and from British Ambassadors and
Ministers and correspondence with foreign diplomatic
representatives in London ("Domestic").

i)    United States of America

FO5/288        To Sir C. Vaughan 1834.

FO5/293        From Sir C. Vaughan. 1834. November-

| | |
|---|---|
| | December. |
| FO5/299 | To Sir C. Vaughan. 1835. |
| FO5/300 | From Sir C. Vaughan. 1835. January-July. |

ii)  Austria

| | |
|---|---|
| FO7/246 | To W. Fox Strangways. 1834. |
| FO7/249 | From W. Fox Strangways and Sir Frederick Lamb. 1834. July-December. |
| FO7/251 | Domestic. 1834. |
| FO7/252 | To W. Fox Strangways and H.E. Fox. 1835. |
| FO7/253 | From W. Fox Strangways. 1835. |
| FO7/255 | Domestic. 1835. |

iii) Belgium

| | |
|---|---|
| FO10/30 | To Sir Robert Adair. 1834. |
| FO10/33 | From Sir Robert Adair and Sir G.B. Hamilton. 1834. July-December. |
| FO10/35 | Domestic. 1834. |
| FO10/36 | To Sir Robert Adair, Sir G.B. Hamilton and H.L. Bulwer. 1835. |
| FO10/37 | From Sir Robert Adair. 1835. |
| FO10/39 | Domestic. 1835. |

iv)  France

| | |
|---|---|
| FO27/479 | To Earl Granville. 1834. July-December |
| FO27/489 | From Earl Granville. 1834. November-December. |
| FO27/494 | To  Prince Talleyrand. 1834. |
| FO27/497 | To A. Aston, Lord Cowley and Earl Granville. 1835. January-July. |
| FO27/499 | From Earl Granville and A. Aston. 1835. January-February. |
| FO27/500 | From A. Aston. 1835. February-March. |
| FO27/501 | From Lord Cowley and A. Aston. 1835. March-May. |

FO27/511        Domestic. 1835. January-June.

v)  Greece

FO32/42         To E. Dawkins. 1834.

FO32/46         From E. Dawkins. 1834. September-
                December.

FO32/50         To E. Dawkins. 1835. January-April.

FO32/52         From Sir Edmund Lyons. 1835. January-
                August.

FO32/55         Domestic. 1835.

vi)  Holland

FO37/190        To G. Jerningham. 1834.

FO37/191        From G. Jerningham. 1834.

FO37/193        Domestic. 1834.

FO37/194        To and from G. Jerningham. 1835.

FO37/197        Domestic. 1835.

vii)  Portugal

FO63/417        To Lord Howard de Walden. 1834.

FO63/423        From Lord Howard de Walden. 1834.
                November-December.

FO63/428        Domestic. 1834.

FO63/433        To Lord Howard de Walden. 1835.

FO63/434        From Lord Howard de Walden. 1835.
                January-March.

FO63/435        From Lord Howard de Walden. 1835.
                March-May.

FO63/443        Domestic. 1835.

viii)  Prussia

FO64/193        To Lord Minto. 1834.

FO64/196        From R. Abercrombie and G. Shee. 1834.

FO64/197        Domestic. 1834.

FO64/199        To R. Abercrombie, Sir Robert Adair and

|  | Lord William Russell. 1835. |
| FO64/200 | From R. Abercrombie. 1835. January-June. |
| FO64/203 | Domestic. 1835. |

ix) Russia.

| FO65/212 | To J.D. Bligh. 1834. |
| FO65/214 | From J.D. Bligh. 1834. July-December. |
| FO65/216 | Domestic. 1834. |
| FO65/217 | To and from J.D. Bligh. 1835. |
| FO65/220 | Domestic. 1835. |

x) Spain

| FO72/419 | To G. Villiers. 1834. |
| FO72/428 | From G. Villiers. 1834. November-December. |
| FO72/434 | Domestic. 1834. August-December. |
| FO72/439 | To G. Villiers. 1835. |
| FO72/440 | From G. Villiers. 1835. January-February |
| FO72/441 | From G. Villiers. 1835. March-April. |
| FO72/450 | Domestic. 1835. January-August. |

xi) Turkey

| FO78/234 | To Lord Ponsonby. 1834. |
| FO78/240 | From Lord Ponsonby. 1834. November-December. |
| FO78/250 | Domestic. 1834. |
| FO78/251 | To Lord Ponsonby. 1835. |
| FO78/252 | From Lord Ponsonby. 1835. January-March. |
| FO78/253 | From Lord Ponsonby. 1835. April-June. |
| FO78/268 | Domestic. 1835. |

Wellington held the office of Foreign Secretary for only six months, during which time the crisis points of European diplomacy were Belgium, following the revolution in 1830, the Iberian Peninsula, and the perennial Eastern

question.  There are scattered references to the Duke in
correspondence with other, minor, powers.

40.        War Office Papers

  a) Correspondence as Commander-in-Chief in the
     Peninsula, Low Countries and France.

  WO1   War Office. In-letters and Papers.

  WO1/228      From General Wellesley.  1808.  June-
               November.

  WO1/415      Papers respecting the Convention of
               Cintra.  General Wellesley's speech.
               1808-9.

  WO1/238      From General Wellesley. 1809. April-
               August.

  WO1/242      From Viscount Wellington.  1809.
               September-December.

  WO1/243      From Viscount Wellington.  1810.
               January-March.

  WO1/244      From Viscount Wellington.  1810.  April-
               June.

  WO1/245      From Viscount Wellington.  1810.  July-
               September.

  WO1/246      From Viscount Wellington.  1810.
               October-December.

  WO1/248      From Viscount Wellington.  1811.
               January-March.

  WO1/249      From Viscount Wellington.  1811. April-
               June.

  WO1/250      From Viscount Wellington.  1811.  July-
               September.

  WO1/251      From Viscount Wellington.  1811.
               October-December.

  WO1/253      From Earl Wellington.  1812.  January-
               March.

  WO1/254      From Earl Wellington.  1812.  April-June

  WO1/255      From Earl Wellington.  1812.  July-
               September.

  WO1/256      From Earl Wellington.  1812.  October-

December.

| | |
|---|---|
| WO1/257 | From Earl Wellington. 1813. January-March. |
| WO1/258 | From Earl Wellington. 1813. April-June |
| WO1/259 | From Marquess Wellington. 1813. July-September. |
| WO1/260 | From Marquess Wellington. 1813. October-December. |
| WO1/202 | From Marquess Wellington. 1814. January-March. |
| WO1/203 | From the Duke of Wellington. 1814. April-June. |
| WO1/205 | From the Duke of Wellington and the Prince of Orange. 1815. January-July. |
| WO1/207 | From the Duke of Wellington. 1815. July-September. |
| WO1/208 | From the Duke of Wellington. 1815. October-December. |
| WO1/209 | From the Duke of Wellington. 1816. January-March. |
| WO1/210 | From the Duke of Wellington. 1816. April-June. |
| WO1/211 | From the Duke of Wellington. 1816. July-December. |
| WO1/214 | From the Duke of Wellington. 1817. |
| WO1/215 | From the Duke of Wellington. 1818. |
| WO1/216 | From the Duke of Wellington. 1819-20. |

Despatches from the front, addressed to the Secretary of State for War and the Colonies, and mostly published in Gurwood's <u>Despatches</u>.

| | |
|---|---|
| WO6 | War Office. Out Letters. |
| WO6/29 | To Lord Wellington. 1810-11. |
| WO6/30 | To Lord Wellington. 1811-12. |
| WO6/31 | To Earl Wellington. 1812-13. |
| WO6/32 | To Marquess Wellington. 1813-15. Part |

one.

| | |
|---|---|
| WO6/33 | To Marquess Wellington. 1813-15. Part Two. |
| WO6/34 | To Lord Wellington. 1809-10. Drafts. |
| WO6/35 | To Lord Wellington. 1811. Drafts. |
| WO6/36 | To Earl Wellington. 1812. Drafts. |
| WO6/37 | To Marquess Wellington. 1813-14. Drafts. |
| WO6/38 | To Lord Wellington and others. 1811-12. Drafts. |
| WO6/39 | To Lord Wellington and others. 1811-12. Drafts. |
| | |
| WO6/41 | Portugal. 1809. |
| WO6/42 | Spain and Portugal. 1808. Drafts. |
| WO6/47 | Spain and Portugal. 1808. June-September Drafts. |
| WO6/48 | Spain and Portugal. 1808. September-November. Drafts. |
| WO6/49 | Spain and Portugal. 1808-09. Drafts. |
| WO6/50 | Spain and Portugal. 1810-12. Drafts. |
| WO6/51 | Spain and Portugal. 1812-13. Drafts. |
| WO6/52 | Spain and Portugal. 1813-14. Drafts. |

b)   Papers as Master General of Ordnance

WO1   War Office. In-letters and Papers.

WO1/967      Increase of the army. 1823-25.

Includes two memoranda from Wellington and other Cabinet papers respecting the size of the army.

WO46   Ordnance Office. Letter Books.

| | |
|---|---|
| WO46/28 | Inspector General of Fortifications. 1818-25. |
| WO46/29 | Inspector General of Fortifications. 1826-27. |

WO46/45          Barracks. Foreign. 1822-25.

WO46/46          Treasury. 1822-35.

WO46/47          Solicitor. 1824-25.

WO46/48          Solicitor. 1825-28.

Letter books containing copies of letters from Wellington and some memoranda by him, as well as numerous other papers emanating from the Master General's office. A wide variety of subjects is covered.

WO55  Ordnance Department. Miscellaneous.

Engineer Papers.

WO55/715.        Northern District. 1812-25.

WO55/716         Northern District. 1826-30.

WO55/720         Midland District. 1819-26.

WO55/735         Eastern District. 1812-25.

WO55/736         Eastern District. 1826-28.

WO55/741         London District. 1804-26.

WO55/742         London District. 1827.

WO55/754         Waltham District. 1819-41.

WO55/757         Woolwich District. 1811-21.

WO55/758         Woolwich District. 1822-30.

WO55/766         Thames District. 1819-35.

WO55/768         Medway District. 1812-25.

WO55/769         Medway District. 1826-28.

WO55/779         Dover District. 1811-19.

WO55/780         Dover District. 1820-27.

WO55/788         Portsmouth District. 1819-24.

WO55/789         Portsmouth District. 1825-27.

WO55/799         Plymouth District. 1819-26.

WO55/800         Plymouth District. 1827-28.

WO55/810         Channel Islands. 1819-27.

| | |
|---|---|
| WO55/819 | Scotland. 1812-25. |
| WO55/820 | Scotland. 1826. |
| WO55/821 | Scotland. 1827. |
| WO55/836 | Ireland. 1816-20. |
| WO55/837 | Ireland. 1821-25. |
| WO55/838 | Ireland. 1826-30. |
| WO55/861 | Canada, Newfoundland, Nova Scotia. 1817-22. |
| WO55/862 | Canada, Newfoundland, Nova Scotia. 1822-25. |
| WO55/863 | Canada, Newfoundland, Nova Scotia. 1826. |
| WO55/889 | Cape of Good Hope. 1819-30. |
| WO55/892 | Mauritius. 1811-30. |
| WO55/894 | Ceylon. 1803-30. |
| WO55/904 | Gibraltar. 1819-25. |
| WO55/905 | Gibraltar. 1826-30. |
| WO55/909 | Malta. 1819-30. |
| WO55/911 | Ionian Islands. 1804-30. |
| WO55/918 | Saint Helena, Sierra Leone, Gold Coast. 1816-30. |
| WO55/923 | Antigua. 1798-1845. |
| WO55/924 | Bahamas. 1792-1830. |
| WO55/926 | Barbadoes. 1798-1830. |
| WO55/928 | Bermuda. 1798-1825. |
| WO55/929 | Bermuda. 1826-30. |
| WO55/931 | Demerera, Berbice, Dominica.  1798-1830. |
| WO55/933 | Grenada. 1798-1845. |
| WO55/934 | Jamaica. 1800-30. |
| WO55/937 | St. Christopher. 1798-1845. |
| WO55/938 | St. Lucia. 1798-1845. |
| WO55/939 | St. Vincent. 1797-1845. |

WO55/940    Tobago 1795-1845.

WO55/942    Trinidad 1819-45.

WO55/944    West Indies 1812-22.

WO55/945    West Indies 1823-30.

A large collection of letters and papers relating to fortifications and other buildings for which the Ordnance Department was responsible. Each box includes some letters and papers by the Duke. These papers give a good impression of the work of the Master General of the Ordnance in peacetime.

WO55/1551(7)    "A copy of a report to His Grace the Duke of Wellington, relative to H.M.'s North American Provinces" by Sir J. Carmichael Smyth, Lt. Col. Sir G. Hoste and Captain Harris. 1825.

c)    Papers as Commander-in-Chief

WO30    War Office. Miscellanea.

WO30/111    Papers. 1806-1848

Includes correspondence between Wellington, the Duke of York and others respecting the issue of medals for the Peninsular war and other engagements, and a series of letters from and to the Duke respecting arrangements made to counter the Chartist "riots" of 1848.

WO30/112    Papers. 1846-47.

Correspondence between Wellington, Fitzroy Somerset, Lord Grey and Lord John Russell respecting the Army Service Act, and between Wellington and others on providing reliefs for regiments serving in the East Indies.

WO30/113    Papers. 1845-50.

Includes correspondence relating to the Royal Hospital Chelsea, the erection of barracks in Ireland, and the Tower of London.

WO30/116    Papers. 1845-46.

Letters from Sir John Le Couteur respecting Channel Islands defences.

WO55    Ordnance Department. Miscellanea

WO55/1548(19) Memorandum by Wellington on works proposed for the Naval Arsenals and Dockyards. 1844.

WO55/1548(20)

Memorandum by Wellington on the Naval Defence of the
Country. 1845.

WO55/1551(7B) Papers on the Defence of Canada, 1841-2

A series of letters and memoranda by Wellington,
mostly to his predecessor, Lord Hill.

WO55/1563(6)   "Observations on the probable results of
a war with France under our present
system of military preparation" by Sir
John Burgoyne. 1846. Reply by the Duke
of Wellington. 1847.

Wellington's reply to Burgoyne was published in
January 1848 and caused the Duke great annoyance.

d)  Papers as Constable of the Tower of London.

WO 94 Tower of London.   Constable's Office. Letter
Books.

WO94/15       1816-31.

WO94/17       1832-36.

WO94/18       1836-40.

WO94/19       1840-48.

WO94/20       1848-58.

Wellington became Constable of the Tower of London at
the end of December 1826.   The letter books include correspondence from and to the Duke on a wide variety of subjects
relating to the Tower.   These include appointments; the
privileges of the Tower; building works; state visits; the
defence of the Tower against an insurrection; the great fire
of 1841 and the admission of tourists to the buildings.

# (ii) Private Collections

Archives Nationales, 60 Rue des Francs-
Bourgeois, 70-Paris-03, France.

41.     Archives de Joseph Bonaparte.

    381 AP34   Wellington letters, 1811-13.

    381 AP35   Wellington letters and papers, 1809-13.

    381 AP36   Papers respecting the Portuguese army,
                 1813-14.

    381 AP37   Papers respecting Wellington in France,
    Dossiers   1814-19.
    1-6.

Included among the intercepted papers of Joseph
Bonaparte, returned by the British Government in the 1950s.
Includes miscellaneous papers by, and to, the Duke, from
the civil and military authorities in Iberia and, later,
France. The latter include papers on provisioning the army,
the payment of the French indemnity and the Duke's
inspection of the "Barrier fortresses" in the Netherlands in
1819.

Bodleian Library, Department of Western
Manuscripts, Oxford, OX1 3BG.

42.     Sir James Graham Papers.
    Microfilm.

    Film 113   Correspondence. 1842.

    Film 118   Correspondence. 1843.

    Film 120   Correspondence. 1844.

    Film 121   Correspondence. 1845.

Includes correspondence with Wellington relating to national defences, especially with regard to the Channel Islands and the formation of a militia force in Britain and Ireland.

43.      Sir Thomas Munro Papers.

Ms Eur F. 151 Piece 1   Letters from Wellington, August 1799 to November 1803.

Ms Eur F. 151 Piece 56 Letters and Papers, Prize Money, 1818-19.

A very useful collection for Wellington's campaigns in India, but also includes official correspondence on the Indian Prize Money controversy of 1818-19 and other miscellaneous and private letters to and from the Duke.

44.      Sir William Napier Papers.

Ms Eng. Lett. c. 250   Correspondence, 1825-48.

Includes correspondence between Wellington and Sir William Napier, the historian of the Peninsular war, dating from 1825, 1839 and 1847-8, mostly about the war.

45.      Benjamin Symons Papers.

Ms Eng. Lett. d. 193   Letters from Wellington, 1844-8.

Thirty letters from the Duke in his capacity as Chancellor of the University of Oxford to Benjamin Parsons Symons, Warden of Wadham College and Vice Chancellor of the University between 1844 and 1848.

British Library, Department of Manuscripts, Great Russell Street, London, WC1B 3DG.

46.      Aberdeen Papers.

Additional Manuscripts

43056   General Correspondence. July 1827-October 1828.

43057   General Correspondence. November 1828-September 1829.

43058   General Correspondence. October 1829-July 1830.

43059   General Correspondence. August 1830-May 1832.

43060    General Correspondence. June 1832-June 1846.

43269    Letter Book. 1827-34.

43270    Letter Book. 1834-41.

Letters and memoranda from and to the Duke, mostly dealing with foreign affairs and dating from Aberdeen's time as Foreign Secretary in Wellington's Ministry. There are also some papers on domestic politics, and on Anglo-French relations during Peel's second ministry.

47.    Bathurst Papers.

Loan 57

Piece 60    Private letters to the Duke of Wellington. 1812.

Piece 61    Private letters to the Duke of Wellington. 1813.

Pieces 62;  Private letters to the Duke of
63          Wellington. 1814.

Piece 89    Letters to and from the Duke of Wellington. 1814-33.

Mostly correspondence relating to the Peninsular war when the third Earl Bathurst was Secretary of State for War and the Colonies, dealing with a wide range of military matters. The final volume includes miscellaneous letters and papers on political events, including the formation of the Duke's Cabinet in 1828.

48.    Beresford Papers.

Additional Manuscripts

21504    Correspondence with Viscount Wellington, November-December 1811.

36306    Correspondence with Wellington. January 1810-December 1811.

Letters from Wellington on military subjects are mostly in Add Ms 36306 but Add Ms 21504 includes some papers by him on the future of the Portuguese army.

49.    Broughton Papers.

Additional Manuscripts

43750    Diary. March-July 1847.

| 43751 | Diary. | July 1847-March 1848. |
| 43752 | Diary. | March-July 1848. |
| 43753 | Diary. | July 1848-April 1849. |
| 43754 | Diary. | March-September 1850. |
| 43755 | Diary. | September 1850-May 1851. |
| 43756 | Diary. | May 1851-April 1852. |
| 43757 | Diary. | April 1852-May 1853. |

Valuable diary of the Russell Cabinet, from 1847 to 1852, reflecting the Duke's relationship with it, especially in matters relating to the national defences and India.

50.      Croker Papers.

Additional Manuscripts

38078      Letters from Wellington, April 1832 -
            September 1852.

38079      Memorandum by Wellington on Ireland,
            c. 1807.

Correspondence covering a wide range of subjects, both political and personal, over the last twenty years of the Duke's life.  Many have been published.

51.      Dropmore Papers.

Additional Manuscripts

58988      Correspondence with Wellington, 1806-14.

Includes some early letters from Wellington, asking Lord Grenville for a job and memoranda relating to a proposed attack on Spain's Latin American colonies in 1807.

52.      Gladstone Papers.

Additional Manuscripts

44363      General correspondence, December 1845-
            March 1846.

44364      General Correspondence, April-August
            1846.

Correspondence on military arrangements, dating from Gladstone's term of office as Secretary of State for War and the Colonies.  There are a few letters in the Gladstone papers pre- and post-dating these papers, but Wellington and the young Gladstone were not close colleagues.

53.     Goderich Papers.

        Additional Manuscripts.

        40862     General correspondence to 1832.

        40863     General correspondence 1832-1842.

        40864     General correspondence January-May 1843.

        40865     General correspondence June-September 1843.

        40866     General correspondence October-December 1843.

        40867     General correspondence January-March 1844.

        40868     General correspondence April-June 1844.

        40869     General correspondence July-October 1844.

        40870     General correspondence November-December 1844.

        40871     General correspondence January-March 1845.

        40872     General correspondence April-June 1845.

        40873     General correspondence July-September 1845.

        40874     General correspondence October-December 1845.

        40875     General correspondence January-March 1846.

        40876     General correspondence April-May 1846.

        40877     General correspondence June 1846-February 1851.

        Includes some papers relating to Goderich's ill-fated Premiership, but most letters date from the period between May 1843 and June 1846, when Goderich was President of the Board of Control, and deal with Indian affairs.

54.     Herries Papers.

        Additional Manuscripts

57368        Correspondence with Wellington, 1812-52.

Comprises letters from the Duke and draft replies on military, political and private subjects.

55.      Hill Papers

Additional Manuscripts

35059        Military correspondence 1801-1812.

35060        Military correspondence 1812-1842.

Includes over 130 letters from the Duke down to March 1812 and some thereafter, detailing the Duke's relationship with his most eminent divisional commander in the Peninsula and, from 1828 to 1842, his successor as Commander-in-Chief of the army.

56.      Huskisson Papers

Additional Manuscripts

38749        General correspondence February-June 1827

38751        General correspondence, September-October 1827

38754        General correspondence January 1828.

38755        General correspondence February-March 1828.

38756        General correspondence April-June 1828.

Significant letters from the Duke in this collection cover the formation of his administration in January 1828, and Huskisson's subsequent resignation and its consequences.

57.      Liverpool Papers

Additional Manuscripts

38196        Correspondence with Wellington, 1807-40

Loan 72

19        Correspondence with Wellington, 1807-8.

20        Correspondence with Wellington, 1809-10

21        Correspondence with Wellington, 1811-14

22        Correspondence with Wellington, 1813-15; 1818.

23          Correspondence with Wellington, 1821-45.

Mostly letters form and to the Duke by the Second Earl
of Liverpool, from 1807 to 1809 Home Secretary; from 1809
to 1812 Secretary of State for War and the Colonies, and
thereafter Prime Minister until 1827. This correspondence
opens with letters and papers on Ireland when Wellington was
Chief Secretary, and continues with much very important
correspondence on the Peninsular war. There are also some
letters on political matters especially the Duke's joining
the Cabinet in 1818-19; the effects of Castlereagh's death
in 1822 and disagreements with Canning in 1826-7.

58.     Melbourne Papers.

Microfilm 859
Reel 8     Correspondence 1837-1840.

Includes correspondence with Wellington, and letters
between the Duke and Lord Howick (later third Earl Grey)
on the question of war office reform, 1836-40. The original
papers are in the Royal Archives at Windsor Castle.

59.     Melville Papers.

Additional Manuscripts

41084     Correspondence 1812-1838.

Includes a series of letters from the Duke to the
Second Viscount Melville, relating mostly to naval affairs.
Melville served as First Lord of the Admiralty between 1812
and 1827 and was President of the Board of Control, and
afterwards First Lord of the Admiralty, in Wellington's
Ministry.

60.     Peel Papers.

Additional Manuscripts

40306     Correspondence with Wellington, January
          1822-1827.

40307     Correspondence with Wellington, January-
          September 1828.

40308     Correspondence with Wellington, October-
          December 1829

40309     Correspondence with Wellington, January
          1830-April 1834.

40310     Correspondence with Wellington, January
          1835-April 1841.

40459     Correspondence with Wellington, May 1841-

                                    1842.

         40460            Correspondence with Wellington, 1843-44.

         40461            Correspondence with Wellington, 1845-
                          September 1846.

        An important collection of manuscripts, covering all
aspects of Wellington's political career and his relations
with Peel, from Peel's appointment as Home Secretary in
1822.  Peel remained Home Secretary until he resigned, with
Wellington, in April 1827.  He then served as Wellington's
Home Secretary between 1828 and 1830, while the Duke was
in Peel's Cabinets of 1834-5 (as Foreign Secretary) and
1841-6 (without office).  Peel was the greatest influence
on the Duke's later political career, and these letters are
central to an understanding of conservative party politics
at this time.

61.      Willoughby Gordon Papers.

         Additional Manuscripts

         49481            Correspondence with Wellington, 1807-
                          1839.

        Includes personal and official letters from the Duke,
mostly relating to Ireland (1807-8) and Portugal (1808-9).
Deal mostly with pensions, appointments and Commissariat
matters.

62.      Marquess Wellesley Papers

         Additional Manuscripts

         13669-13674      Papers relating to the Commission
                          on the Affairs of Mysore, 1799.

         13772-13778      Papers relating to Indian affairs,
                          1800-1804.

         37286-37288      Papers as Ambassador Extraordinary
                          to Spain, 1809

         37292            Correspondence as Foreign Secretary
                          1810-11.

         37304            Correspondence with Wellington and
                          Lord Liverpool. 1826.

         37307            Correspondence with Wellington,
                          1834-5.

         37415            Private correspondence with
                          Wellington and Lord Cowley, 1806-42.

The main collection of Marquess Wellesley's papers, including correspondence with Wellington throughout his official career, beginning in India and the Peninsula. Later papers cover the Duke's political career. The private letters include not only letters from Wellington, but also from other members of the Wellesley family.

British Library - India Office Library and Records, 197 Blackfriars Road, London, SE1 8NG.

63.     Major General George Scott Papers

Mss Eur. D 828   Correspondence. 1801-4.

Correspondence respecting the administration of the gun carriage factory at Seringapatam.

64.     Wellesley Papers.

Home Miscellaneous series.

Scattered letters from and to the Duke, dating from 1803 to 1805.

Cefntilla Court, Usk, Gwent (Lord Raglan).

65.     Raglan Papers.

Boxes 1 & 2     Secretary of Embassy in France, July 1815-December 1818.

Box 3     Correspondence. Military Secretary to the Commander-in-Chief

Bundle A     Letters from Wellington to William Wellesley-Pole, 1807-17.

Bundle B     Copies of letters from William Wellesley-Pole to Wellington, 1808-14.

Boxes 1 and 2 contain thirty-nine letters from the Duke when Commander-in-Chief in France and Box 3 thirty-seven letters from Wellington as Commander-in-Chief. These deal with general military arrangements.

Wellington's correspondence with his brother William Wellesley-Pole, third Earl of Mornington, comprises eighty-nine letters from and thirty-nine copies of letters to, the Duke, dealing with personal and family matters, as well as more public events relating to the Duke's campaigns.

Cleveland Public Library, 325 Superior Avenue, Cleveland, Ohio 44114, U.S.A.

66.     John G. White Collection.

"Documents relating to the history of British India."

Includes sixteen letters from Wellington to Lieutenant General James Stewart dating from 1802-3, and dealing with miscellaneous military matters.

Clwyd Record Office, The Old Rectory, Hawarden, Deeside, CH5 3NR.

67.    Peel of Bryn-y-Pys Manuscripts

Includes twenty-eight letters from the Duke, dated between 1824 and 1846, to Charlotte, Duchess of Northumberland, mostly of a social nature, with occasional political comment.

Devon Record Office, Castle Street, Exeter, EX4 3PU.

68.    Sidmouth Papers

C1820/OM          Correspondence. 1819-33.

Correspondence from Wellington as Master General of the Ordnance to Sidmouth, the Home Secretary, dealing with the militia and Ordnance Department matters.

Durham County Record Office, County Hall, Durham DH1 5UL.

69.    Londonderry Papers

D/LO/C 113        Correspondence with Wellington, 1809-27.

D/LO/C 122        Letters on the death of Canning and Goderich's government, 1827-8.

D/LO/C 123        Letters on Catholic emancipation 1828-9.

D/LO/C 127        Letters on Wellington's resignation 1830.

D/LO/C 129        Letters on the Wellington memorial. 1838-47.

Military and political letters and papers of the third Marquess of Londonderry, an high Tory colleague and, later, political opponent of the Duke. Comprises some 400 letters, half from the period before 1827 and the remainder after that date.

Durham University Library, Department of Special
Collections, Palace Green, Durham, DH1 3RN.

70.      Grey Papers

The papers of the third Earl Grey contain 100 letters
to, and ninety from, the Duke, on subjects of mutual
official interest, especially army reform.  Grey was
Secretary for War and the Colonies between 1846 and 1852 and
a keen army reformer, and frequently crossed swords with
Wellington on this question.  The letters mostly date from
1839 to 1852. (See also Melbourne Papers).

Gloucestershire Record Office, Clarence Row off
Alwin Street, Gloucester, GL1 3RN.

71.      Redesdale Papers

D. 2002 C. 39    Correspondence with Wellington,
[Microfilm       1840-51.
361/3]

Forty-one letters from the Duke and eight draft
replies, on political matters which date from Lord
Redesdale's time as Conservative chief whip in the House of
Lords.

Greater London Record Office, 40 Northampton
Road, London EC1R 0HB.

72.      Sarah, Countess of Jersey Papers

Acc 510.

Includes fifteen miscellaneous letters from the Duke
on political and social matters.

The Huntington Library, 1151 Oxford Road, San
Marino, California 91108, U.S.A.

73.      Beresford Papers

HM21095-21128    Correspondence with Wellington,
                 1809-10.

Thirty-five letters from Viscount Beresford to
Wellington, written between June 1809 and July 1810,
relating to military events during that period.  Beresford
commanded the Portuguese army.

74.      Elrington Papers

Includes over 270 letters from Wellington as
Constable of the Tower of London, to his deputy, Tower Major
J.H. Elrington, dating from 1827 to 1849.  Included in this
collection are two manuscript articles relating to

Wellington as Constable of the Tower: "The Duke, the Tower and the Beefeaters" by Frank B. Maggs and "The Duke and the Beefeaters" by Ralph Partridge.

75.      Stowe Collection.

         Grenville Family Papers - General Correspondence.

     Includes a series of letters from Wellington to the first and second Dukes of Buckingham and Chandos, dating from the 1820s and 1830s, covering a wide range of political and social matters.

         The Institution of Civil Engineers, 1-7 Great George Street, Westminster, SW1P 3AA.

76.      James Walker Papers

         627.2           "Wellington Letters and Notes from the Duke to James Walker and Memoranda of Observations by his Grace."

     Papers dating from the 1840s and mostly relating to the defence of the Channel Islands.  Walker was civil engineer in charge of the building of the Harbours of Refuge in the Islands and the Duke was keenly interested in their progress.

         Kent Archives Office, County Hall, Maidstone, ME14 1XQ.

77.      Pratt Manuscripts

         C 266       Letters of Wellington to the first and second Marquesses Camden. 1795-6; 1828-45.

     Includes some very early letters from Wellington to the first Marquess Camden about Wellington's leaving Ireland and some later letters on general social and political matters to the second Marquess.

78.      Stanhope of Chevening Manuscripts

         C407/1-20   Papers relating to the Duke of Wellington, 1829-66.

         C408/1-11   "Notes on Conversations with the Duke of Wellington."

         C409        Another draft of "Notes ..."

         C410        Memorandum by Wellington on the Defence of Canada. 1841.

C411          Lithographed form letters from the Duke.

Includes a variety of original letters and copies of
papers by the Duke on various political matters; papers
relating to the Duke, including stories about his father
by the second Duke; tickets for Wellington's funeral; a lock
of his hair and two drafts of Stanhope's book "Notes on
Conversations with the Duke of Wellington" eventually
published in 1888.

> Lincolnshire Archives Office, The Castle,
> Lincoln, LN1 3AB.

79.    Revesby Abbey Papers.

R.A. 4/A/2    Letters to Emily, Viscountess Mahon,
              (later Countess Stanhope), 1836-51.

Eighty-four letters from the Duke, mostly of a social
nature, and detailing some of his problems with charitable
requests.

> Liverpool Record Office and Local History
> Department, City Libraries, William Brown Street,
> Liverpool, L3 8EW.

80.    Derby Papers.

Box 27/5    Miscellaneous Memoranda by Wellington.
            1845.

Box 42/1    Papers respecting Wellington's funeral.

Box 123/2   Correspondence with Wellington, 1838-
            1852.

Letters dealing mostly with political and military
matters, and some more personal papers, at least until the
Duke's personal and political estrangement from Lord Derby
in 1846.  Derby was Prime Minister at the time of the
Duke's death and burial.

> McGill University Library, Department of Rare
> Books and Special Collections, 3459 McTavish
> Street, Montreal, P.Q., Canada, H3A 1Y1.

81.    Hardinge Papers.

Includes letters to and from the Duke, dating from
1808 to 1851.  The bulk of the letters date from the
Peninsular war, but Hardinge was a political colleague of
the Duke in 1828-30, and there was some general correspondence between the two men thereafter.

National Army Museum, Department of Records,
Royal Hospital Road, London SW3 4HT.

82.      D'Urban Papers.

Loan 6502.

Includes memoranda by Wellington on the seige of
Badajoz in 1812; letters from the Duke on the 1812 campaign
and one letter from him, in Portuguese, on handing over
command of the Portuguese army in May 1814.

83.      Sir Frederick Maitland Papers.

7902-13

Pieces 197-201   Correspondence with Wellington.
1812.

Piece 202        Letter Book. 1827-46.

The letters from 1812 relate to the war in Spain and
Maitland's war in Sicily. The letter book includes forty-
three notes from the Duke "mostly of a social nature".

National Library of Ireland, Kildare Street,
Dublin 2, Eire.

84.      Maurice Fitzgerald Papers.

Mss 2077   Correspondence with Wellington, 1796-
1849.

Primarily letters and papers on political subjects
dating from 1824-49.  Some personal letters are included.
Xerox copies of these papers are held at the Public Record
Office of Northern Ireland, Belfast (reference T3075/1-95).

National Library of Scotland, Department of
Manuscripts, George IV Bridge, Edinburgh,
EH1 1EW.

85.      Lynedoch Papers

Ms 3863   Letters from Wellington, 1810-1813.

Letters from Wellington to one of his divisional
commanders, Sir Thomas Graham, on military operations in the
Peninsula.  There are some miscellaneous letters in the
main body of the correspondence (Ms 3606-12; 3615-21) dating
from 1810 to 1836.

86.      Sir George Murray Papers.

Adv. Ms 46

46.1.22 -46.4.9.       Papers relating to the
                       Peninsular War, 1807-14.

46.6.7. - 46.7.13;     Papers as Chief of Staff of
46.7.23. - 46.8.1.     the Allied Army of Occupation
                       in France 1815-18.

46.8.12 - 46.8.15      Letter Books. Colonial Office.
                       1828-30.

46.8.16. - 46.9.19.    Letters Books. Ordnance. 1841-
                       45.

Murray was Wellington's effective chief of staff in
the Peninsula as well as in France after the battle of
Waterloo, and this is reflected in his papers.  Murray was
also a close political colleague of the Duke, acting as
Colonial Secretary after Charles Grant's resignation in 1828.
During Peel's second Ministry Murray was Master General of
the Ordnance and was responsible for home defence (see under
Public Record Office).

          National Library of Wales, Department of
          Manuscripts and Records, Aberystwyth, SY23 3BU.

87.       Aston Hall Correspondence.

          1099-1104; 6818-6844 Correspondence of William
                       and Louisa Lloyd of Aston Hall
                       1815-39.
     A series of letters of a social nature from Wellington
to Louisa Lloyd.

88.       Powis Castle Archives.

     Includes twelve letters from Wellington to the Earl of
Powis (with five replies) and two letters to Rev. R.W.
Huntley (with replies), dating from May 1844 to May 1846,
and concerned with ecclesiastical matters - the proposed
separation of the Dioceses of St. Asaph and Bangor.

          National Register of Archives (Scotland),
          HM General Register House, Edinburgh, EH1 3YY.

89.       Viscount Colville of Culross Muniments.

     Includes among the papers of General Sir Charles
Colville, a divisional commander in the Peninsula, a series
of private letters from Wellington from 1810 to 1843, and
offiical returns, orders and other papers on the Peninsula
campaign from 1810 to 1830.

Nottingham University Library, Manuscripts
Department, University Park, Nottingham, NG7 2RD

90.      Cavendish Bentinck Papers.

PWJD 5346-5408          Correspondence. Wellington
                        and Lord William Bentinck,
                        1811-14.

Some sixty-three pieces, concerning intelligence
relating to the Peninsular war. Lord William was Ambassador
to the Sicilian Court, and well placed to provide the Duke
with information.

91.      Newcastle Papers.

Ne. C. 5052-5072         Correspondence. 1839.

Ne. C. 5290-5328         Correspondence with Wellington
                        1825-40.

The 1839 correspondence concerns the Fourth Duke of
Newcastle's dismissal as Lord Lieutenant of Nottinghamshire;
the general correspondence contains thirty-nine letters
from, and draft replies to, Wellington, on political matters.
Newcastle was an Ultra-Tory.

Plas Newydd, Llanfairpwull, Isle of Anglesey,
LL61 6DZ (The Marquess of Anglesey).

92.      First Marquess of Anglesey Papers.

Includes papers on military subjects, dating from
1824-5 and the 1840s, the latter including copies of
Wellington's correspondence with Sir Robert Peel on the
national defences.

Public Record Office, Ruskin Avenue, Kew,
Richmond, Surrey, TW9 4DU.

93.      Colchester Papers.

PRO30/9/4/1             Correspondence of the First
                        Earl of Ellenborough, the
                        Duke of Wellington etc.,
                        1828-30.

One bundle, dealing mainly with Indian affairs during
the Duke's administration.

94.      Cowley Papers

FO 519

FO 519/33               Letters to Wellington, March-
                        May 1810.

FO 519/34          Letters to Wellington, June-August
                   1810.

Two volumes of "very faded" letters to Wellington
from his younger brother, Henry Wellesley, mostly relating
to the Peninsular war.

95.       Ellenborough Papers.

          PRO 30/12/5/1    Letters to Wellington. 1846.

          PRO 30/12/6/6    General correspondence, 1835-52.

          PRO 30/12/21/9   Correspondence with Wellington,
                           1828-52.

          PRO 30/12/28/13  General correspondence, 1841-44.

          PRO 30/12/29/5   Correspondence with Wellington,
                           1834-5.

          PRO 30/12/37     In Letters. India. 1841-44.

          PRO 30/12/89     Out Letters. India. 1842-44.

Includes official and private correspondence between
the first Earl of Ellenborough and Wellington, mostly
relating to India, when Ellenborough was Governor-General
(1841-44) and also to naval affairs when Ellenborough was
First Lord of the Admiralty (1845-6). Also includes
letters on a wide range of political questions, as well as
more personal material.

96.       Murray Papers.

          WO 80/2          Correspondence with Wellington,
                           1824-45.

          WO 80/8          Correspondence with Wellington,
                           1844-5.

          WO 80/9          Ordnance Papers. 1836-48.

          WO 80/11         Correspondence respecting Canada,
                           1815-46.

          WO 80/13         Miscellanea.

The second half of Murray's papers (see the National
Library of Scotland). Includes many papers from the Duke on
various questions relating to the national defences in the
mid-1840s, when he was Commander-in-Chief and Murray was
Master General of the Ordnance. Also includes the Duke's
views on the defence of Canada and drafts of Murray's
replies to his observations.

97.          Russell Papers.

          PRO 30/22/5A-G     General correspondence. 1846.

          PRO 30/22/6B-F     General correspondence. 1847.

          PRO 30/22/7A-F     General correspondence. 1848-9

          PRO 30/22/8A-E     General correspondence. 1849-
                             50

          PRO 30/22/9C-H     General correspondence. 1851

          PRO 30/22/10A-B    General correspondence. 1852

     Numerous letters from the Duke during Russell's first
premiership.  A wide variety of subjects is covered,
especially relating to national defence and other military
questions, and the preparations for the Great Exhibition.

          Public Record Office of Northern Ireland, 66
          Balmoral Avenue, Belfast, BT9 6NY.

98.     First Marquess of Anglesey Papers.

          D619/26    Correspondence as Lord Lieutenant of
                     Ireland. 1828-9.

     Some forty letters from Wellington relating to Irish
affairs.

99.     Londonderry Papers.

          D3030      Correspondence with the Duke of
                     Wellington (1805-21) and others.

     A chronologically arranged collection.  The main body
of the correspondence includes many letters from Wellington
to Lord Castlereagh, afterwards second Marquess of Londonderry.  Wellington was a close friend and political
colleague of Castlereagh and this is reflected in the
correspondence.  There are also a few letters from the Duke
in the collection of Castlereagh's brother, the third
Marquess of Londonderry (see also Durham County Record
Office).

          Royal Archives, Windsor Castle, Berkshire.

100.      Queen Victoria Papers.

          R.A. E1    "Army. 1848. 1852"

          R.A. E42/1 "National Defences, 1847-8".

     Includes letters from the Duke, primarily on the
administration of the army and on the question of home

defence.   These papers are only open to established scholars.

    John Rylands University Library of Manchester,
    Deansgate, Manchester, M3 3EH.

101.   Sir Henry Clinton Papers.

   A collection of thirty-nine letters from Wellington
to General Sir Henry Clinton, mostly dating from 1812 and
relating to the Peninsular war.

    St. John's College, Oxford, OX1 3JP.

102.   Philip Wynter Papers.

    Ms Dep. d. 4   Correspondence with
            Wellington, 1841-44.

   Letters from, and draft replies to, the Duke on
University matters, dating from Wynter's time as Vice-
Chancellor of the University.

    Sheffield Record Office, Surrey Street,
    Sheffield, S1 1XZ

103.   Wharncliffe Papers.

    WhM516 General correspondence.

    WhM516 Correspondence from Wellington, 1831-2
    (d)

    WhM516 Letters from Wellington, 1820, 1836-44.
    (h)

   Includes a series of miscellaneous general correspondence with Wellington between 1830 and 1834, as well as
other letters from him, dealing with parliamentary reform
and other political matters.   The reform letters were all
published by the second Duke of Wellington.

    Shetland Library, Archives Section, Lower
    Hillhead, Lerwick, ZE1 0EL

104.   Edmonston of Buness Papers.

   A series of personal and private correspondence
between the Duke and Thomas Edmonston of Buness, dating
from 1829 to the Duke's death in 1852.

    Slane Castle, Slane, County Meath, Eire
    (The Earl of Mount Charles).

105.   Conyngham Papers.

   Includes twenty-two letters of a private nature to

the first Marquess Conyngham and his wife, and to the
second Marquess, dating from 1817 to 1838.

>            Southampton University Library, Highfield,
>            Southampton, SO9 4XR

106.      Broadlands Papers.

>    GC/WE/28-46;    Letters from Wellington, 1820-41.
>    49-53.

>    GC/WE/54-59.    Letters to Wellington, 1820-8.

The correspondence relating to military arrangements,
dates mostly from 1820 to 1828, when Palmerston was
Secretary at War, and ends almost completely with his
resignation from Wellington's Cabinet in May 1828.

107.      Carver Manuscripts.

>    Section 36.     Letters of Wellington to Richard
>                    Wellesley 'II', 1819-29.

>    Sections 43,    Letters of Wellington to Mrs. Jane
>    64-66.          Wellesley, 1830-50.

>    Section 99      Copy of "Observations on the
>                    Convention of Cintra by Sir Arthur
>                    Wellesley. 1809."

>    Section 115     Transcripts of correspondence
>                    between Marquess Wellesley and Sir
>                    Arthur Wellesley, 1805-8 [British
>                    Library Additional Manuscript
>                    37286]

A series of letters, mostly private and personal, to
Wellington's nephew, Richard Wellesley, and his wife.

>            Suffolk Record Office, County Hall, Ipswich,
>            IP4 2JS.

108.      Bunbury Family Papers.

>    E18/740.

>    Bundle 131.     Letters from the Peninsular, 1811-
>                    13.

>    Bundle 135.     Letters from the Low Countries,
>                    1815.

Includes letters from the Duke adding some information
respecting the Peninsular and Waterloo campaigns.

Surrey Record Office, County Hall, Penrhyn Road,
Kingston-upon-Thames, KT1 2DN.

109.    Goulburn Papers.

Includes letters from the Duke, mostly from 1828, when
Goulburn was Wellington's Chancellor of the Exchequer, but
including some letters from both before and after that
period, down to 1850.  Subjects covered include a wide range
of domestic political questions.

West Sussex Record Office, County Hall,
Chichester, PO19 1RN.

110.    Goodwood Estate Archives.

Includes a volume of correspondence of a personal
nature with Charlotte, Duchess of Richmond, dating from 1809
to 1842 and sixteen letters from Wellington to her son,
and his Peninsular comrade, the fifth Duke, on miscellaneous
matters.  The collection also includes seventy-two letters
from Wellington to Algernon Greville, his Private Secretary
dating from 1829 to 1841.

West Yorkshire Archives, Chapeltown Road,
Sheepscar, Leeds, LS7 3AP.

111.    George Canning Papers.

Bundle 98a.      Includes correspondence between
                 Wellington and Canning, 1814-15.

Bundle 104.      Correspondence. Wellington and
                 Canning. 1822-25.

Bundle 104a.     Correspondence. Wellington and
                 Canning. 1825-27.

Bundle 105.      Additional correspondence.
                 Wellington and Canning. 1821-27.

Bundle 105a.     Additional correspondence.
                 Wellington and Canning. 1816-27.

Correspondence relating to both foreign affairs during
Canning's tenure of office as Foreign Secretary, and on
domestic affairs, including the formation of Canning's
Ministry and the Duke's resignation in 1827.

# Section D
# Other Published Papers
## (i) Official Papers

112.   "Abstract of Parliamentary Proceedings connected
with the army and navy." <u>United Service Journal</u>,
10 (1833): 270-82.
  Extracts from the Select Committee on appointments
(1833) with a letter from Wellington to Lord Hill of 7
March 1833, complaining about it and defending purchase and
the royal appointment of officers as just and necessary.

113.   <u>"Dispatches have been received from the Marquess
of Wellington, dated Ostiq, the 3d July ..."</u>
London, [1813].
  A broad sheet digest of allied operations in the
Peninsula at the end of June 1813, issued by the War Office
on 19 July.

114.   <u>Instructions given to the Duke of Wellington, on
Proceeding to St. Petersburg, in February 1826.</u>
[London, 1826].
  A confidential document printed for the use of the
Cabinet, comprising a long letter from the Foreign Secretary,
George Canning, to the Duke, respecting his policy toward
Russia and Turkey over the Greek revolt.  This is supported
by despatches to and from British diplomats, and various
papers on the Greek question and Stratford Canning's mission
to Greece.

115.   <u>[Lord Wellington's Circular Letter to commanding
officers on regimental discipline, 28th Nov. 1812].</u>
[Frenada, 1812].
  A copy of Wellington's notorious General Order issued
to officers commanding Brigades after the retreat from
Burgos, complaining of indiscipline in the army and outlining specific measures to prevent it.

116.   [Stockdale, J.J., ed.], <u>A narrative of the
Campaign which preceded the Convention of Cintra in
Portugal to which is annexed the report from the
Board of Enquiry to the King.</u>  London, 1809.
  Includes maps of operations in Portugal, Wellington's

despatches on the subject, his submission, taken verbatim, to the Board of Enquiry, and the final Report of the Board.

117.  Wellington, Duke of, Marquess of Dalhousie, and Sir Charles Napier, <u>Minutes on the Resignation of the Late General Sir Charles Napier of the Command of the Army in India</u>. London, 1854.
Wellington's memorandum of 30 July 1850 is one of several reprinted. He concludes Napier made mistakes in dealing with a "mutiny" at "Weizeerabad", the Governor-General was right to censure him, and his resignation must be accepted.

118.  <u>The Whole Proceedings of the Court of Enquiry upon the Conduct of Sir Hew Dalrymple, late Commander-in-Chief of his Majesty's forces in Portugal, relative to the Convention of Cintra ... with an introductory account of the Campaign</u>. London, 1808.
Includes a brief introductory account of the campaign and a verbatim report of the ten days' public proceedings in the "Great Hall of Chelsea College".

# (ii) Parliamentary Debates

119. The most convenient reference to Wellington's Parlia-
mentary speeches from 1792, when he entered the Irish
House of Commons, to 1852, is the compilation by Lieutenant
Colonel Gurwood and W. Hazlitt, completed in 1854 [19].

This collection is complete for the Duke's major
speeches, but others are not noted; equally little is said
about the context of the speech.  Consequently, the best way
to see Wellington's contribution to Parliamentary debates,
at least between 1806 and 1852, is to consult the reports
published by T.C. Hansard (and others).

Wellington's official career spans part of three
series of Hansard's Parliamentary debates:

> The Parliamentary Debates from the Year 1803 to
> the Present Time  40 vols., London, 1812-19 .

> The Parliamentary Debates. New Series:
> commencing with the accession of George IV. 25
> vols., London, 1820-30.

> Hansard's Parliamentary Debates: forming a
> continuation of "The Parliamentary History of
> England from the Earliest Period to the year 1803".
> Third Series: commencing with the accession of
> William IV.  350 vols., London, 1831-91.

The reliability of these series as a verbatim record
increases as time passes.

The following list includes all speeches made by the
Duke of more than one column in length: other, brief,
comments by Wellington have not been included.

In each case the subject of the speech is given,
followed by the date, the volume number and columns
occupied and a brief resume of the argument.  Speeches on the

same subject are listed together.

### 1806

Lord Wellesley's conduct. 22 April [6, 863-4].  28 April. [945].  A defence of Wellington's brother's - and his own - conduct.

Indian Budget.  10 June [6, 1060-82].  Requested leave to bring in the budget, and defended himself against attack. Later published as a pamphlet [See No. 287].

### 1808

Copenhagen expedition.  1 February [10, 192-3]. Reply to a vote of thanks.

Irish expenses.  28 March [10, 1275-8]. Defence of expenses incurred by his administration.

### 1809

Duke of York's administration of the army.  27 January [12, 188-90], 22 February [1030-31]. Defence of the Duke of York's conduct as Commander-in-Chief.

Irish Militia Bill.  6 February [12, 365-6]. Introduced the Bill.

Personal conduct.  6 February [12, 369-70]. Defended himself for having occupied a civil and military post simultaneously (as Commander in Portugal and Chief Secretary for Ireland).

Convention of Cintra.  21 February [12, 928-36]. Defence of the signature of the Convention.

Inland Navigation (Ireland).  28 March [13, 489-90]. Introduced the Bill to encourage it.

### 1814

Vote of thanks. 1 July 1814 [28, 489-90]. Returned the thanks of the House of Commons for his military services.

### 1819

Roman Catholic Relief.  5 May [40, 115-6], 17 May [446-48]. Presented a petition against Catholic emancipation (5 May) and spoke and voted against an Emancipation Bill.

### 1822

Law and Order, Ireland. 9 February [New series, 6, 208-9]. Speech in favour of severe measures to keep the peace.

1823

Congress of Verona. 24 April [8, 1222-27]. Defence of his, and the government's, conduct at the Congress.

1825

Spring Guns. 7 March [12, 937-38]. Speech against a Bill outlawing spring guns to protect game.

1827

Resignation from Canning's Ministry. 2 May [17, 454-67]. Justification of his resignation, including extracts from correspondence on the subject.

Vote of Thanks. Indian army. 14 May [17, 770-71]. Supported the vote.

Corn Laws. 12 June [17, 1229-31]. Opposed to changes in the law.

Warehoused Corn Bill. 25 June [17, 1384-91]. Opposed to Bill. Speech included quotations from correspondence with Huskisson.

1828

Address from the Throne. 29 January [18, 25-27]. Explained his government's policy respecting corn, and tried to explain away the King's reference to the battle of Navarino as an "untoward event".

Foreign Policy. 11 February [18, 285-92], 16 July [19, 1733-38]. Defence of the government's Near Eastern policy.

Corn Law. 31 March [17, 1364-70]. Introduced a new measure.

Repeal of Test and Corporation Acts. 17 April [18, 1502-5], 21 April [1583-84], 28 April [19, 167-8, 178]. Speeches in favour of repeal as an act of social justice.

State of Ireland. 1 May [19, 257-59]. Declared that the situation was not as bad as some people claimed.

Pensions Act Amendment. 6 June [19, 1100-02]. In favour of it, to give relief to Canning's family.

Roman Catholic Relief Bill. 10 June [19, 1286-92]. Opposed measure: "securities" were required from Ireland first.

West Indian Slavery. 23 June [19, 1465-67]. In favour of gradual abolition.

Scotch Small Notes Bill. 3 July [19, 1597-99, 1605]. In favour: the Bill would prevent small Scottish banknotes circulating in London.

1829

Address from the Throne. 5 February. [20, 13-15, 39-41].
Government would introduce a Catholic Emancipation Bill.

Roman Catholic Claims. 10 February [20, 166-69]. Must
grant concessions. 2 March [641-43] 10 March [935-37], 13
March [1042-44], 16 March [1074-76] - defence of the
government against Ultra Tory attacks. Bill introduced on
31 March [21, 1, 5-6]; 2 April [41-58], 3 April [226], 4
April [389-92], 6 April [407-10, 439-40] - in favour of
second reading; 7 April [481-83] - on committee stage; 10
April [688-94] third reading: defence of his conduct. Bill
passed.

Associations Suppression (Ireland) Bill. 19 February [20,
388-95], 24 February [515-17]. In favour - a matter not
connected with Catholic relief.

Coal Trade. 24 March [20, 1411-12]. Sounded a note of
caution respecting alterations in coal import duties.

Qualification of Freeholders (Ireland) Bill. 6 April [21,
407-10, 439-40] 9 April [588]. Favoured the measure which
would regularise the registration of Irish freeholders
qualified to vote.

Militia Staff Reductions. 7 April [21, 467-68]. In favour.

Release of Eneas MacDonnell. 13 April [21, 731-33].
Defended this action, on the grounds of the prisoner's ill-
health.

Recall of Lord Anglesey. 4 May [21, 1021-30]. Defended his
decision to recall Anglesey from Ireland. Included a copy
of the letter of recall.

Corporation of London petition. 25 May [21, 1567-64].
Against import duties. Opposed to it, as an attack on
Parliamentary privilege.

Metropolitan Police Bill. 5 June [21, 1750-52]. In favour
of the second reading.

Foreign relations. 19 June [21, 1805-12]. Defence of the
government's conduct respecting Portugal.

1830

Address from the Throne. 4 February [22, 34-41]. Proposed
address to the Crown, stressing the country's prosperity.

East India Company. 9 February [22, 257-58]. Defence of

the government's conduct towards the company.

Greece. 12 February [22, 419-24]. Defence of government's policy.

"The state of the nation". 25 February [22, 937-39], 18 March [23, 528-33], 13 May [24, 662-64]. Defence of the government's conduct. The government was taking steps to alleviate distress, which was lessening.

"Affair at Terceira". 23 March [23, 766-72]. The government was right not to prevent the Portuguese government from landing trops there: it would have been against the law of nations.

Lord King's motion, Corn Laws. 29 March [23, 981-85]. Against the motion calling for easing of restrictions on the import of corn.

National Debt. 6 May [24, 441-42]. The government was trying to reduce the national debt.

King's Illness; Royal Accession. 24 May [24, 986-88], 27 May [1134-35], 19 June [25, 707-10], 30 June [724-26]. Speeches on various arrangements necessitated by the illness and death of George IV and the accession of William IV.

Revenue. 8 July [25, 1220-22]. Surplus would be smaller than hoped.

East Retford Disfranchisement Bill. 20 July [25, 1272-73]. Expressed regret at the introduction of this measure, but the Lords' duty was to pass it.

Speech from the Throne. 2 November [Third series, 1, 44-53] A review of the government's conduct and aims, including the famous declaration against the reform of Parliament.

Royal Visit to the City of London. 8 November [1, 250-53, 260-61], 11 November [366-70]. Ineffective defence of the decision to advise the King not to attend a dinner in the City.

Resignation. 16 November [1, 558-59]. Very brief statement: because of an adverse vote in the House of Commons.

Arson. 29 November. [1, 683-84]. Attacks were the work of British, not foreign, criminals.

Distress. 10 December [1, 958-59; 960; 962-63]. Admitted the existence of distress, and need for cuts in government expenditure.

New government. 13 December [1, 1030-38]. Attack on the Whig government appointments.

1831

Portuguese Commercial Treaty. 21 February [2, 770-72].
Criticised the Treaty for sacrificing Britain's large
Portuguese trade in favour of the small amount of trade with
France.

Government policy. 24 March [3, 854-55]. The government was
too radical, and would cause a revolution.

Parliamentary Reform. 28 March [3, 1064-73], 14 April
[1321-22]. Strongly opposed to the Reform Bill, which was
unnecessary. 4 October [7, 1186-1205], 5 October [1327-28].
Reform was opposed by the country. 7 October [8, 338-39]
Voted against the second reading. The speech of 4 October
was later published as a pamphlet. [see No. 284].

Civil List. 19 April [3, 1594-97]. Objection to the
reductions proposed.

Foreign Policy. 24 June [4, 316-19]. Stressed the need to
act cordially with France over Belgian and Portuguese
questions.

Mr. Michael Stokes. 4 July [4, 640-41]. This man was a
perjurer, and should not be a magistrate.

Irish County Lieutenants. 4 July [4, 645-46], 7 July [948-
50]. Argued they should be military men, but supported the
government's proposals.

Belgian revolution. 26 July [5, 317-22]. Argued for the
retention of the barrier fortresses. 9 August [5, 1000-04].
Complained that Britain had abandoned her old allies, the
Netherlands. 29 August [6, 746-49]. Conceded that if the
Dutch withdrew, the French would, too. 29 September [7,
807-10]. On the danger of French influence in Belgium.

Portuguese affairs. 5 August [5, 808-11]. Portugal must be
ruled by those friendly to Britain. 5 September [6, 1116-
21], 19 September [7, 117-19]. French influence in Portugal
was increasing and had to be countered.

Coal Duties Bill. 11 August [5, 1175-77, 1179]. Not much in
favour of the Bill, but would have to vote in favour of it.

Wine Duties Bill. 30 September [7, 873-75]. Pleased to
support this, which would help Anglo-Portuguese relations.

Conduct of the Bishops. 11 October [8, 479-80]. Defence of
the Bishops in the House of Lords, in daring to defy the
government.

Galway Franchise Bill. 13 October [8, 680-81]. No need for
this Bill.

Consolidated Fund. 17 October [8, 836-43]. Warned the
government to act on the economy, which was "falling into
confusion".

1832

Belgian affairs. 26 January [9, 874-84]. Further object-
ions to the British government's treatment of the King of
Holland. 16 March [9, 302-09, 314-15]. A warning against
French activities in Belgium.

Tithes in Ireland. 27 February [10, 732-33, 735-37].
Clergy of the Church of Ireland deserved protection and
their tithe. 8 March [1294-97, 1305]. Approved of a
Select Committee on Ireland and declared support for the
government's policy toward Ireland - even for commutation of
tithes.

Irish education. 28 February [10, 881-82], 3 July [13,1273-
75]. Disapproved of the government's proposals, because
they were not founded on religion.

Glove making. 9 March [11, 21-22]. Declared that free
trade would never be possible for Britain and hoped help
could be given to distressed glove makers.

Lord Chancellor Eldon. 12 March [11, 103-04]. Defended the
Chancellor's nepotism in regard to law appointments.

Parliamentary Reform. 26 March [11, 869-70]. Questions respecting the government's proposals. 10 April [12, 159-75].
Strong speech against second reading of the Bill. 13 April
[459-62]. Voted against it and entered a protest in the
House of Lords Journal. 7 May [697-99]. In favour of major
amendments to the Bill. (The government resigned on 10 May).

Sacking of the Westmeath Magistrates. 6 April [11, 1323-28]
They should not have been dismissed for doing their duty and
calling out the Yeomanry.

West India Interest. 7 May [12, 697-99]. Expression of
sympathy for the Planters.

Failure to form a Ministry. 17 May [12, 993-99]. An explanation of his failure to form a ministry, following the
resignation of Lord Grey.

State of Ireland. 2 July [13, 1206-12]. Agitators, led by
priests, caused the trouble and firm action was needed.

Irish Reform Bill. 23 July [14, 626-29]. Objected because
an English Bill was not suited to Ireland. 26 July [772],
27 July [821-23]. Further objections to details.

Russo-Dutch Loan Convention. 30 July [14, 906-12]. Regretted
Britain's poor relations with Holland, but ministers needed

Parliamentary approval for the Dutch loan. Approved of the
loan to Russia.

Loan to King of Greece. 13 August [14, 1343-44]. No
objections to the loan, but disapproved of the presence of
French troops in Greece.

Juries (India) Bill. 14 August [14, 1355-56] Strong
opposition because it would allow Indians to judge Britons.

Consolidated Fund Bill. 15 August [14, 1379-82] Used as a
means to attack the government over the British blockade of
the Tagus.

1833

Speech from the Throne. 5 February [15, 122-33]. Strong
attack on the government's foreign (Portuguese) and domestic
(Church reform) policies.

Suppression of Disturbances (Ireland). 15 February [15,
745-48] , 18 February [848-50]. Supported the government's
Coercion Bill but regretted their failure to act sooner.
1 April [16, 1300-02] House of Commons amendments would ruin
the Bill and ought to be rejected.

Juries (Ireland) Bill. 26 April [17, 671-75] In view of
the Coercion Act just passed, this Bill was inappropriate.

Abolition of Slavery. 2 May [17, 837-39], 17 May [1339-41],
30 May [18, 103-04], 4 June [368-70] Presented petitions
against the measure. 25 June [1180-94] Long speech against
abolition, [1228-29] Entered a protest against it in
Journal of the House. 12 August [20, 502-03] Tried, but
failed, to present petition from Jamaica against abolition.
[504-5], 14 August [587-88, 590, 591, 593, 594], 15
August [627-28, 632], 19 August [753-55]. Further
opposition to the Bill in the Committee stage.

Relations with Portugal. 3 June [18, 238-49, 296-98]. Long
review of British policy towards Portugal, calling for
strict neutrality. 30 July [20, 105-07] British blockade,
if it existed, ought to be effective.

Tithes (Ireland). 21 June [18, 1042-46]. Not sure of what
government proposals were, but they seemed unwise. Another
attack on loyal Protestants.

Church Temporalities (Ireland) Bill. 11 July [19, 551-52]
Attempted to present a petition against it, and argued that
the King had to give permission for the Bill to be discussed.
19 July [948-61] Government should conciliate Protestants.
Announced his intention to amend the Bill in Committee.
23 July [1084, 1091-92], 24 July [1156-57] Objections to
detailed clauses of the Bill. 30 July [20, 116-18] Would
now support the amended Bill, to help the Protestant Church

of Ireland.

Revision of the East India Company's Charter. 5 July [19, 196-204]. Opposed to the measure, because the Company was already a perfectly administered organisation. 9 August [20, 442, 444, 446]. Objected to details in the Bill.

1834

Address from the Throne. 4 February [21, 9-16] Critical of the government, which evidently wanted to do nothing on the problems in Europe, or at home, or in Ireland.

Admission of Dissenters to University of Cambridge. 21 March [22, 507-11] Presented a petition in favour, but spoke against it. 21 April [22, 988-89, 993-94] Presented a petition against it. 1 August [25, 832-40]. Declaration against the admission of Dissenters to any University.

Lord Ellenborough and the King of Oude. 5 May [23, 500-02] Attack on Ellenborough for arrogating excessive powers to himself.

Sir John Campbell. 6 May [23, 601-03] Government should rescue this officer from a Portuguese prison.

Church of England. Pluralities and Non Residence. 23 May, [23, 1263-66]. Too late to discuss this measure.

Church of Ireland. Committee of Inquiry. 6 June [24, 293-98]. Opposed the Committee as an attack on the Royal Prerogative, and defended the Church of Ireland.

Captain Aitchison. 24 June [24, 815-17]. This officer should not be reinstated.

Resignation of Earl Grey. 9 July [24, 1319-23]. Sorry for this, and, with so many difficulties, Grey should not have resigned.

Irish Coercion Bill. 17 July [25, 40-44] Renewal of this Bill was immediately necessary. 29 July [665-69]. Should be renewed in its entirety.

Poor Law Amendment Bill. 21 July [25, 268-70]. Pass second reading, and amend in committee.

1835

Address from the Throne. 24 February. [26, 82-87]. Defended himself against charges that he brought about Grey's resignation, and then stood in Melbourne's way.

Ambassador to Russia. 16 March [26, 1006-08]. A defence of his appointment of Lord Londonderry to the post.

Poor Law Amendment Bill. 17 March [26, 1259-60]. Petitions against it should not yet be heard.

Conviction of Steyne for Murder. 31 March [27, 455-56]. Justified.

Resignation of the Ministry. 8 April [27, 974] A brief statement on the resignation of Peel's ministry.

Church of Ireland. 2 June [28, 352-53] Presented a petition. The main problem facing the Church was the failure to pay Tithes. 16 July [662-63, 626-28]. Further defence of the Church of Ireland. 24 August [30, 874-5, 877, 932-34], Proposed amendment to the Tithes and Church (Ireland) Bill. 3 September [1295-96] Pleased the government had decided to drop the measure.

Admission of Dissenters to University. 14 July [29, 529-33] Speech, and vote, against the proposal.

Municipal Corporation Reform. 28 July [29, 1135-36], 30 July [1242-43], 3 August [1419-21]. Pressed for hearing of counsel against the Bill before going into Committee. 12 August [30, 356-61] Would amend the Bill in Committee. 13 August [444-45, 464-65], 14 August [492], 17 August [599-601], 25 August [962-63]. Proposed amendments. 4 September [1363-67] objected to Commons amendments of Lord's amendments to the Bill.

Spain. 26 August [30, 999-1000]. Opposed Don Carlos' decree.

Re-registration (Ireland) Bill. 2 September [30, 1256-57] Opposed it.

1836

Appointment of Borough Magistrates. 23 February [31, 747-49]. Should not rest with the new Municipal Corporations.

Spain. 18 March [32, 396-99] The Government should withdraw British troops immediately.

Municipal Corporation Reform Bill. 29 March [32, 756-57] Expressed dislike of the government's haste in passing the measure.

Constabulary Force (Ireland) Bill. 12 April [32, 882-85], 2 May [33, 486-87] Would propose amendments in Committee.

Disfranchisement of Stafford Borough. 15 April [32, 1068-74], 4 August [35, 887-88]. Opposed and voted against the measure, because charge of corruption had not been proven.

Municipal Corporation (Ireland) Bill. 9 May [727-29]. Proposed amendments. 27 June [948-55]. The Lords should persist in their amendments.

Railways 3 June [34, 1-4], 14 June [498-99].  Parliament
should have the power to amend Railway Acts.  16 June
[540-41, 549-51].  A clause to this effect should be added
to the Birmingham and Bristol Railway Bill.

Irish Roman Catholic Priest's Petition.  7 June [34, 153-55]
The Lords should hear it.

Legal Reforms.  13 June [34, 479-89].  Opposed to these,
which were an attack on the dignity of the Lord Chancellor.

Imprisonment for Debt.  11 July [35, 69-74].  Disapproved of
it, but some security was needed.

Tithes and Church (Ireland) Bill.  25 July [35, 454-55].
Disapproved .

Charitable Trustees.  4 August [35, 893-95], 11 August [1107-
09].  Disapproved.

Post Office Commissioners Bill.  12 August [35, 1167-69].
A major change was proposed: this measure should be postponed.

Church Temporalities (Ireland) Bill.  12 August [1170-71].
Proposed amendments.

Greek Loan.  16 August [35, 1242-44].  Approved - but
Britain should not act alone.

Conduct of the House of Lords.  18 August. [35, 1309-12].
Defence of the Lords' conduct.  Later printed as a pamphlet.
[see No. 288].

1837

Address from the Throne.  31 January [36, 12-15].  Defended
his conduct in the previous session.

Poor Law Amendment Bill.  7 April [37, 851-52].  Further
amendments were not needed.

Oxford and Cambridge University Statutes.  11 April [38,
1022-26], 8 May [664-69], 21 December [39, 1392-99].
Speeches against the revisions proposed by Lord Radnor:
Parliament ought not to interfere in this case.

Municipal Corporations (Ireland) Bill.  13 April [37, 1156-
57].  Proposed postponement. 21 April [38, 271-74].  Bill
should be amended in Committee.  25 April [550-56, 598-99]
English conditions could not be applied to Ireland.  The
question could only be settled when the Church of Ireland
question was dealt with.

Spain. 21 April [38, 137-50, 169]. Approved of the Quad-
ruple Treaty of 1834, but Britain should not intervene in
Spain.

Canada. 9 May [38, 744-48]. The government proposals were
too vague to be fully satisfactory.

The New Reign. 22 June [38, 1550-51] Seconded a message to
the new Queen. 7 July [1839-40] Opposed Regency Bill.
21 December [39, 1380-82]. Civil list should be increased.

State of Ireland. 27 November [39, 262-68]. Figures and
papers were needed to show the true state of Ireland.

Imprisonment for Debt. 5 December. [39, 596-97]. Opposed
to it, but security was needed.

                              1838

Affairs of Canada. 16 January [40, 3-4], 18 January [223-
29], 2 February [693-701]. Urged action on the government
to deal with the insurrection in Lower Canada.  7 August
[44, 1032-33] Durham should not have issued his deportation
ordinance.  9 August [1096-1101].It was the government's
fault Durham was sent - he ought to be recalled.

Negro Emancipation. 20 February [40, 1341-45]. The slave
trade ought to be abolished, but foreign interests needed to
respected.  13 March [41, 820-22].  Abolition of Slavery Act
ought only to be amended if local legislatures were not
doing their job.

The Ballot. 23 February [41, 51-53].  Opposed it.

Importation of Hindus into Guyana.  6 March [41, 454-59].
Acceptable, but only if agreements freely entered into and
adhered to.

Parliamentary Elections and Freemen Bill.  8 March [41,
694-96]. Opposed this amendment to the Reform Act.

Church of Scotland.  30 March [42, 146-50].  The government
should help the Synod of the Church of Scotland, who had
asked for it.

Church of Ireland.  6 April [42, 448-50].  Question must be
settled.

Free Press in Malta.  3 May [42, 812-16].  No need for a
free press on the island.

Poor Law (Ireland).  21 May [43, 19-24].  The New Poor Law
worked in England, and ought to be extended to Ireland.
28 May [358-60], 31 May [477-81].  Supported the Bill in
detail.

Education in Ireland. 25 May [43, 358-61]. Need to discuss
this, because the government might propose a Bill.

Oaths Validity Bill. 15 June [43, 763-64]. An oath was
needed as the basis of the administration of justice. Some
could affirm. 12 July [44, 145, 148]. Supported Bill to
this effect.

Spain. 19 June [43, 863-67]. Reviewed British policy:
strict neutrality was needed. 10 July [44, 63-69, 74-75, 77]
Asked whether there was a blockade of the coast of Spain.

The Magistracy. 5 July [43, 1278-81], 17 July [44, 267-74].
The Lord Lieutenant ought to appoint magistrates, and the
Lord Chancellor ought not to interfere.

Oxford University Statutes. 9 July [44, 5-7, 9]. The
Senate was working on a revision: Parliament should not
interfere.

Westmeath Election. 24 July [44, 569-70]. An attack on
Lord Plunkett and on government appointments in Ireland.

Church Discipline Bill. 26 July [44, 627-28]. Ought to be
postponed.

Municipal Corporations (Ireland) Bill. 27 July [44, 710-15]
10 August [1135-36]. Was now evident the Bill had to be
passed, but it could be amended in Committee.

Commercial relations. 14 August [44, 1198-1203]. An
important question. British merchants should be protected,
and the blockade of the coast of Spain abandoned.

1839

Address from the Throne. 5 February [45, 18-24]. Seconded
the address, but ran through many pressing domestic and
international questions needing solutions.

Corn Laws. 18 February [45, 565-71]. Agreed to hear
evidence, but not necessarily to a change in the law.  14
March [46, 592-97, 604-05]. Strong speech against any
alteration in the law.

Lord Ebrington's conduct. 4 March [45, 1156-58]. Satisfied
with the explanation of his conduct as Lord Lieutenant of
Ireland.

Strength of the Royal Navy. 7 March [46, 6-10]. Argued for
an increase, to build up reserves.

Pardons at Mullingar, Ireland. 7 March [46, 18-20] A
serious case and the Lords should be interested in it.
Pardons ought not to have been issued.

Government of Ireland. 21 March [46, 1012-15]. This was
not a party matter, but something would have to be done
about law and order in Ireland. 8 August [50, 60-63, 85-86]
Approved of the Bill to outlaw oath-taking. There was a
conspiracy in Ireland.

Free Press in Malta. 30 April [47, 670-74]. Opposed to it:
it was not needed.

Ministerial explanation. 14 May [47, 1015-21], 31 May
[1186-7]. Explanation of the Conservative failure to form a
Ministry ("the Bedchamber crisis"). Melbourne must do his
duty as Prime Minister.

Canada - Conduct of Colonel Prince. 30 May [47, 1099-1102].
The Lords should wait until his trial was over before
passing judgement.

Arming the People. 11 June [48, 136-37]. Questions who the
government circular was aimed at. Disapproved of it.

The Poor Law. 13 June [48, 188-92]. Supported the efforts
of the Commissioners, who were more honest than local
authorities.

Ballot and Universal Suffrage. 25 June [48, 826-27].
Agreed with Melbourne and disapproved of this.

Government of Jamaica Bill. 1 July [48, 1049-53]. The
Assembly must do its duty - or be restricted in its rights.
The Lords should amend the Bill in Committee.

Education. 5 July [48, 1325-28]. Disapproved of the plan to
allow the Treasury to give grants for education, which was
an attack on the Clergy.

Riots in Birmingham. 16 July [49, 373-77, 382-84], 18 July
[450-53, 463-66], 22 July [586-93]. Strong attack on the
government for failing to repress extremely serious riots:
defended himself vigorously against well-founded arguments
that he was exaggerating.

Municipal Corporations (Ireland) Bill. 22 July [49, 615-18]
Accepted the need for them and therefore approved the second
reading - aimed to amend it in Committee. 25 July [748,
762-3]. Successfully proposed amendments.

Government of Lower Canada. 26 July [49, 871-75, 883]. The
government ought to act immediately to preserve peace there.

Portuguese Slave Trade. 1 August [49, 1063-67]. Disapproved of the trade, but the present proposed Bill was not
the best way to tackle it. 2 August [1130-32, 1134-35].
Justified his vote against the government's proposals. 15
August [50, 304-11], 19 August [382-85]. Spoke and voted
against the Bill.

Penny Postage.  5 August [49, 1215-21].  Long speech stressing objections to the scheme, but recommended voting for it.

Worship in India.  12 August [50, 233-34].  The British government ought not to interfere with the religion of their Indian subjects.

Birmingham Police Bill.  15 August [50, 292-4].  Favoured this, especially in view of the recent riots.

Manchester Police Bill.  19 August [50, 377-78], 20 August [425-26].  Disapproved of the Bill: the new police would not be as efficient as the old one - but then withdrew opposition to the measure.

Police in Bolton.  20 August. [50, 432-33].  Praised their recent conduct.

Business of the Session.  23 August [50, 553-55]  A general attack on the government.

1840

Address from the Throne.  16 January [51, 11-14].  Satis-factory announcement, but an explicit reference to Prince Albert's Protestantism ought to be made.

Address from the Throne: Relations with Portugal.  20 January [51, 235-36].  Criticised the government policy in Portugal and called for papers.

Socialism.  24 January [51, 544-46], 3 February [1095], 4 February [1210-11].  The government must take steps to combat this new menace.

Prince Albert's naturalisation.  27 January [51, 576-60].  Called for postponement. 31 January [924, 927] Brief, favourable comments on the proposed measure.

Vote of thanks to the Army of the Indus.  4 February [51, 1173-74].  Praised the skill with which recent military operations in India were carried out.

State of the Navy. 6 February [51, 1302-08].  The fleet was now too weak and comparisons with 1829 were not valid.

Queen's Message - Lord Seaton.  [53, 165-66].  Approved of Lord Seaton's conduct in Canada.

Canada -Clergy reserves.  31 March [53, 277-78], 7 April [663-64], 10 April [960-61].  Expressed disapproval of an Act passed by the Canadian Parliament, encouraged by the Governor General.

Privilege Bill.  6 April [53, 583-87], 10 April [978-79]

Approved of the Bill to preserve immunity from libel
proceedings arising from debates in Parliament, but disapproved of selling Parliamentary Papers by the authority of
Parliament.

Poor Laws Guardians (Ireland). 13 April [53, 1014-17], 14
April [1086]. Disapproved of changes to the law proposed by
the recent commission and wanted correspondence relating to
it printed. 4 May [1178-79]. Commons should have amended
the law. 3 July [54, 416-18]. Disappointed by the
Commissioner's refusal to enquire fully into the question.

Municipal Corporations (Ireland) Bill. 4 May [53, 1164-71].
Approved of the second reading, but disliked the idea of
new corporations and proposed to amend it in Committee. 12
June [54, 1110-11]. Proposed postponement of the measure.
6 July [55, 446]. Expressed fears of the democratic element
in the Dublin Corporation, which should be reformed by this
Bill. 20 July [815-16]. New corporations power to tax
should be limited.

War with China. 12 May [54, 34-43]. The Lords ought to
leave it to the responsible authorities to determine the
rights and wrongs of the situation.

Government of Canada. 30 June [55, 239-46], 7 July [506-10]
13 July [657-59]. Strong opposition to the proposed union
of Upper and Lower Canada, which culminated in a 27-clause
protest in the Journal of the House.

Ecclesiastical Revenues Bill. 23 July [55, 903-04], 30
July [1131-33]. Presented a petition against it, but
approved of the measure to redistribute the Church's
income among poorer parishes.

Affirmations. 4 August [55, 1247-48]. Oaths were the only
acceptable form.

Case of John Thorogood. 7 August [55, 1386-7]. He lost his
case in the Ecclesiastical Court, so he must pay costs.

1841

Address from the Throne. 26 January [56, 32-37]. Supported
it, but expressed concern at developments in the Near East.

Vote of thanks to Sir R. Stopford. 4 February [56, 253-4,
256]. Highly approved this reward to a great feat of arms
(at Acre).

Canada - St. Sulpice. 4 March [56, 1334-36]. Disapproved
of Canadian government aid for the seminary at St. Sulpice,
which attacked the whole reformation settlement. [57,
230-33]. Changed his mind, because he had forgotten his
own membership of Cabinets approving similar measures.

Poor Law Commission (Ireland) Clonmel Union.  3 May [57, 1398-1400].  Attacked corruption in the Clonmel Union; falsified papers had been presented to the House.

Corn Laws.  7 May [58, 9-11], 11 May [183-84], 17 May [494], Strong defence of the existing Corn Law.  25 May [737-39] The present system of duties worked well.  4 October [59, 1101-02].  Present financial problems were Melbourne's fault, not that of the Corn Laws.  5 October [1108-10]. Admitted the existence of distress, but amending the Corn Laws would not alleviate it.

Address from the Throne.  24 August [59, 72-83].  Strong attack on Melbourne's government at the opening of the new session on the grounds of it financial incapacity and poor foreign relations.

1842

Address from the Throne.  3 February [60, 38-39]. Defended himself and the government from charges of inconsistency respecting the Corn Laws.

Poor Law Chaplains (Ireland).  17 February [60, 628-31]. The position of the Chaplains should be regulated - the Poor Law Commissioners had not done enough.

Forgery of Exchequer Bills. 4 March [61, 39-41].  Defended Lord Monteagle: the Commons ought to investigate this matter.  12 April [62, 292-93].  Introduced a Bill to appoint Commission of Inquiry into forgeries.

Corn Law.  14 April [62, 457-58]. Defended Peel against charges that he was not helping farmers.  19 April [62, 781-90].  Long speech in support of the government's amendments to the Corn Law - repeal would not solve anything.

Sunderland Magistrates.  9 May [63, 267-68].  Defended the appointment of Lord Londonderry as Lord Lieutenant of Durham.

The Queen's Letter on National Distress.  26 May [63, 771-72] Was not aware of this.  Distress was caused by a shortage of money to buy grain, not by a shortage of grain itself.

Attack on the Queen.  31 May [63, 995-96].  Gave details of the assault on the Queen on 30 May.

National Distress.  2 June [63, 1131-36], 16 June [1604-05]. Defended the government's efforts to relieve distress, which had to be given time to work.  Corn Law repeal was not contemplated.

Income (Property) Tax.  17 June [64] Insisted on the necessity of this tax as an emergency measure.

Irish Magistracy. 21 June [64, 279-80]. Approved of the reappointment of Mr. St. George.

Mines and Colleries Bill. 8 July [64, 1167-68]. Expressed unease at the way the evidence was collected. 14 July [65, 116-17] Still unhappy, but voted in favour.

Poor Law Amendment Bill. 26 July [65, 619-21]. Introduced second reading. The Act worked, but some elements of it, such as construction of prison-like workhouses, were too harsh.

Slave Trade (Brazil). 2 August [65, 950-52]. Agreed with the need to repress this trade, and supported Lord Brougham's proposed measure.

Outrages (Ireland). 8 August [65, 1114-16]. Approved production of returns of crime rates, but what was really needed was better policing.

1843

Address from the Throne. 2 February [66, 29-33, 52-53]. A strong defence of the government's policy in China, India and North America.

China. 4 February [66, 525-27] Proposed the vote of thanks to the army and navy for their conduct of operations in China.

Afghan war. 17 February [66, 763-64]. Laid papers on the war before the House. 20 February [892-93] Proposed a vote of thanks to the army, but commented most on events leading to the disaster of 1841-42.

Poor Laws. 7 March [67, 345-47]. Opposed vague opposition motions on the subject.

Lord Ellenborough's Proclamations, Somnauth. 9 March [67, 526-36[. Defended Lord Ellenborough's conduct, and argued that the desecration of the Temple at Somnauth would not affect the Indian army.

Poor Law (Scotland). 20 March [67, 1122-24]. A Commission was looking into the matter and would report in due course.

Duties on Cotton and Wool. 6 April [68, 478-80]. Pressed for the cautious reduction of duties.

Addresses of Condolence on the late Duke of Sussex. 27 April [68, 997-98], 13 June [69, 1399-1400[.

Poor Law (Ireland). 8 May [68, 1366-69]. Amendments would be made to the law: there was no need for a Select Committee of Inquiry. 15 August [71, 918-19, 920-24] Explained some details of the government's measure.

Repeal of the Union (Ireland). 9 May [69, 7-9]. Strongly opposed to this.

Scinde. 22 May [69, 681-82]. Would not comment on a rumour that British troops had invaded Scinde. Gave details of negotiations leading to the war.

Sees of St. Asaph and Bangor. [69, 774-80]. These sees, only recently united should not now be separated.

Dismissal of Magistrates (Ireland). 30 May [69, 1072-74] Lord Ffrench deserved to be sacked, because he organised a repeal meeting. 9 June [1291-93]. Others had to go too. 14 July [70, 1113-21]. Strong defence of the government's policy.

Marriage of Princess Augusta. 13 June [69, 1396-7]. Pleased to vote an increased grant.

Archdeaconry of Armagh. 15 June [69, 1553-56]. Did not know any details, but defended the policy of the government and the Church of Ireland.

Church of Scotland Benefices.Bill. 17 June [70, 372-73]. Agreed with the Bill.

Processions (Repeal) Ireland. 8 August [71, 371-74]. The Irish situation was very bad. The processions Act must be repealed, or upheld.

Financial State of the Country. 14 August [71, 609-16]. There probably would be a surplus, but it was not time to discuss the budget.

Arms (Ireland) Bill. 15 August [71, 690-91]. This law was now fifty years old, and had to be renewed.

Dismissal of the Earl of Lucan as a J.P. 21 August [71, 968-72] Defended Lucan, who had apologized and ought to be reinstated.

Chelsea Out Pensioners. 21 August [71, 973-74]. Proposed a measure to make the pensioners more efficient as Special Constables.

1844

Scinde. 12 February [72, 498-501]. Proposed, in extravagant terms, a vote of thanks to Sir Charles Napier and the army.

Board of Charitable Bequests (Ireland). 4 March [73, 503-05] Commented on the case of Mr. Bermingham, accused of fraud in setting up a school. Defended the government's actions.

Anti-Corn Law League meeting in Somerset. 11 March [73, 789-90] Recommended a calm approach.

Maynooth College. 12 March [73, 857-58]. The House ought not to hurry into the details of this question.

The Church of Ireland. 18 March [73, 1170-73]. Strong defence of the Church of Ireland. No measure of reform was needed or contemplated.

Recall of Lord Ellenborough. 29 April [74, 340-44]. Very critical of the East India Company Directors for taking this step, but they had the right to take it. 7 May [778-80]. Would not reform the East India Company because of this.

Public Works (Ireland). 10 May [74, 892-94]. An enquiry would be held, but no more money would be available.

Lancaster and Carlisle Railway. 23 May [74, 1437-38]. Gates should be provided where railways crossed roads.

St. Asaph and Bangor Dioceses Bill. 11 June [75, 493-96]. Opposed the Bill to separate the two Dioceses. 1 July [76, 124-26, 128, 131], 11 July [603-09, 617-18]. Opposed the third reading because it infringed the Royal Prerogative. The Bill ought to be abandoned.

Home Office opening letters. 17 June [75, 975-78, 985], 25 June [1328-29], 4 July [76, 306-11, 313-14]. Defended the practice as long-established and vital to national security.

Workhouses (Ireland). 27 June [76, 13-15]. The government would appoint a committee to investigate the question, but the Lords could do so if they wished.

Party Processions (Ireland) Bill. 26 July [76, 1457-60]. Defended the Bill as necessary and not an innovatory measure.

State of the Navy. 5 August [76, 1741-43]. The navy was stronger because the country was at peace. The Tahitian problem would soon be settled.

Business of the Session. 6 August [76, 1799-1802]. The government was doing its best, but there was much to do.

Poor Law Amendment Bill. 6 August [76, 1828-32]. An important Bill, which the Lord's should dispose of as quickly as possible.

1845

Law enforcement (Ireland). 7 March [78, 417-23]. Opposed Lord Normanby's motion on the actions of troops and police in Ireland. 7 April [79, 246-48]. Corrected some mis-statements in the previous speech.

St. Asaph and Manchester Diocese Bill. 2 May [80, 52-60]. Opposed to another attempt to separate the dioceses of St. Asaph and Bangor.

Maynooth College Bill. 2 June [80, 1160-69]. Introduced
the second reading and warmly commended the Bill, giving
additional money to the College in perpetuity. 3 June
[1336-37]. Denied the government was influenced by popular
meetings. 16 June [81, 567-75]. Argued that Catholic
Priests should be properly educated and denied the measure
was injurious to the Church of Ireland.

Church Education Society (Ireland). 17 June [81, 660-63]
Announced the Duke's conversion to support of a national
education system in Ireland. Clergymen should now uphold
the law.

Decorations for Peninsular officers. 21 July [82, 719-26].
Argued that the Lords should not discuss this matter, that
adequate rewards had been provided and that Indian medals
were not comparable.

1846

Address from the Throne. 22 January [83, 23-24]. Defended
Peel.

Ministerial explanation. 26 January [83, 166-71].
Explained the Duke's decision to stand by Peel and do his
duty to his Sovereign. Peel's proposed measures would not
damage the landed interest.

Public Works (Ireland) Bill. 9 February [83, 532-33]. The
government must pay the Irish police force.

Campaign on the Sutlej. 2 March [84, 370-72]. Praised the
military operations there, especially the conduct of Lord
Hardinge.

Corn Importation Bill. 18 May [86, 728]. Introduced the
measure (in one sentence). 28 May [86]. The Bill had to
be passed; this was his duty to the Crown.

Customs Duties Bill - Silk Trade. 22 June [87, 780-81].
This was a finance Bill and the Lords should not interfere
with it.

Resignation of the Ministry. 29 June [87, 1039-40]. A
brief statement.

Annuities to Lord Hardinge and Lord Gough. 16 July [87,
1154-58]. This was a money Bill, so the Lords should not
have increased Hardinge's grant.

Flogging in the army. 11 August [88, 600-02]. Favoured the
abolition of flogging, but some form of punishment was
necessary.

Intervention in Cracow. 11 August [88, 616-18]. The
Russians, Prussians and Austrians were justified in

occupying Cracow to repress a revolutionary conspiracy.

### 1847

Army Service Bill. 26 April [91, 1337-42]. In support of
the Bill, stressing that old soldiers would be retained in
the service. 18 May [92, 1027-29]. Confused speech in favour
of the Bill.

Landed Property (Ireland) Bill. 4 May [92, 367-69], 11 May
[687-88]. Argued strongly in favour: Irish labourers should
be paid in cash.

Railways in Kent. 20 May [92, 1094-95]. The matter ought
to be referred to the Railway Commissioners.

Portugal. 15 June [93, 579-84].' The government policy
towards Portugal - a blockade - was fully justified.

### 1848

Diplomatic Relations with the Court of Rome. 17 February
[96, 778-80], 18 February [875, 881, 894, 896]. Supported
the Bill establishing relations, with some reservations.

Public Order. 10 April [98, 71-72], 19 April [498-501].
Supported government measures to deal with the threat posed
by large public meetings.

The State of Ireland. 3 August [100, 1110-11]. This was not
bad at present, but the government had to be vigilant.

Unlawful Acts (Ireland) Bill. 14 August [101, 114-17].
Supported this government measure.

### 1849

Address from the Throne. 1 February [102, 70-72]. Favoured
the government, but felt there was no need to lay papers
respecting foreign policy before the House.

Affairs of Sicily. 6 March [103, 241-42]. Britain must
remain neutral.

The Army in India. 24 April [104, 721-26]. Praised the
operations of the army in the Punjab. 6 July [106, 1238-40]
The government was not ungenerous to the army.

Pilotage Bill. 20 July [107, 969-71]. Opposed to it,
because it would adversely affect the Cinque Port Pilots.

Medals. 23 July [107, 829-30]. A confused speech,
respecting campaign medals for the services.

Regimental Benefit Societies Bill. 24 July [107, 878-80].
Proposed the second reading of the Bill abolishing these

Societies.

1850

Medals. 21 February [108, 1141-2, 1145]. Proposed to give medals to all men involved in actions for which principal officers received them, but could not afford to have them engraved with their names.

Party Processions (Ireland) Bill. 4 March [109, 310-12]. Disliked the measure, which did not go far enough. 8 March [109, 526-27]. Moved an amendment regarding people carrying arms at these meetings.

University Reform. 13 May [110, 1373-74]. Opposed to change.

Lord Lieutenancy of Ireland. 27 June [112, 468-71]. Opposed to its abolition, on military grounds. Later printed as a pamphlet [see No. 286].

Sir Robert Peel. 4 July [112, 864-65]. A brief eulogy.

1851

Affairs of Ceylon. 1 April [115, 880-81]. Nowhere should be governed by martial law. Papers were needed.

Ecclesiastical Titles Assumption Bill. 21 July [118, 1113-16] Supported the Bill: the Pope had launched an attack on the Church of England.

1852

Kaffir War. 5 February [119, 174-76]. Praised Sir Harry Smith's conduct of operations.

Captain Warner's Inventions. 21 May [121, 855-56]. There was no need for the House of Lords to form a Committee to investigate this subject.

The Militia Bill. 15 June [122, 728-31]. Strongly supported the Bill to reestablish the militia, which was essential, given the weakness of the country's defences.

The Birkenhead. 22 June [122, 1130]. The Duke's last speech. Moved a motion with regard to the state of discipline of the troops on board the Birkenhead.

Funeral of the Duke of Wellington.

The Queen's message relating to the State Funeral was presented to both Houses of Parliament on 12 November [123, 127, 129-30]. The major obituary speeches on the

Duke were delivered by Disraeli in the Commons on 15
November [149-54] (this was the infamous plagiarised
speech) and Derby in the Lords on 19 November [239-43].
On 16 November [212-23] the indefatigable Joseph Hume
complained about the cost of the funeral. He was supported
by S. Carter. On 6 December Hume and Carter voiced
further criticism in the Committee of Supply [1040-11].
Colonel Charles Sibthorpe condemned the unseemly discussion,
and the money was duly voted.

# (iii) Parliamentary Papers

The following section comprises Parliamentary papers which contain letters from Wellington or significant reference to him. It is chronologically arranged.

The form of reference begins with the title of the paper, followed by the date of the Parliamentary session, the number assigned to the paper by the House of Commons (in parentheses) and the volume number within the sessional series.

120.     Copies and extracts of all dispatches or correspondence received from India ... relative to hostilities between the British Government and ... Jeswunt Rao Holkar and the causes thereof...

     1805 (19) X.
Includes correspondence between Arthur Wellesley and the Marquess Wellesley, relating to the third Mahratta war.

121.     Papers ... relating to East India Affairs - Dowlut Rao Scindia and Jeswunt Rao Holkar.

     1806 (231) XVI.
Reproduces despatches from General Wellesley and other papers relating to the Treaty with Scindia and instructions from the Marquess Wellesley to Arthur Wellesley, respecting the campaign against Holkar.

122.     Papers ... relating to East India affairs (financial and political state of India, 1798-1805).

     1806 (257) XVI.
Reproduces despatches from General Wellesley respecting military events subsequent to the battle of Assaye and negotiations for peace with the Mahratta chiefs, the Rajah of Berar and Scindia.

123.     Copy of the Proceedings upon the inquiry relative to the armistice and convention, etc.

made and concluded in Portugal, in August 1808 ...

1809 (17) XII.
The official report of the Board of Inquiry into the
Convention of Cintra.  Includes much direct evidence from
Wellington: his address to the Board; his written
explanation of events; his interrogation by the Board and
despatches relating to the signature of the Convention and
its aftermath.

124.       ... Copies of, or extracts, from the instructions to the Commanders ... of his Majesty's forces
in Spain and Portugal in the year 1808; together
with such communications as have been received
from the said commanders ... relating to the
execution of the said instructions...

1809 (66) XI.
Reproduces much correspondence between Lord Castlereagh, the Secretary of State for War and the Colonies,
from June 1808, and Wellington: includes the instructions
issued to Wellington on his departure for Portugal, details
of the battle of Vimeiro, and Wellington's replacement in
command.

125.       Papers relating to Spain and Portugal.

1810 (140) XV.
Includes Wellington's correspondence with the British
Ambassador to Spain and the Spanish authorities from April
to August 1809, and correspondence with the Marquess
Wellesley (envoy extraordinary to the Spanish government)
and others from July to September 1809.  All relate to the
progress of military operations.

126.       Papers relating to Spain and Portugal.

1810 (154) XV.
Correspondence between Foreign Secretary Canning and
Marquess Wellesley on the question of whether the British
army should remain in the Peninsula.  Includes many
references to Wellington, to whom the decision was finally
left.

127.       Papers relating to Spain and Portugal.

1810 (210) XV.
Correspondence between the Marquess Wellesley and
Wellington in October 1809 and a long letter from the
Spanish authorites giving details of the Talavera campaign,
and the Wellesleys' response to it.

128.       Papers relating to Spain and Portugal.

1810 (211) XV.
Further correspondence between Castlereagh and

Wellington, from April to September 1809, giving details of
the crossing of the Douro and the Talavera campaign, and
estimates of the current strategic situation.

129.      Papers relating to Spain and Portugal

          1810 (245) XV.
      Further correspondence between Castlereagh and
Wellington together with letters from Wellington to other
Generals, dating from August 1809 and indicating movements
by the French and Spanish armies.

130.      Papers relating to Spain and Portugal

          1810 (247) XV.
      Correspondence between the Commisary General, John
Murray, and William Huskisson of the Treasury, between April
and September 1809. Mostly concerned with the supply of
money to the army, in which Wellington was closely involved.

131.      Copy of a dispatch from Viscount Wellington to
          the Earl of Liverpool, dated Pero Negro, 27th
          October 1810.

          1810-11 (115) X.
      On the evacuation of parts of Portugal and an appeal
to Britain to aid the people of Portugal who had lost their
harvest because of the war.

132.      Copy of the Memorial of Colonel Sir William
          Rule and others, on behalf of His Grace the Duke of
          Wellington ... respecting the claims of His Grace
          and the army for captures.

          1814-15 (406) IX.
      Claims the army is entitled to over £900,000 in Prize
Money for booty captured in Spain and the South of France.

133.      Second Report from the Select Committee on the
          public income and expenditure of the United
          Kingdom.  Ordnance Estimates.

          1828 (420) V.
      Wellington, who was a former Master General of the
Ordnance, appeared before the Committee as a witness on 18
April 1828 (pages 83-88).  He was questioned about the
constitution of the Ordnance Office, the duties of the
Staff, and on ways in which money could be saved.

134.      Copy of the letter from the Trustees of the
          Deccan Prize, to the Secretary of the Treasury ...
          and of the minutes of the Lords of the Treasury
          thereon ...

          1833 (589) XXVI.
      Wellington and Charles Arbuthnot were the Trustees of

the Deccan Prize Fund.  This correspondence deals with
difficulties arising from establishing what was captured
and where, and how the booty should be distributed.

135.       Report from the Select Committee on Cinque Ports
           Pilots with the minutes of evidence and an appendix

       1833 (636) VII.
   The appendix includes (on pages 767-9) a long letter
from Wellington, in his capacity as Lord Warden of the
Cinque Ports, to Lord Auckland, opposing changes in the
regulations governing pilotage in the Downs.

136.       Report from the Select Committee on army and
           navy appointments, with minutes of evidence and
           appendix.

       1833 (650) VII.
   Includes as an appendix (on pages 273-8) a memorandum
by Wellington on military governors of castles etc.
Justifies their continuance as a way of rewarding generals
for meritorious service.

137.       Deccan Booty.

       1833 (701) XXVI
   Includes further letters from Wellington (July 1825
and August 1823), Arbuthnot and others on the question of
Deccan prize money.

138.       Deccan Prize Money.  Copy of a Memorandum of
           date 10th September 1825 on the subject of the
           Deccan Prize Money; signed by the Duke of
           Wellington, and sent to the First Lord of the
           Treasury.

       1833 (702) XXVI.
   Reviews the whole subject and concludes that both
armies involved in the campaign in the Deccan (commanded by
Sir Thomas Hislop and Lord Hastings) deserve a share of the
prize money.

139.       Report from the Select Committee on Dover
           Harbour with the minutes of evidence and appendix.

       1836 (398) XX.
   Includes frequent mention of the Duke in his capacity
as Lord Warden of the Cinque Ports, with comments on his
administration.  Wellington did not give evidence to this
committee personally.

140.       A return of the Booty captured as Prize Money
           by the Army in the Deccan in 1817-18; the amount
           which has been distributed ...

       1837-8 (556) XLI.

A list, signed by Wellington and Arbuthnot on 20 June 1838, showing money collected and disbursed.

141.        <u>Report from the sub-committee of the Wellington Military Memorial: with the appendix.</u>

1846 (553) XLIII.
Includes a description of a visit by the sub-committee to Wellington, informing him of the decision to place a statue on Decimus Burton's arch, outside Apsley House, at Hyde Park Corner, and his response, together with correspondence (not with the Duke) on the question.

142.        <u>Correspondence on the Wellington Statue.</u>

1847 (577) LVII.
Much futher correspondence about the statue on Burton's Arch.

# (iv) Private Collections

143.     Aspinall, Arthur, ed., The Later Correspondence
         of George III. Volumes 4 and 5, London, 1968, 1970.
Volume four includes letters on Wellington becoming
Chief Secretary for Ireland; volume 5 covers his appoint-
ment to command in the Peninsula, and his campaigns down to
February 1810.

144.     Aspinall, Arthur, ed., The Letters of King
         George IV, 1812-1830. Introduced by C.K. Webster.
         3 vols., Cambridge, 1938.
Volume 1 covers the years from 1812 to 1815, and
includes some mention Wellington.  Much more material, both
by and about the Duke, is in volumes 2 (1815-23) and 3
(1823-30).  These deal with all matters relating to the
private and public life of the King, and the political life
of the nation.

145.     Aspinall, Arthur, ed., "The Correspondence of
         Charles Arbuthnot." Camden Society, Third Series,
         volume LXV.  London, 1941.
Contains a few letters from Wellington, but a great
many about him.  The correspondence starts in 1817 and goes
on to 1848, dealing with all aspects of Tory foreign and
domestic policy during this period, often giving the Duke's
views on developments.

146.     Aspinall, Arthur, ed., "The Formation of
         Canning's Ministry, February to August 1827."
         Camden Society, Third Series, volume LIX.  London,
         1937.
Extracts from numerous letters - including fifteen
from and twenty-one to the Duke, and many others about him.
The correspondence and scholarly introduction reflect
Wellington's part in Canning's Ministry, and his quarrel
with it.

147.     Bamford, F. and Wellington, Seventh Duke of, eds.
         The Journal of Mrs. Arbuthnot. 2 vols., London,

1961.
An intimate record of conversations with the Duke
by a very close friend, covering the years from 1820 to
1831, dealing with a wide variety of matters affecting him,
public and private.  Volume 1 covers the years from 1820 to
1825, and volume 2, from 1826 to 1831.

148.          Barker, G., The Impunity of Military Insolence
and Licentiousness exhibited in a correspondence
between George Barker of the Theatre Royal, Drury
Lane, and Captain Sutton, of the 7th Hussars, and
the Commander-in-Chief, His Grace the Duke of
Wellington.  London, 1845.
Contains one brief letter from Fitzroy Somerset and
one, even briefer, from Wellington, declining to interfere
in a quarrel over Captain Sutton's relations with Barker's
wife.

149.          Benson, Arthur Christopher and Viscount Esher,
eds., The Letters of Queen Victoria: A Selection
from Her Majesty's Correspondence between the
years 1837 and 1861.  3 vols., London, 1907.
Volumes 1 and 2 cover the years to Wellington's death,
and amply reflect the Duke's role in national life, and
reproduce some of his correspondence with the Queen.

150.          Bessborough, Earl of and Arthur Aspinall,
Lady Bessborough and her family circle.  London,
1940.
Includes letters from Sir Frederick Ponsonby during
the Peninsula war and a few letters from, and about, the
Duke thereafter.

151.          Browne, George Lathom, Wellington: or, The
Public and Private Life of Arthur, First Duke of
Wellington, as Told by Himself, his Comrades, and
his Intimate Friends.  London, 1888, reissued 1889.
A very useful collection of extracts, carefully edited,
overall giving more space to the Duke's post-Waterloo career
and private life than to his years of active military
service.  Based mainly on Greville, Larpent and Wellington's
despatches.

152.          Bruce, H.A., ed., Life of General Sir William
Napier, K.C.B.  2 vols., London, 1864.
The life of the historian of the Peninsular war.  The
Duke was involved throughout Napier's career.  Reproduces
correspondence and a conversation with the Duke about the
war.

153.          Buckingham and Chandos, Duke of, Memoirs of the
Court and Cabinets of George the Third from
original family documents.  4 vols., London, 1853-4.
Volume 4 includes some letters from Wellington in the
Peninsula in 1809 and 1810, but there is more information on

the Duke's eldest brother, the Marquess Wellesley.

154.        Buckingham and Chandos, Duke of, <u>Memoirs of the</u>
            <u>Court of George IV.</u>  2 vols., London, 1859.
    A collection of letters, with some additions from
memory, about political events between 1820 and 1830, in
which Wellington figures prominently.

155.        Buckingham and Chandos, Duke of, <u>Memoirs of the</u>
            <u>Courts and Cabinets of William IV and Victoria.</u>
            <u>2 vols., London, 1861.</u>
    Volume 1 reproduces many letters from the Duke during
the reform bill crisis, volume 2 has some letters on
political matters dating from 1833 to 1838.

156.        Chancellor, E. Beresford, ed. and trans., <u>The</u>
            <u>Diary of Philipp von Neumann, 1819-1850.</u>  Volume 1,
            <u>London, 1928.</u>
    Recounts some conversations with Wellington while
Neumann was resident in England between 1819 and 1830,
including recollections and comments on current affairs.

157.        Colebrooke, T.E., <u>The Life of the Honourable</u>
            <u>Mountstuart Elphinstone.</u>  2 vols., London, 1884.
    Volume 1 contains useful information on Wellington in
India; volume 2 recounts conversations with the Duke on the
affairs of India in 1830-1.

158.        Combermere, Mary, Viscountess and W.W. Knollys,
            <u>Memoirs and Correspondence of Field Marshal</u>
            <u>Viscount Combermere, G.C.B. etc., from his family</u>
            <u>papers.</u>  2 vols., London, 1866.
    Volume 1 covers Combermere's service as cavalry
commander in the Peninsula, including orders from Wellington;
volume 2 includes only a few anecdotes of the Duke.

159.        Delavoye, Alex M., <u>Life of Thomas Graham, Lord</u>
            <u>Lynedoch.</u>  London, 1880.
    Includes a journal of campaigns from 1810 to the end
of the war, as well as a number of letters to and from
Wellington during this period.

160.        [Eaton, Charlotte M.] <u>The Battle of Waterloo ...</u>
            <u>from a variety of authentic and original sources.</u>
            <u>London, 1815.</u>
    Includes the "Waterloo despatch" and some despatches
from the duke written on the advance to Paris, as well as a
description of Wellington by a German officer.

161.        Gooch, G.P., ed., <u>The Later Correspondence of</u>
            <u>Lord John Russell, 1840-1878.</u>  2 vols., London,
            <u>1925.</u>
    Correspondence with Wellington is concentrated in
volume 1, with letters from the Duke on personal matters,
such as his remaining Commander-in-Chief in 1846, and
public ones like national defence, military appointments,

and the state of Europe.

162.        Harriott, Lieutenant, ed., <u>An Autobiographic</u>
            <u>Memoir of the Services of the late Major J.C.</u>
            <u>Francke ...</u>  Madras, 1833.
        Interesting letters from Wellington on military
matters in India between 1799 and 1802.

163.        Haydon, Frederic Wordsworth, <u>Benjamin Robert</u>
            <u>Haydon: Correspondence and Table Talk, with a</u>
            <u>Memoir.</u>  2 vols., London, 1876.
        Various letters by, and anecdotes about the Duke.
Haydon and his son were not especially sympathetic to the
Duke.

164.        <u>History of the Indian Administration of Lord</u>
            <u>Ellenborough, in his correspondence with the Duke</u>
            <u>of Wellington [and] letters to the Queen.</u>  London,
        Includes letters from Wellington respecting general
matters arising during Ellenborough's stay in India as
Governor-General, in particular on wars with China and
Afghanistan; papers on the Indian army and Scinde, relations
with Burma and attacks on Ellenborough in England.
Reproduces more letters to the Duke than from him.

165.        Hodder, Edwin, <u>The Life and Work of the Seventh</u>
            <u>Earl of Shaftesbury.</u>  3 vol., London, 1886.
        Volume 1 contains some letters from the Duke on
personal and political matters.  Shaftesbury was a junior
member of Wellington's 1828-30 ministry.

166.        Jennings, Louis J., ed., <u>The Croker Papers. The</u>
            <u>Correspondence and Diaries of the late Right</u>
            <u>Honourable John Wilson Croker, LL.D., F.R.S.,</u>
            <u>Secretary to the Admiralty from 1809 to 1830.</u>
            3 vols., London, 1884.
        Well-known memoirs, by a High Tory associate of
Wellington.  Volume 1 begins in 1808, and Croker loyally
followed the Duke down to the passing of the 1832 Reform
Act; they still corresponded, and visited each other
occasionally down to the Duke's death.

167.        Lloyd, Christopher, ed., <u>The Keith Papers:</u>
            <u>selected from the papers of Viscount Keith.</u>  3 vols.,
            London, 1955.
        Volume 3 contains invaluable material on naval
operations on the northern coast of Spain between 1812 and
1814.

168.        Lushington, S.R., <u>The Life and Services of</u>
            <u>General Lord Harris, G.C.B., during his campaigns</u>
            <u>in America, the West Indies, and India.</u>  London,
            1840.
        Includes comments and correspondence relating to
Wellington's service in India, between 1798 and 1800.

169.        Martin, Robert Montgomery, ed., The Despatches,
            Minutes and Correspondence of the Marquess
            Wellesley, K.G., during his administration in
            India. 5 vols., London, 1836-7.
    Volumes 3 and 4 cover the Mahratta war and its after-
math, while volume 5 supplements these. They include
private and official letters to, from and about Wellington,
highlighting the relationship between him and his eldest
brother.

170.        Martin, Sir Theodore, The Life of His Royal
            Highness the Prince Consort. Volumes 1 and 2,
            London, 1875-6.
    Volume 2, in particular, well reflects the Prince's
association with the Duke, and includes letters from, to,
and about him, on a wide variety of matters concerned with
public business.

171.        Martin, Sir Theodore, A Life of Lord Lyndhurst
            from letters and papers in the possession of his
            family. London, 1883.
    Includes much correspondence between the Duke and
Lyndhurst, dating from the late 1820s and early 1830s, on
legal matters as well as more general political matters,
such as Roman Catholic emancipation.

172.        Melville, Lewis, ed., The Wellesley Papers. The
            Life and Correspondence of Richard Colley
            Wellesley, 1760-1842. 2 vols., London, 1914.
    Includes letters from Wellington while in India and
in the Peninsula and later.

173.        Melville, Lewis, ed., The Huskisson Papers.
            London, 1931.
    Most valuable for political events in the 1820s,
including the formation of Wellington's 1828 ministry.

174.        Mitford, Rev. J., "Conversations with the Duke
            of Wellington." Temple Bar, 82 (January-April
            1888): 507-13.
    Extracts from a "commonplace book", contains the
Duke's opinions on personalities and events in his career.

175.        Napier, Sir William, The Life and Opinions of
            General Sir Charles James Napier, K.C.B. etc., etc.
            4 vols., London, 1857.
    Some mention of Wellington in the Peninsula in
volume 1; volumes 3 and 4 cover Napier's service in India,
and include the Duke's actions and opinions relating to
that country.

176.        Oman, Carola, The Gascoyne Heiress. The Life and
            Diaries of Frances Mary Gascoyne-Cecil, 1802-39.
            London, 1968.
    A valuable diary, especially for the mid-1830s, by an
intimate friend of the Duke, covering both personal and

public matters.

177.         Owen, Sidney J., ed., A Selection from the
        Despatches, Treaties, and other Papers of the
        Marquess Wellesley K.G., during his Government of
        India.  Oxford, 1877.
A selection primarily intended for students.  Some
papers taken from the Wellington Despatches, while the Duke
figures strongly in some sections of the book.

178.         Palmerston, Third Viscount, Selections from
        Private Journals of Tours in France in 1815 and
        1818.  London, 1871.
Contains records of conversations with Wellington on
various subjects, the qualities of British and allied
troops in war and peace, military tactics and the removal
of French works of art in 1815, and from 1818, Wellington
on how he had defeated the French in battle.

179.         Parker, Charles Stuart, ed., Sir Robert Peel
        from his Private Papers.  3 vols., London, 1899.
Includes letters to and from the Duke, on all manner
of political subjects.  Volume 1 ends in 1817; volume 2
covers the years from 1827 to 1843 and volume 3 covers the
years from 1843 to 1850.

180.         Parker, Charles Stuart, The Life and Letters of
        Sir James Graham, Second Baronet of Netherby, P.C.,
        G.C.B., 1792-1861.  2 vols., London, 1907.
Volume 1 reproduces much valuable correspondence
between the Duke and Graham during Peel's Ministry of
1841-6.  Incidental mention is also made elsewhere.

181.         Phipps, Hon. Edmund, Memoirs of the Political
        and Literary Life of Robert Plumer Ward, Esq. ...
        Vol. 2, London, 1850.
Includes a useful diary for 1819 and 1820 when Ward
was Clerk of the Ordnance, in close contact with Wellington,
the Master General.

182.         Raikes, Harriet, ed., Private Correspondence of
        Thomas Raikes with the Duke of Wellington and other
        distinguished contemporaries.  London, 1861.
Letters to and from the Duke, dating mainly from the
early 1840s and dealing mostly with foreign affairs.

183.         Simmons, J.S.G., "The Duke of Wellington and the
        Vice-Chancellorship in 1844." Bodleian Library
        Record, 5 (1954-5): 37-52.
An account of the Duke's role in settling a disputed
election to the Vice-Chancellorship of Oxford University.
Based on primary sources: two of the Duke's letters are
printed in full.

184.         "Sin embargo de que el Gobierno annuncio en
        Gazeta di 28 de Mayo."  Manila', 1814.

A letter of thanks to Wellington following the capture of San Sebastian.

185.        Stanhope, Fifth Earl, Notes of Conversations with the Duke of Wellington, 1831-1851. London, 1888.
Records written down within hours of the conversations having taken place. Stanhope relentlessly questioned the Duke about all matters relating to his career, and this is a very valuable record of Wellington's opinions on all matters from Kings of England to Spanish generals, to Corn Laws and Catholics, the public and the British army.

186.        Stanhope, Fifth Earl and Edward Cardwell, eds., Memoirs by the Right Honourable Sir Robert Peel, Bart., M.P.  2 vols., London, 1856.
Includes much correspondence from the Duke and comments about him, dealing with Roman Catholic emancipation, Peel's ministry of 1834-5 and the repeal of the Corn Laws.

187.        Strachey, Lytton and Roger Fulford, eds., The Greville Memoirs, 1814-1860.  8 vols., London, 1938.
The most complete edition of the famous memoirs, containing many records of conversations with the Duke and thoughts on his sayings and actions.  Greville was a fairly impartial witness and is not always favourable to Wellington.

188.        Strafford, Countess of, ed., Personal Reminiscences of the Duke of Wellington by Francis, the First Earl of Ellesmere. London, 1903.
A collection of letters to, from and about the Duke; a long reminiscence on him by Ellesmere (and one on Ellesmere by his daughter); extracts from contemporary memoranda about the Duke, and Ellesmere's account of the battle of Waterloo.  Arranged haphazardly, not by chronological order or subject, and public and private letters are inextricably mixed up.  Covers the period from 1820 to 1852.

189.        Taylor, Tom, ed., The Autobiography and Memoirs of Benjamin Robert Haydon (1786-1846) edited from his journals.  2 vols., London, 1853.
Volume 2 contains a good description of a visit to Walmer Castle, and some other anecdotes about, and correspondence with, the Duke, by a persistent artist.

190.        Vane, Charles, Marquess of Londonderry, ed., Memoirs and Correspondence of Viscount Castlereagh, Second Marquess of Londonderry. 12 vols., London, 1848-1853.
Volumes 6 to 12 contain much correspondence from the Duke, a close friend and colleague of Castlereagh.  Volumes 6 to 10 deal with the war years.

191.        Weigall, Lady Rose S.M., ed., The Correspondence of Lady Burghersh with the Duke of Wellington.

London, 1903.
Comprises, primarily, letters from the Duke to Lady
Burghersh, his niece, but also includes some letters to her
husband, and a memorandum by her about the Duke's character.
The letters cover the period from 1815 and 1852, and are
mostly of a personal nature, published to show the Duke's
private character in a favourable light.

192.       Wellesley, Colonel the Hon. F.A., ed., The
           Diary and Correspondence of Henry Wellesley, First
           Lord Cowley, 1790-1846.  2 vols., London, 1930.
Concentrates on the official career as a diplomat in
India, Spain and France of Wellington's youngest brother.
Little mention of the Duke or Cowley's private life.

193.       Wellington, Seventh Duke of, ed., The Conver-
           sations of the First Duke of Wellington with
           George William Chad.  Cambridge, 1956.
A series of notes of conversations by Chad, from 1820
to 1848, covering such topics as Wellington's battles and
recent national and international politics, from a Tory
point of view.

194.       Wrottesley, George, The Life and Correspondence
           of Field Marshal Sir John Burgoyne, Bart., Volume
           1, London, 1873.
Contains a great deal of information on the Peninsular
war, including letters from the Duke, as well as later
correspondence relating to the national defences.  Burgoyne
was Wellington's chief Engineer in the Peninsula.

195.       Yonge, Charles Duke, The Life and Administration
           of Robert Banks Jenkinson, Second Earl of Liverpool
           K.G.,late First Lord of the Treasury.  3 vols.,
           London, 1868.
Volume 1 covers the Peninsular war from the point of
view of the home government; volume 2 goes down to 1820,
and includes some material on Wellington's appointment as
Master General of the Ordnance; volume 3 deals with
Wellington as a diplomat and politician, down to April 1827.

# Section E
# Contemporary Pamphlets

196.       An Account of the Entertainment Given to the
           Duke of Wellington by the Corporation of London in
           the Guildhall, on the 9th of July 1814. London,
           1816.
    The official account, lavishly presented, listing all
those able or unable to attend a banquet, and reproducing
the speech of welcome made to the Duke.

197.       Aednr-Nos, S.I., The Chronicles of Reform of
           the Children of the Isles in the Days of Arthur,
           the Chief Ruler of the Land, and his Colleagues.
           Edinburgh, 1832.
    A blasphemous account of the Reform Bill crisis,
written in the style of the Authorised Version of the Bible.
Unfriendly to Wellington.

198.       Angerstein, J.J., Victory of Waterloo,
           eighteenth June 1815. [London, 1815].
    A large broadsheet, with an impressive coat of arms
depicting the Duke's victory, sending him the congrat-
ulations of the City of London and subscribers for the
benefit of the wounded, and including a lithograph of
Wellington's reply.

199.       Batty, R.E., Wellington and the Pulpit. A Reply
           to a Sermon on the 'Life and Character of
           Wellington'. London, 1853.
    An outspoken attack on admirers of the Duke and those
who felt his military life was worthy of emulation.

200.       Brewster, Patrick, Wellington 'Weighed in the
           Balance' or, War a Crime, Self-Defence a Duty.
           With a brief reference to the Claims of Hungary
           and Italy. Paisley, 1853.
    A sermon, using Wellington's death to comment on
"just" and "unjust" war and unnecessary cruelty. Some
words of praise for the Duke.

201.       A Brief Exposition of the foreign policy of

Mr. Canning, as contrasted with that of the
existing administration. London, 1830.
Criticises Wellington for supporting absolutist
monarchies and fears it may lead to general war. Contrasts
this with Canning's wise, liberal, policy.

202.        'Britannicus', A Letter to Samuel Whitbread,
            Esq., M.P., upon the Military Conduct of Lord
            Wellington, with some remarks upon the Marquess
            Wellesley's Government in India, and the fatal
            effects of party spirit. London, 1810.
Strong defence of Wellington's conduct in Spain
against ignorant attacks made out of party spite in Parliament and the press. Includes an equally strong defence of
Marquess Wellesley.

203.        Brougham, H.P., The Speech of Lord Brougham
            at the Dover Festival. London, 1839.
A pamphlet of Brougham's eulogy on the Duke, given at
the Wellington Banquet in Dover in 1839.

204.        [? Brougham, H.P,], The Result of the General
            Election; or, What has the Duke of Wellington
            gained by the dissolution. 2nd ed., London, 1830.
Argues that the Duke, because of his failures, has
lost the 1830 election, and will shortly be defeated. This
pamphlet went through at least four editions.

205.        Bush, Robert Wheler, England's Two Great
            Military Captains: Marlborough and Wellington. A
            Lecture delivered to the Church of Englands Young
            Men's Society at Islington, December 17, 1852.
            London, 1853.
A survey of the characters, as soldiers, diplomatists
and in private life, of both men, and generous to both.

206.        'Caleb', Vox Populi or the Naked Truth.
            London, 1830.
A strong attack on Wellington and his government
(unfortunately published after it had fallen), calling for
drastic cuts in public spending.

207.        Camden, Theophilus, The History of the Present
            War in Spain and Portugal with memoirs of the
            life of the Marquis of Wellington. London, 1813.
A brief and very favourable memoir of Wellington's
life up to January 1814, with a full account of the war in
Spain and Portugal, and Wellington's involvement in it.

208.        Caravita and Liverati, Il Trionfo di Cesare
            sopra i Galla; Cantata as represented at The King's
            Theatre, in the Haymarket, In Honour of the
            glorious victory obtained by the Immortal
            WELLINGTON over the French Army, June 18, 1815.
            London, 1815.
The words, in English and Italian, to an operatic

ballet, with Caesar's return to Rome overshadowed at the
end by the rise of Britannia - and Wellington.

209.         'A Citizen of London.' Letters to the Duke of
          Wellington from 1828 to 1830 on currency.
          London, 1831.
          Seven letters, written between February 1828 and
March 1830, calling on the Duke to abandon the gold
standard and cut taxes as a means of relieving distress.

210.         'Clergyman of the Church of England', A Letter
          to His Grace the Duke of Wellington.  London, 1828.
          Argues in favour of Catholic Emancipation, as a
measure of social justice and as a means of attaching
Ireland more securely to the British connection.

211.         The Country Well Governed; or plain questions on
          the perplexed state of the parties in opposition.
          London, 1830.
          Contends that the country needs a strong government,
and that the Duke is the best man to provide it.

212.         The Country without a Government or plain
          questions upon the unhappy state of the present
          adminstration.  London, 1830.
          A strong attack on the Duke's administration:
Wellington is the only man of talent among them, and so he
tries to do everything and ends up doing nothing.

213.         Devereux, James E., The Duke of Wellington, Lord
          Killeen, and Lord Plunkett.  1828.
          Reprint of an article in the Morning Chronicle
calling on the Duke to give immediate and unconditional
relief to Roman Catholics.

214.         The Duke of Wellington and the Whigs.  London,
          1830.
          A Tory view of the Duke's actions: argues that
Wellington should govern firmly, and that he alone can deal
with the pressing domestic and international problems.

215.         The Duke's Coat, or the Night after Waterloo;
          a Dramatic Anecdote; Prepared for Representation on
          the 6th September, at the Theatre Royal, Lyceum,
          and Interdicted by the Licenser of Plays.  London,
          1815.
          A farce with music, banned by the censor, it concerns
an A.D.C. and his coat, staying at La Belle Alliance farm,
and mistaken for Wellington.

216.         England's Pre-Eminence in Arms: A New Song
          addressed to the Honourable Lieut. Gen. Sir Arthur
          Wellesley. [? 1808].
          Written in celebration of Wellington's victory at
Vimeiro.

217.        'An Englishman and Civilian', The Invasion of
England, considered in a letter and postscript to
The Times, dated 30th January, and 5th February
1852, containing the opinions of the Duke of
Wellington and of other officers of distinction.
London, 1852.
Writes in support of, and quotes extensively from,
Wellington's letter to Sir John Burgoyne of 1847, on the
state of the national defences.

218.        Flanagan, L., The Wellington Prosecution
developed in a letter addressed to the Duke of
Wellington ... London, 1831.
The author defends himself against charges of inciting
a riot outside Apsley House, claiming he was trying to
prevent an outrage rather than start one.

219.        Flesher, Gilbert, For the anniversary of the
memorable Battle of Waterloo (June 18, 1815).
[? 1820].
A poem, written prior to the battle, reissued to
celebrate the Duke's latest triumph.  Date of publication
uncertain.

220.        Forster, William, Rev., The Life of Wellington:
its lessons to young men.  A Discourse.  London,
1852.
Wellington's life seen as the perfect example to
follow: young men should emulate his character, and be
prepared to follow his profession.  This is the pamphlet
to which Batty's is a reply.

221.        Gentili, M.A., L'Uomo dell'Europa. Arturo
Wellesley, Wellington, Pari e duca della Gran
Brettagna. Florence, 1815.
A brief, laudatory, pamphlet, outlining  Wellington's
life and career to date.

222.        Gordon, J.T., Eloge on Field Marshal The Duke of
Wellington Pronounced Before the Philosophical
Society of Edinburgh on Thursday, 18th November.
Edinburgh, 1852.
This eulogy on Wellington from a political opponent,
concentrates on his greatness as a soldier, but recognises
his work as a politician.

223.        Gore, Montague, Letter to his Grace the Duke of
Wellington on the present state of affairs in
India.  3rd ed., London, 1843.
A pamphlet stressing the importance of India to Britain
on political and moral grounds, and arguing that Britain's
prestige must be reasserted following recent events in
Afghanistan.

224.        Gore, Montague, Lecture on the character of the

late Duke of Wellington delivered at Wells,
September 1852, during the meeting of the North
Somerset Yeomanry. London, 1852.
   A brief eulogy, stressing the "Englishness" of the
Duke's character in its simplicity, directness and
resolution: a good example to follow.

225.      Government without Whigs, being an answer to
          the "Country without a Government" and the
          Edinburgh Reviewer. London, 1830.
   Defends Wellington against charges that he runs a one-
man government, and argues that the united, Tory, government of the Duke is better than a factious Whig one.

226.      Govion Broglie Solari, A. and Catherine Hyde
          Solari, Wellington. Poemetto del Marchese Antonio
          Solaris, and Wellington Proved to be the Greatest
          Warrior of Ancient and Modern Times. London, 1820.
   Privately printed. An epic poem in Italian and a
survey of warfare from Ancient Greece to 1815 in English,
combine to form a eulogistic appraisal of the Duke's career.

227.      'Graduate of the University of Oxford, Reply to
          a Pamphlet entitled: "What has the Duke of
          Wellington gained by the dissolution?". London,
          1830.
   Written by an ultra Tory supporter of the Duke,
defending him against charges of interfering in the 1830
elections and arguing that the Tory party did well in it.

228.      Grattan, W., The Duke of Wellington and the
          Peninsular Medal. London, 1845.
   A strong attack on Wellington and the Horse Guards for
refusing to issue, or support the issue of, a medal to
Peninsular War veterans.

229.      The Great Duke's Motto, "Duty". London, 1853.
   A one page tract, urging people to follow Wellington,
and do their "duty" to God and Man.

230.      Host, Richard, The Horse Guards by the two
          mounted sentries. 2nd ed., London, 1850.
   A strong attack on Wellington's administration of the
army, both on personal grounds, but above all because of
faults in the system. Argues the Duke should now retire.

231.      'Hippolyte', Observations d'un Francais, sur
          l'enlèvement des Chefs-d'oeuvres du Museum de Paris,
          en reponse a la lettre du duc de Wellington au Lord
          Castlereagh, sous la date du 3 Septembre 1815.
          Paris, 1815.
   Includes a French translation of the Duke's despatch
to Castlereagh, approving the decision to take by force, if
necessary, paintings belonging to the King of the
Netherlands.

232.        Histoire du singe de Napoleon. Paris, 1822.
A brief, unflattering, life of the Duke, making
comparisons between him and a monkey.

233.        Hughes, Thomas, Wellington. A Lecture on his
            career and character. London, 1853.
Reflections on the Duke's life and death, with lessons
to be learned from these events, from a Christian point of
view.

234.        'Jamaica Proprietor', Negro Emancipation No
            Philanthropy. A Letter to the Duke of Wellington.
            London, 1830.
Recounts a series of arguments in favour of negro
slavery, and outlines the likely disastrous consequences of
its abolition.

235.        James, George Payre Rainford, An oration on the
            Character and services of the late Duke of
            Wellington: Delivered before the British Residents
            of Boston and Vicinity, and their American friends,
            at the Melodeon, Nov. 10, 1852. Boston [Mass.],
            1853.
An English speaker addressing an English audience. A
fairly detailed study of the Indian campaigns, less on the
Peninsula, and nothing on politics, except to show the
Duke's humanity and generosity.

236.        Keble, J., et al, Congratulatory Addresses
            received in the Theatre, Oxford, at the Install-
            ation of His Grace the Duke of Wellington,
            Chancellor of the University. Oxford, 1834.
A collection of eighteen addresses, poems and essays
written in English, Latin, Greek and other languages,
praising the Duke's great achievements in war and peace.

237.        The King and his Prime Grey Cock; and the
            destruction of the Waterloo Black Bantam. London,
            1830.
A strong condemnation of Wellington's government,
believing them fools, if nothing worse, and looking forward
to Lord Grey's administration.

238.        King, Ebedmelech, A Letter to George IV.
            London, [1828].
An appeal to the King to save the country from the
Roman Catholics, and to prevent Wellington, with their help
and that of the army, overthrowing the monarchy and
becoming dictator.

239.        The Leading Articles on the death of the Duke
            of Wellington, which appeared in "The Times" of
            September 15th and 16th. London, 1852.
A cheap reprint of two leading articles, for popular
circulation.

240.       A Letter to his Grace the Duke of Wellington
           K.G. on Branch Banks. London, 1828.
Defends the Bank of England's branch banks, and urges
Wellington not to abandon the policy of allowing only those
banks to issue coin.

241.       A Letter to the Duke of Wellington, on the
           propriety and legality of creating Peers for life,
           with precedents. 2nd ed., London, 1830.
The author is worried that too many poor men are
created hereditary Peers, so the Peerage loses dignity: he
suggests Life Peerages should be introduced as a reward for
good public conduct.

242.       Lewis, J.H., Lewis's Oration on the Battle of
           Waterloo and the rise and fall of Buonaparte.
           London, 1815.
Includes two speeches and a poem, portraying the Duke
as the embodiment of virtue. Privately printed.

243.       L'Eveque, Henry, Campaigns of the British Army
           in Portugal, under the command of General the Earl
           of Wellington, K.B. London, 1812.
A large format work, illustrating in engravings
Wellington's triumphs in Portugal between 1808 and 1810.

244.       The Life and Martial Achievements of the Most
           Noble Arthur, Duke of Wellington, Commander in
           Chief of the Combined Army at the Battle of
           Waterloo. Falkirk, 1817.
A very small and cheaply produced pamphlet, but a
nicely written, straightforward account of Wellington's
career down to the occupation of Paris in 1815.

245.       Love at Headquarters, or a week in Brussels.
       A mock epic poem, carefully mentioning no names,
dealing with Wellington's relationship with Lady Frances
Webster. Place and date of publication unknown.

246.       May, Walter Barton, A Panegyric in honor of the
           Duke of Wellington. Taunton, 1854.
Written as a letter to a friend, this work is as
favourable to Wellington as the title suggests.

247.       'Member of the House of Commons', A short letter
           to his grace the Duke of Rutland, K.G., on the
           present aspect of political life. London, 1830.
Expresses fear of Wellington's "liberal" tendencies:
would like to support him, but fears what he might do next.

248.       'A Minister of the Establishment', A letter to
           the Duke of Wellington on the reasonableness of a
           Church Reform and its peculiar fitness to the
           present time. 3rd ed., London, 1830.

Very lengthy call for Wellington to exert his great
talents and reform the Church of England, by redistributing
income from bishoprics, and improving the clergy.

249.       Muntz, George F., Three letters to the Duke of
       Wellington in 1829 and 1830, upon the distressed
       State of the Country. Birmingham, 1830.
Three letters, dated between April 1829 and February
1830, outlining the author's proposals to revive the
economy, primarily by abandoning the gold standard.

250.       Musa Victoriae. An irregular ode with notes ...
       respectfully dedicated to Field Marshal the Duke
       of Wellington. Chelmsford, 1814.
A bad poem optimistically celebrating the return of
peace and France's gratitude to her conquerors.

251.       Observations on Two Pamphlets, lately published
       attributed to Mr. Brougham. London, 1830.
Defends Wellington at some length from the attacks in
Brougham's two pamphlets published this year.

252.       Ode for the Encænia at Oxford, June 11, 1834,
       in honour of his Grace, Arthur, Duke of Wellington,
       Chancellor of the University. Oxford, 1834.
An ode, intended for public performance, celebrating
the Duke's installation as Chancellor and his martial
prowess.

253.       'An old soldier', The Gentle Sponge: being a
       safe, easy, certain, and just mode of reducing,
       to any desirable extent, the National Debt of
       England, in a letter to His Grace the Duke of
       Wellington. London, 1829.
A rambling piece, proposing that 1% of their capital
should be taken from every landowner in the country
annually, the funds collected being used to pay off the
National Debt.

254.       'One of the old school', Tory Union our only
       safeguard against revolution. London, 1830.
Expresses great alarm of "the revolution", centred
in Paris, and argues only a united Tory Party under
Wellington can defeat the revolutionary Whigs.

255.       Parties and Factions in England, at the
       Accession of William IV. London, [1830].
A survey of various groups which sees Wellington's as
a truly liberal government, prepared to grant gradual reform,
which all true patriots ought to support.

256.       Phillipart, Mrs. John, Victoria. [1813].
A poem to celebrate the Duke's success at Vitoria.

257.       Phillips, Charles, Historical Sketch of Arthur,

Duke of Wellington. Brighton, 1852.
A brief and rather absurd eulogy on the Duke, anxious
to stress his greatness as an Irishman.

258.        Plan of Finance for the Reduction of the
National Debt and Relief of Prevailing Distress in
a letter addressed to the Duke of Wellington.
London, 1830.
An attempt to encourage Wellington to alleviate
distress by regulating the stock market and increasing
government spending on productive investments.

259.        Political Life, Fortunes and Character of the
Military dictator, Duke of Wellington.  Glasgow,
[? 1834].
A cheap tract, strongly attacking Wellington for
rigidity and harshness during, and especially after, the
war, and for greed at the wars end.  Indicative of the
Duke's low popular esteem in the early 1830s.

260.        Principal Characters in the New Piece entitled
The Man Wot Drives the Sovereign.  [? London,
1828].
A satirical broadside, with an illustration of Arthur,
or "Nosey" or "Achilles, the man wot drives the sovereign",
and his unsavoury cronies, i.e. Wellington as Prime
Minister and his Cabinet.

261.        Rees, A.A., The Death of Wellington and the
resurrection of Napoleon, being a Lecture, Critical
Historical, and Prophetical, delivered at Bethseda
Free Chapel, on Thursday, the 18th November, 1852,
the day of the Funeral of the late Duke.
Sunderland, 1852.
Really has little reference to Wellington beyond
mentioning his death, and is more alarmed at the coming of
the Napoleonic "beast".

262.        The Result of the Pamphlet: Or, What the Duke
has to look to.  London, 1830.
A defence of the Wellington government's policies on
specific issues, such as Poor Laws, Corn Laws, Parliamentary
Reform and the Civil List.

263.        'Roman Catholic Barrister', A Letter to his
Grace the Duke of Wellington ... on the justice
and expediency of Catholic Emancipation, at the
present important crisis, in which is discussed
the question of securities.  Dublin, 1828.
A reasoned call on the Duke to grant Catholic
Emancipation in the interests of peace and social justice,
especially for Ireland.

264.        'Roman Catholic Barrister', A Short Letter to
his Grace the Duke of Wellington [etc.] on the
subject of "Securities" as connected with the

removal of Catholic Disabilities. Dublin, 1829.
A moderate supporter of Catholic emancipation, who is
prepared to accept certain restrictions on Catholics to
secure it.

265.       'Scotch Catholic', A Letter to his Grace the
           Duke of Wellington, K.G., respecting the
           "securities" necessary towards emancipation.
           Edinburgh, 1828.
Argues that the Pope has no temporal power and therefore Catholic emancipation would pose no threat, and reminds
the Duke of the services of his Irish Catholic soldiers.

266.       The Sphynx. London, 1835.
An attack on Peel's Ministry of 1834, with the Duke
seen as the leading Tory in it.

267.       'Syntax, Dr.', The Wars of Wellington. A
           Narrative Poem, embellished with thirty engravings.
           London, privately printed, 1819.
A very poor poem celebrating the Duke's triumphs from
Assaye to Waterloo. The engravings, usually showing the
Duke in dramatic action, are coloured.

268.       Two great men: one in the highest position that
           was due to him, the other in a very humble station
           in Life; but both of them Uomuni! London, 1861.
An extraordinary work, praising the Duke and a
Spanish peasant who brought him a message at great personal
risk. Factually unreliable.

269.       A Voice from the Tomb. A Dialogue between
           Nelson and Wellington, overheard at St. Paul's
           London, 1859.
A series of forty-two cheap broadsides, these
"conversations" use the characters to launch bitter attacks
on contemporary issues, as much as to comment on past
events.

270.       Webster, James Webster Wedderburn, The
           Important Trial in the Common Pleas, Friday
           February 16, 1816, Webster v. Baldwin, for a libel
           charging adultery between the most noble Arthur,
           Duke of Wellington and Lady Frances C.W. Webster,
           at Brussels, after the Battle of Waterloo.
           London, 1816.
A verbatim account of the proceedings, culminating in
victory for the plaintiffs - Webster and Lady Frances - over
the defendant, Charles Baldwin of the St. James' Chronicle
- and the award to them of £2,000 damages.

271.       Wellington and Uncle Tom: or a hero of this
           world contrasted with the Hero in Jesus Christ.
           London, 1853.
A rather unfair contrast between Wellington and the

hero of Miss Beecher Stowe, to whom this tiny pamphlet, a sermon, is dedicated.

272.    The Wellington Almanack, 1841.   London, 1841.
A small, single, sheet, noting the dates of all of Wellington's, and some other, battles, illustrated, and with an account of the battle of Waterloo.

273.    The Wellington Almanack, 1853.   London, [1852].
A ld pamphlet, which includes not only an almanack for the year, but also a memoir, illustrated with engravings, of the Duke's life, and the order of the procession at his funeral.  The memoir was afterwards reprinted separately.

274.    Wellington Anecdotes.  A Collection of the Sayings and Doings of the Great Duke.  London, 1852.
A cheap pamphlet recounting, more or less in chronological order, stories about, or sayings of the Duke.  No sources are given, and reliability is not always great.

275.    The Wellington Banquet at Dover, Friday, 30 August 1839.  London, [1839].
A description of the banquet in the Duke's honour, with verbatim reports of the speeches made.  Lord Brougham's speech made on this occasion was later reprinted separately as a pamphlet and, with verbal changes, as an appendix to an anonymous life of the Duke of Wellington in 1852.

276.    Wellington dans l'eau jusqu'au cou: il n'en sortira pas.  [Paris, 1815].
A broadside published shortly before Waterloo, attacking the allies, and declaring Wellington to be a bad general, before predicting his downfall.

277.    The Wellington Souvenir.  A Golden Record.  London, 1852.
A brief chronological survey of the Duke's life, produced at the time of his funeral.  Printed in gold and illustrated.  Very brief comments on his political career.

278.    Wellington's Address; To which are added, The Banks of Clyde, The Wells o'Weary, Hand awa frae me Donald.  Edinburgh, 1824.
A very cheap song sheet.  "Wellington's Address" celebrates the victory at Waterloo.

279.    Wellington's Laurels.  Being a choice collection of the newest songs, now singing at all the Public Places of Amusement.  London, [?1815].
A cheap song sheet, printing the words to sixteen songs, seven of which, including "Wellington's Laurels" and "British heroism in Spain", directly relate to Wellington and his Peninsular victories.

280.          'Whig Commoner', <u>A letter respectfully
          addressed to his Grace the Duke of Wellington on
          the question of reform</u>.  London, 1831.
     Hopes that the Lords will reject the current Reform
Bill, and that a more moderate measure, presumably to be
introduced by Wellington, will be approved.

281.          'Wholesale Grocer', <u>A letter to the Duke of
          Wellington on the Expediency of an Income tax</u>.
          London, 1829.
     A very sensible, and well presented case, for
abolishing indirect taxes, and replacing them with direct
ones.

# Section F
# Contemporary Newspapers

282. The life and career of the Duke of Wellington featured
in a great many newspapers for many years.  This section was
compiled from the following newspapers: all, with one
exception, were published in London.

The Age (1828-35) (Tory)
The Courier  (1809-41) (Liberal-Tory)
The Daily News (1852) (Liberal)
The Examiner (1809-52) (Whig-Radical)
The Globe (1827-52) (Conservative)
The Manchester Guardian  (1827-52) (Radical-Liberal)
The Morning Advertiser  (1809-52) (Whig)
The Morning Chronicle  (1809-52) (Whig)
The Morning Herald (1809-52) (Tory)
The Morning Post (1809-52) (Conservative)
The News of the World (1852) (Radical)
The Observer (1809-52) (Radical)
The St. James' Chronicle (1809-52) (Tory)
The Spectator (1852) (Liberal)
The Standard (1828-52) (Tory)
The Sun (1809-52) (Whig)
The Sunday Times (1827-52) (Radical)
The Times (1809-52) (Liberal-Conservative)
The Weekly Despatch (1827-52) (Radical)

Each newspaper was examined for evidence of its
attitude towards the Duke at key moments in his career.

## The Convention of Cintra

The findings of the Court of Enquiry into the signature
of the Convention were reported in the most important London
daily papers.  The Courier (4 January 1809) strongly condemned the Convention, as did the Morning Advertiser (3
January) and The Times (4 January).  The Examiner (8 January)
pointed out no-one favoured the Convention, while The
Morning Chronicle  (January) criticised all operations in
Portugal.  The St. James' Chronicle (January) was more
interested in the scandal surrounding the Duke of York.

However, Sir Arthur Wellesley's reputation survived.
The Courier (4 April) and The Morning Advertiser (26 May)
both believed he was a good general: only The Examiner
(4 June), which declared Sir Arthur to be a brave man, had
doubts about his ability to defeat the French.

### The Peninsular War

As the war progressed, opinions of Wellington rose to
an ever higher pitch of admiration. The Courier (16 May
1809) never wavered in its support for the war, nor did The
Sun (28 August 1809; 13 July 1813).  The Morning Advertiser
(11 August 1810) considered Wellington's army the best in
Europe, while the St. James' Chronicle strongly supported
the campaign.  The Times (11 August 1813) decided Wellington
had a "genius" for war.  The Morning Post (16 August 1809)
proudly declared that it stood by Wellington while others
doubted, and (7 September 1809) defended him from attacks,
real and imagined, at home.  On 6 July 1813 the paper
enthused over the victory at Vitoria.  Some were more
cautious.  The Morning Chronicle (27 January 1813) expressed
doubts about the justice of the war, but (15 July) forgot
this when rejoicing over Vitoria. The Examiner (30 January,
3 April 1814) thought progress was not good enough.

### Waterloo

The Courier (20 June 1815) was most optimistic about
the outcome of the campaign.  The Morning Chronicle (21
June) reported hopefully that a victory had been won even
before news arrived of the battle on 18 June.  The Sun
(14 June) did not doubt Wellington was ready for anything,
nor did The Times (9 May) which scorned French reports that
the Duke had been beaten (16 June 1815).  The Morning Post
(17 April) was fully confident the Duke would win.

All papers reported in triumphal terms the defeat of
Napoleon.  This news was confirmed in England on 22 June.

### The succession to Lord Liverpool

On 17 February 1827 Lord Liverpool, the Prime
Minister, suffered a stroke.  When George Canning eventually
succeeded him as Prime Minister in April, Wellington
resigned all his offices.  The newspapers had much to say
on these events.  Some had approved of the Duke's appointment as Commander-in-Chief when it was announced  (see The
Morning Chronicle (24 January 1827), The Sun (24 January),
The Morning Post (24 January)). Others had had reservations
about it. (The Morning Herald (25 January) and The Sunday
Times (22 April)). Only The Examiner (14 January) expressed
total disapproval.
The Duke's resignation from office also occasioned
mixed feelings. The Sun (14 April) strongly criticised his
resignation from the Cabinet.  The Globe (13 April) was
pleased with his retirement from the Cabinet, but not as

Commander-in-Chief. The Times (13-15 April) was pleased
with both decisions, and doubted whether Wellington should
ever have been apppointed Commander-in-Chief. The St.
James' Chronicle (14 April) also approved of the Duke's
resignation - to get away from Canning. The Weekly
Despatch (22 April) strongly attacked the Duke, whose
actions revealed his true character. The Morning Advertiser
(14, 16 April) considered Wellington's decision to resign
from all his offices as "extraordinary" but was not dis-
pleased to see him go.

## Prime Minister

Wellington's becoming Prime Minister occasioned much
comment. His supposed High Tory views meant the appointment
was welcomed by some newspapers and fiercely opposed by
others. The Courier (26 January 1828), The Morning Post
(12 January), The St. James' Chronicle (22 January) were
all strongly in favour of it. The Sun (12 January) did not
take to the idea of an ultra-Tory government, but (25
January) became reconciled to the Duke. The Morning Herald
(19 January) thought he would at least take a commonsense
line. Other papers expressed equally strong opposition to
developments. The Weekly Despatch (27 January) thought the
move "an insult" to the British people: The Sunday Times
(27 January) was also highly critical. The Morning Chronicle (22, 24 January) thought it was not a good idea. The
Times (15 January) hoped the Duke would not be Prime
Minister and (21-23 January) attacked him for remaining
Commander-in-Chief. The Examiner (27 January) thought the
Wellington would now try and become Archbishop of Canterbury
as well. The Manchester Guardian (2 February), The Sunday
Times (3 February) and The Times (4, 5, 7 February) believed
the Duke's resignation as Commander-in-Chief effectively
left him still in command of the army.

## Repeal of the Test and Corporation Acts

This measure also occasioned comment in the press.
The Courier (22 April) and the St. James' Chronicle (22
April) saw why the decision to repeal the Acts had been
taken and gave it guarded approval. The Morning Chronicle
(1 May) thought Wellington gave way at just the right
moment, and expressed hope for the future, as did The
Examiner (2 March). The Globe (19 March) was surprised at
the Duke's "manly course" respecting the measure. The
Morning Advertiser (28 February) also expressed its approval.
The Sunday Times (2 March) was also pleased, but did not
see in the measure any great hope for the future.

## Roman Catholic Relief

The first intimation of this to reach the newspapers
was Wellington's letters to two eminent clerics, Dr. Doyle
and Dr. Curtis. The Morning Herald (2 January 1829)

thought the letter to Dr. Doyle had caused "a sensation" in
Ireland, but (3 January) doubted if it would help Roman
Catholics.  The Globe (1 January) thought the correspondence with Dr. Curtis proved agitation on the question
was overdone.  The Morning Chronicle (2 January), on the
other hand, criticised Wellington.  The Times (1 January)
believed the Duke had been "outflanked" by the clerics.
The announcement in the King's Speech that a measure of
emancipation was proposed was greeted with outrage by the
Tory papers.  The Morning Post (6 January, 3 February) had
argued this would never occur.  The St. James' Chronicle
(24 January) had believed Wellington was not weakening: was
horrified at the "change" (7 February) and became bitterly
critical of the Duke and Peel (14 February, 2, 4 April), as
did The Age, in whose pages between 22 February and 5 March
the Duke descended from being "a GREAT man" to a "dictator".
This experience was paralleled in The Standard, when the
"illustrious premier" of 23 January became "the most
remorseless dictator" of 4 March.
     The Morning Herald (7 March, 4 April) accepted the
Duke's judgement that concession was necessary.  The Courier
(5 April) tried not to comment at all. The Sunday Times
(8 January) thought Wellington and Peel had shrunk from
danger, and had given way.  The Examiner (8, 22 February)
The Globe (3 February, 28 March), The Morning Advertiser
(7 February, 4 March), The Morning Chronicle (4 February)
and The Observer (8 February) were all in favour of the
measure, while The Manchester Guardian (7 February) and The
Weekly Despatch (8 February) greeted in enthusiastically.

Parliamentary Reform

     On 2 November the Duke declared outright opposition
to the idea of Parliamentary Reform.  Only a few papers,
such as The Morning Advertiser (4 November) and The Sunday
Times (7 November)picked up the importance of this when it
occurred.  The Manchester Guardian (6 November) could well
understand why the Duke's declaration caused laughter.
More typical was the reaction of The Times (4 November)
which commented on the speech in negative terms and (5
November) was "surprised" at the opposition it aroused.  It
was only after the Duke's government had fallen that the
speech aquired greater importance in the papers.  This line
was followed by The Morning Chronicle (11 November) and The
Globe (16 November).
     After the Duke had resigned, opinions of his ministry
varied.  The Times (17 November) thought Wellington had done
his best.  The Observer (22 November) was also sorry the
Duke's ministry had fallen, as was The Courier (17 November)
and, for differeent reasons, the St. James' Chronicle (18
November).  The Age (24 November), on the other hand, was
pleased to see the Duke go. The Morning Herald (18 November)
declared that he should have stuck to his profession as a
soldier.

## Proposed Ministry

In May 1832, following the defeat of the Reform Bill and the resignation of the Whigs, Wellington was invited, and attempted, to form a government. This was strongly attacked by the pro-reform newspapers, including The Sun (12, 14, 15, 24 May 1832), The Manchester Guardian (19 May) The Morning Advertiser (15, 16, 18 May), The Weekly Despatch, (13, 20, 27 May) and The Times (14-17 May). The Courier (14, 16 May) pardoned Wellington on the grounds of his political ineptitude. The Tory Morning Herald (15, 18 May) actually supported the Reform Bill, and was confident that Wellington could not stand in the way of it. The Examiner (18, 27 May) praised the Duke as a general, but not as a politician, and declared he should not have tried to form a government. The Age (13 May) was pleased the Duke was coming back into office, and (20 May) blamed Peel for his failure to form a cabinet. The Standard (12, 14 May) thought the Duke could now reunite the Tory Party and pass a moderate Reform Bill, as did The Morning Post (10, 15 May) and the St. James' Chronicle (15, 17 May). The Morning Post lavished extravagant praise on the Duke for his action.

## "Caretaker" Prime Minister

On 15 November 1834 the Duke was appointed caretaker Prime Minister. The Times (17-19, 21-22 November) argued he would have to govern on reforming principles, and only slowly realised he was only standing in for Peel. The Globe (18, 19, 21 November) paid tribute to the Duke as a man, but opposed him as Prime Minister. The Morning Advertiser (17 November) was pleased the enemy was now out in the open and (21, 25 November) firmly opposed the Duke. The Weekly Despatch (23, 30 November, 7 December) launched a strong attack on "the Dictator" for taking office and The Morning Chronicle (18 November) and The Sunday Times (16, 23, 30 November) also expressed concern at the "military dictatorship".

The St. James' Chronicle (20, 27 November) strongly defended the Duke against these charges: the arrangement was only temporary. The Morning Post (17-20 November) and The Standard (19, 20, 27 November) took the same line.

## Fall of Peel's Ministry

This occasioned little comment on the Duke. The Courier (28 March 1835) was very pleased to see the country was to be rescued from the chaos caused by Peel and Wellington's government. Wellington's conduct of foreign policy occasioned some comment in The Times (17 March), but (9 April) although it expressed regret at Peel's fall, it did not mention the Duke.

Peel's Return to Office

By September 1841, when Peel again became Prime
Minister, his ascendancy over Wellington was clearly
reflected in newspapers comments, which make relatively
little mention of the Duke. The Times (2 September) was
pleased to see Wellington's reputation and experience added
to the Cabinet. Other newspapers that commented on the Duke
expressed a different view. The Globe (18, 19 November)
felt Wellington was not a great threat, but he was still a
Tory. The Morning Advertiser (8 September) launched a
strong attack on the Duke's age and reactionary politics.
The Weekly Despatch (10 October) praised the Duke as a
soldier, but not as a politician.

The Repeal of the Corn Laws

When discussion of the question first arose in
November-December 1845, the Duke (along with Lord Stanley)
was seen as the leading opponent of repeal. The Morning
Chronicle (20 October 1845), The Manchester Guardian (12
November), The Weekly Despatch (21 December), The Sunday
Times (9 November) and The Morning Advertiser (26 November)
all believed this, and strongly attacked the Duke as a
result. Only The Morning Post (15 December) argued that he
and Stanley were right in opposing repeal. The Standard
(10 December) argued that there was no division in the
Cabinet on the question anyway.

The Times (4, 5, 11, 12 and 23 December) first reported
that the Corn Laws would be repealed - a fact The Standard
(31 December) was anxious to deny. Wellington's change of
mind on the question - he would now support repeal - was
published in The Morning Chronicle (29 January 1846) -
because it was his duty to the Queen to do so - and The
Examiner (31 January). Wellington's decision exposed him to
covert (in The Morning Post, 24 December 1845) and overt
(in The Globe, 19 December) attack. Those who favoured
repeal would have agreed with the summing up of The
Weekly Despatch (31 May 1846): the Duke had done his last
great service to his country. The Times (1, 11, 29 June),
however, was somewhat critical of the Duke's attitude to the
change.

Death and Funeral

News of Wellington's death was first published in a
late edition of The Sun (14 September 1852). It was published more widely the next day. The Duke's greatness as a
soldier was admitted by all the leading newspapers of the
day, but his political career occasioned some controversy.
Whatever their differences in the past, on 15 September 1852,
The Examiner, The Globe, The Morning Advertiser, The Morning
Post, The St. James' Chronicle and The Weekly Despatch all
praised the Duke's conduct in politics unreservedly. The
assessment of The Morning Chronicle was very balanced and

judicious.  The Morning Herald  cautiously praised the
Duke's politics.  The Sun praised the Duke's sense of Duty,
but The Sunday Times and The Observer both reminded their
readers of the Duke's illiberalism.  The Standard, while
praising the Duke as a man and as a soldier, declared he
was "certainly not" a statesman.  Most newspapers took at
least part of their obituaries from those in The Times
(15, 16 September).

   The character of the Duke's funeral occasioned some
comment.  The Daily News (17 September) thought Wellington
ought to have a "soldier's funeral" - simple and dignified,
and The Morning Post (18 September) agreed.  The News of
the World (19 September) believed he ought to be interred at
"Strathfieldsaye".  The Morning Chronicle (21 September)
declared that the Duke should have a really public funeral.
The Morning Advertiser (18 September) called for a public
funeral, and this was the judgement of most other papers.
When the announcement was made, The St. James' Chronicle
(21 September) expressed full approval, and The News of the
World (26 September), which was critical of public funerals
in general, made an exception for this one, as did The
Daily News (20 September).  The Times (21 September)
accepted the long delay before the funeral because it would
ensure the obsequies were suitably impressive.

   The actual funeral was fully described in all the
papers on 19 November.  Most, like The Times approved -
although even The Times described the "car" carrying the
coffin as "a ponderous vehicle".  The Morning Advertiser
considered the ceremony uniquely impressive, and The St.
James' Chronicle thought it was almost worthy of the Duke.
Only The Examiner went so far as to say that "the pageant
failed".  All the other papers agreed that the Duke's
funeral was a truly national occasion, and fully appropriate
for the Great Duke.

# Part Two
## Speeches and
## Public Writings

283.        National Defences: Letters of Lord Ellesmere
and the Duke of Wellington and the Speech of
Richard Cobden, Esq., M.P. at the Free Trade
Meeting in Manchester. London, 1848.
    Includes Wellington's alarmist letter to Sir John
Burgoyne of 24 January 1847, and contrasts it with two
other views of the subject.

284.        Speech of the Duke of Wellington on the motion
for the Second Reading of the Reform Bill, in the
House of Lords, Tuesday, 4th October 1831.
London, 1831.
    A verbatim report of a speech, attacking Lord Grey
for inconsistency in proposing a reform bill, predicting
dire consequences - such as democracy, secret ballots and
the end of the Union - following its passage, and urging
Peers to reject the measure.

285.        Speeches of Eminent British Statesmen During the
Thirty Years Peace. First Series: From the Close
of the Great War to the Passing of the Reform
Bill. London & Glasgow, 1854.
    Includes a temperate speech by Wellington justifying
his change of policy on the question of Roman Catholic
Relief, comprising a review of the proposed measure, its
expediency, the lack of any realistic alternative and the
"securities" that still existed for the Protestants.

286.        Speeches of the Marquess of Londonderry and the
Duke of Wellington on the presentations of
petitions against the Bill for the abolition of
the Lord Lieutenancy of Ireland. London, 1850.
    Verbatim reports of speeches strongly deprecating the
proposed abolition of the Lord Lieutenancy - in the Duke's
case on the grounds of military and bureaucratic expediency.

287.        Substance of Sir Arthur Wellesley's Speech

delivered in the Committee of the House of Commons, on the India Budget, on Thursday, July 10th, 1806. London, 1806.
A detailed account of the economic situation of British India, and a defence of Marquess Wellesley's conduct there, in particular with relation to the cession of the fortress of Gwalior.

288.    Summary of the Session.  Speech of the Right Hon. Lord Lyndhurst, Delivered in the House of Lords, on Tuesday, August 18, 1836, to which is added, the substance of the Speech of His Grace the Duke of Wellington upon the same occasion.  26th edition, London, [1836].
A brief defence of Lyndhurst and the Lords by Wellington, against accusations of "wrecking" Bills passed by the Commons, for party reasons.

289.    "Wellington's warning of invasion." Fort, 9 (Supplement) (1981): 57-76.
A copy of the Duke's letter to Sir John Burgoyne of 1847, with an introduction and notes.

# Part Three
# General Biography

290.　　　　Adams, W.H.D., and W. Pairman, Great Generals.
　　　　London, 1905.
　　A brief survey of Wellington's life, coupling his
name with other 'great generals', Charlemagne, Edward III,
Gustavus Adolphus, Marlborough and Roberts. A standard
account.

291.　　　　Aldington, Richard, The Duke. Being an Account
　　　　of the Life and Achievements of Arthur Wellesley,
　　　　First Duke of Wellington. New York, 1943.
　　A detailed account of Wellington's life, including
apposite quotations from primary sources and some
illustrations. Deals at length with the war years, less
with the period after 1815. Reissued in London in 1946.

292.　　　　Alexander, Sir James, Life of Field Marshal his
　　　　Grace the Duke of Wellington, embracing his Civil,
　　　　Military and Political Career to the Present Time.
　　　　2 vols., London, 1839-40.
　　A long work, mainly concerned with the Duke's military
career and based on his despatches. An interesting view of
contemporary attitudes to the Duke, and displays a marked
partiality for him.

293.　　　　"Anecdotes of Wellington." The New Quarterly
　　　　Review, 2 (1853): 51-7.
　　A collection of rather unlikely anecdotes, drawn from
the author's personal recollections and from four volumes
of reminiscences published at the time of Wellington's
death.

294.　　　　Azcarate, Pablo de, Wellington y España.
　　　　Madrid, 1960.
　　A careful survey, in Spanish and based on printed
primary sources, of Wellington's involvement with Spain
(and some notable Spaniards), not simply during the
Peninsular War, but also in the turbulent politics of the
1820s and 1830s.

295.          Bernard, Henri, <u>Le duc de Wellington et la</u>
             <u>Belgique</u>. 1973.
     Deals in general terms with the strategic position of
the Low Countries, and Wellington's life both before and
after Waterloo, but devotes most attention to the campaign
of 1815 and Wellington's thoughts on the "Barrier
Fortresses".

296.          Brett, O., <u>Wellington</u>. London, 1928.
     A full life, not going into detail, but trying to
present a general view of the Duke's personality. Based on
primary printed sources.

297.          Brialmont, A.H., <u>Histoire du duc de Wellington.</u>
             3 vols., Paris, 1856.
     An objective survey by a Belgian soldier. Volumes 1
and 2 comrpise a chronological study of Wellington's
military career; and include very good maps. Volume 3 gives
some consideration to the Duke's civil life, and an assessment of his character.
     Some original correspondence is included.

298.          Brialmont, A.H. and Gleig, G.R., <u>The Life of the</u>
             <u>Duke of Wellington.</u> 4 vols., London, 1858-60.
     Based on Brialmont's work of 1856. Volumes 1 and 2
follow Brialmont almost exactly, although with some added
comments. Volumes 3 and 4 relate to the Duke's civil life.
This is entirely new work, based on Wellington's papers and
Gleig's personal knowledge. Generally discreet, but
coloured by Gleig's admiration for the Duke.

299.          "Brialmont's 'Duke of Wellington.'" <u>Dublin</u>
             <u>University Magazine</u>, 51 (1858): 146-56; 309-19;
             450-58.
     An appreciative review of Brialmont's book,
criticising it simply because, although favourable, it is
not favourable enough to the Duke.

300.          Casadesus Vila, J., <u>Tres grandes Ingleses.</u>
             <u>Moore, Wellington, Shakespeare.</u> Barcelona, 1918.
     Three lectures: that on Wellington is extremely
favourable to the Duke, but really adds nothing new.

301.          Cecil, Algernon, "The characters of Napoleon
             and Wellington compared." <u>The Quarterly Review</u>,
             249 (July-October 1927): 215-33.
     Contrasts Wellington's and Napoleon's private and
public conduct: greatly favourable to the former - a
patriot who always did his duty.

302.          Charles, Alex., "Ministers and Maxims: V.
             Wellington. 'Do Your Duty'." <u>Temple Bar</u>, 50
             (1877): 30-46.
     A survey of the Duke's career, approving of his
conduct as a soldier and admiring of his personality: does

not like his politics.

303.        Chastenet de Castaing, J.A.A.G., <u>Wellington.</u>
<u>1769-1852.</u>  Paris, 1945.
    A scholarly life based on primary sources.  Gives a
balanced coverage of Wellington's military and civil life.
Produced in difficult circumstances.

304.        'Citizen of the World', <u>The military and</u>
<u>political life of Arthur Wellesley, Duke of</u>
<u>Wellington.</u>  London, 1852.
    An unpretentious survey of Wellington's life,
illustrated with engravings.  The author believes Wellington
to have been the world's greatest general, and Waterloo its
most notable event.

305.        Cooke, Alfred R., <u>Wellington: The Story of his</u>
<u>Life, his Battles and Political Career.</u>  London,
<u>1852.</u>
    Relies heavily on Maxwell's 1839-41 <u>Life</u>, but gives
some space to Wellington's career in peace time.  Straightforward narrative, adds nothing new.  More hostile to the
Spaniards and Prussians than the French.

306.        Cooper, Leonard, <u>The Age of Wellington.  The</u>
<u>Life and Times of the Duke of Wellington, 1769-1852.</u>
<u>London, 1964.</u>
    An attempt to place Wellington's life in its broader
context, but ends up as a 'standard life', with little new
material, and little to say about the years after 1815.

307.        Cruttwell, C.R.M.F., <u>Wellington.</u> London, 1936.
    A brief and laudatory life: one in the publisher's
series of 'Great Men'.  Adds nothing new.

308.        Cumming, John, <u>Wellington.  A Lecture.</u>  London,
1853.
    A review of the Duke's career, occasioned by his death.

309.        Cumming, John, <u>Wellington. A new and enlarged</u>
<u>edition.</u>  London, 1853.
    An enlarged lecture, designed to 'help the reader form
some opinion of the moral grandeur ... of the illustrious
hero.' Very fervent, and very Protestant.

310.        Davies, G., "Wellington the Man." <u>Journal of the</u>
<u>Society for Army Historical Research</u>  XXX, (1952):
<u>96-112.</u>
    A scholarly investigation of Wellington's character,
covering the whole of his career and strongly defending him
against attacks, old and new.

311.        Davies, George Jennings, <u>The Completeness of the</u>
<u>Late Duke of Wellington as a National Character.</u>
<u>Two Lectures.</u>  London, 1854.
Outlines the many noble facets of Wellington's

character for others to follow.  Based primarily on recent obituaries of the Duke.

312.         De Grey, Earl, <u>Characteristics of the Duke of Wellington, apart from his military talents.</u> London, 1853.
A compilation of extracts from the Duke's published despatches, arranged by character trait rather than chronologically.  A useful collection, despite the author's partiality.

313.         "The Duke of Wellington."  <u>Blackwood's Edinburgh Magazine</u>, 22 (July-December 1827): 222-37.
An eulogistic survey of the Duke's military career, together with a brief justification of his resignation from Canning's Ministry and as Commander-in-Chief.

314.         "The Duke of Wellington." <u>Dublin University Magazine</u>, 40 (July-December 1852): 506-8.
An eulogy of the Duke, published shortly after his death.

315.         "The Duke of Wellington." <u>Dublin University Magazine</u>, 60 (July-December 1862): 259-70.
Uses a review of Brialmont's <u>Life</u> as the basis for an eulogy on the Duke.  Dismisses the <u>Supplementary Dispatches</u> as valueless.

316.         "The Duke of Wellington." <u>Fraser's Magazine</u>, 46 (July-December 1852): 365-73.
A panegyric on the Duke's career, prompted by his death.

317.         "The Duke of Wellington." <u>Littell's Living Age</u>, 32 (January 1852): 145-60.
A biographical essay, written for a popular audience, praising the Duke's achievements as a soldier, but not as a politician.  Written by a radical.

318.         "The Duke of Wellington." <u>Littell's Living Age</u>, 36 (January 1853): 1-28.
From the obituary in the <u>Morning Chronicle</u>.  Similar in tone and content to the article in <u>Littell's Living Age</u>, volume 32.

319.         "The Duke of Wellington." <u>The Southern Review (Baltimore)</u>, 5 (January-April 1869): 36-62.
Review of Brialmont and Gleig's <u>Life</u>.  Very critical of Wellington's conduct at Waterloo, and overall written in reaction to British eulogies on the Duke.

320.         "The Duke of Wellington." <u>United Service Journal</u>, 23 (1840): 145-57.
A review of the Duke's life, with comments on his success as a soldier, his excellent private character, and

his skilful political conduct.

321.      "The Duke of Wellington." United Service
          Journal, 25 (1841): 145-53.
     An eulogy on Wellington, praising his conduct as a
soldier but especially as a politician. Written from an
ultra-Tory viewpoint.

322.      "The Duke of Wellington." Colburn's United
          Service Magazine, 33 (1845): 161-71.
     A review of the latest volumes of despatches and a
character sketch of the Duke, praising his moderation,
uprightness, success as a soldier and conduct as a
politician.

323.      "The Duke of Wellington." Westminster Review,
          new series, 2 (July-October 1852): 531-49.
     An eulogy of Wellington, concentrating on the
Peninsular War, and enlarging on his greatness.

324.      "The Duke of Wellington, by J. Maurel." The
          Quarterly Review, 92 (January-April 1853): 507-52.
     A review of Maurel's work interspersed with Croker's
"Notes of Conversations" with the Duke. Both the book and
the review are favourable to the Duke.

325.      Fortescue, J.W., A History of the British Army.
          Volumes 4-13, London, 1906-30.
     The standard history of the British army. Volumes 4
and 5 cover the Duke's career in India; volumes 6 to 10
deal with the Peninsular War and the Waterloo campaign;
volumes 11 to 13 take the story of the British army to 1852.

326.      Fortescue, John, Wellington. London, 1925.
     A life by the historian of the British army, which
concentrates mostly on Wellington's years of active service.

327.      French, George Russell, The Royal Descent of
          Nelson and Wellington from Edward I. London, 1853.
     The second half of this work gives Wellington's family
descent from Edward I.

328.      Fuller, Major General J.F.C., "The Duke of
          Wellington." Britain To-day, 198 (October 1952):
          6-11.
     Very brief and very favourable outline of the Duke's
career, by a leading military intellectual.

329.      Gleig, George Robert, The Life of Arthur, First
          Duke of Wellington. London, 1862.
     A condensed version of Gleig's edition of Brialmont's
Histoire du duc de Wellington.

330.      Gower, Lord Francis Leveson, Earl of Ellesmere,
          On the Life and Character of the Duke of Wellington
          London, 1852.

A potted biography by a colleague of the Duke, defending him from some attacks, and presenting a view of his honest and upright character. Hardly mentions Wellington's political career, on the grounds of its controversial nature.

331.     Griffiths, Arthur George Frederick, The Wellington Memorial. Wellington, His Comrades and Contemporaries. London, 1897.
A lavishly produced, adulatory biography of the Duke, principally in war, but devoting some space to his civil and private life. Also covers the careers of some of Wellington's Peninsular lieutenants.

332.     Griffiths, Arthur George Frederick, Wellington and Waterloo. London, 1898.
In fact, a straightforward, complete life of the Duke, concentrating on its military side, but fully illustrated with and enlivened by characters and incidents from his life and times.

333.     Guedalla, Philip. The Duke. London, 1931.
An elegantly written survey of Wellington's life by a sympathetic author. Based on such printed primary material as was available at the time of publication.

334.     Hamley, Sir Edward Bruce, Wellington's Career: Military and Political Summary. Edinburgh & London, 1860.
An interesting and generally friendly, but not uncritical, summary of Wellington's career, based heavily on Brialmont and Gleig's Life, by a Captain at the Army Staff College.

335.     Harding, James, The Duke of Wellington. London, 1968.
A brief 'profile' of Wellington, covering all aspects of his career. Nicely produced and well illustrated.

336.     Head, Charles O., Napoleon and Wellington. London, 1939.
A narrative account of Wellington's life, concentrating on his active military career, comprises half the work, written by an ardent admirer. Based on secondary sources.

337.     Historical Celebrities. Oliver Cromwell, George Washington, the Emperor Napoleon, Duke of Wellington. London & Edinburgh, 1887.
Includes a reprint of an earlier, anonymous, pamphlet, providing an outline life of the Duke.

338.     Hope, Felix, "Wellington." Parent's Review, 42 (December 1931): 771-92.
A rather confused survey of the Duke's life.

339.        Howard, Michael, ed., <u>Wellingtonian Studies.</u>
      <u>Essays on the First Duke of Wellington by five Old</u>
      <u>Wellingtonian historians.</u>  Wellington, Somerset,
      <u>1959.</u>
      A collection of five thoughtful essays covering
Wellington's personality, his achievements as a general,
diplomatist and statesman, and his influence on the British
army.

340.        <u>"The Iron Duke". Memoirs of the Duke of</u>
      <u>Wellington from authentic sources.</u>  York, 1852.
      A straightforward, chronological, survey of
Wellington's life, based on obituraries in <u>The Times</u> and
<u>Daily News</u>.

341.        Johnston, Otto, "Wellington and the Germans."
      <u>The International History Review</u>, XI (1989): 109-
      <u>18.</u>
      A review of the Duke's enduring reputation among
German politicians, soldiers, poets and scholars, and the
changes in it since 1815.

342.        Johnston, Otto, "Wellington and the Germans."
      in Gash, Norman, ed., <u>Wellington Essays.</u>
      (forthcoming).

343.        Knight, A.E., <u>Wellington.  The Record of a</u>
      <u>Great Military Career.</u>  London, 1900.
      A brief life based on W.H. Maxwell: hardly anything
on Wellington's civil life.  Published to coincide with
the increased interest in military matters occasioned by
the Boer War.

344.        Lemoinne, J., <u>Wellington: From a French Point</u>
      <u>of View.</u>  London, 1852.
      A brief critique of Wellington's character.  Contains
some insights.  Adapted from material published in the
<u>Journal des Debats</u>.

345.        <u>Life and Funeral procession of the Duke of</u>
      <u>Wellington.</u>  [London, 1852]
      A narrative account of the Duke's life, with a full
description of his funeral.

346.        "The Life of Arthur, Duke of Wellington, by G.
      R. Gleig." <u>The Quarterly Review</u>, 120 (July-
      October 1866): 1-38.
      A critical review of Gleig, pointing out that the
Duke, although a great man, was not as perfect as his
biographer claimed.  Also critical of Gleig's accuracy.

347.        <u>The Life of the Duke of Wellington, with Lord</u>
      <u>Brougham's Oration Delivered at Dover, October</u>
      <u>1839.</u>  London, 1852.
      A straightforward survey of Wellington's life down to
the battle of Waterloo, together with Lord Brougham's speech

made at the Wellington Banquet in Dover in October 1839.
The main text was reprinted in 1853 as The Military
Achievements of the Duke of Wellington.

348.          The Life of his Grace the Duke of Wellington,
          with Anecdotes of the Battle of Waterloo.
          London, 1850.
          A brief survey of Wellington's life down to Waterloo,
with a summary of his political career, including extracts
from his speech on Catholic relief.

349.          "The Life of Wellington by Sir Herbert Maxwell;
          The Campaign of 1815 by William O'Connor Morris."
          The Edinburgh Review, 192 (July-October 1900):
          91-146.
          A lengthy review, primarily of Maxwell's work.  Very
critical, especially of Maxwell's treatment of the Duke's
political career. The reviewer felt Wellington was always
a politician, and that his political career was not a
failure.

350.          Longford, Elizabeth, Wellington: The Years of
          the Sword.  London & New York, 1969.
          A detailed study of Wellington's life based on a wide
range of source material, both published and unpublished.
Takes the story to 1815.

351.          Longford, Elizabeth, Wellington: Pillar of
          State.  London, 1972.
          The concluding volume of Lady Longford's biography
covering the years from 1815 to 1852.

352.          Lucke, T., Wellington, der eiserne Herzog.
          Berlin, 1935.
          A detailed and balanced life of Wellington, covering
fully both his military and political career.

353.          Macfarlane, Charles, A Memoir of the Duke of
          Wellington.  Revised edition, London, 1853.
          An eulogy on the Duke, relating primarily to his
active military career, with a brief concluding chapter on
his life after 1818, based on The Times obituary.

354.          MacMunn, Lieutenant General Sir George, "The
          Ever Green Wisdom of the Duke of Wellington."
          Journal of the Royal Artillery Institution, 65
          (April 1938-January 1939): 368-90.
          Comments on various aspects of the Duke's "wisdom"
taken from the printed Despatches, and applied, to some
extent, to contemporary problems.

355.          Maurel, J., Le Duc de Wellington.  Brussels,
          1853.
          A balanced survey of Wellington's military career,
countering French attacks on him.  Says almost nothing

about the Duke's life after Waterloo.

356.       Maxwell, Sir Herbert, <u>The Life of Wellington.</u>
           <u>The Restoration of the Martial Power of Great</u>
           <u>Britain.</u>  2 vols., London 1899 and later editions.
      A first class survey of Wellington's life, based on
much primary source material and covering both his military
and civil life in depth and judiciously.
      <u>3rd edition</u>  Some small corrections acknowledged in a
new introduction.
      <u>6th edition</u>  A one volume reissue.

357.       Maxwell, W.H., <u>The Life of Field Marshal his</u>
           <u>Grace the Duke of Wellington.</u> 3 vols., London,
           <u>1839-41.</u>
      Only covers Wellington's military career, but in great
detail.  Based in part on Napier's <u>Peninsular War</u>.  Provides
many quotations from printed primary sources.  Gives much
background information not directly affecting the Duke.
Illustrated.

358.       Maxwell, W.H., <u>The Life of Wellington: New</u>
           <u>Editiion, Revised, Condensed and Completed.</u>  ed.
           by 'H.M.S.', London, 1883.
      Adds only a brief concluding chapter to the original
edition, omitting quotations from primary sources. A well
produced and well illustrated study.

359.       Maxwell, W.H., <u>Life of the Duke of Wellington.</u>
           <u>Revised and Abridged from the larger work, with an</u>
           <u>additional chapter.</u>  London, 1885.
      An illustrated 'popular' edition of the 1839-41 <u>Life</u>
with a brief final chapter on the Duke's civil career.

360.       Maxwell, W.H., <u>The Life of Wellington.</u> Abridged
           & ed. by Rev. L.T. <u>Dodd, London, 1904.</u>
      An abridgement of the 1839-41 <u>Life</u>, with very brief
notes on Wellington's post-Waterloo career and editorial
comments on Maxwell's <u>Life</u>.

361.       Maxwell, W.H., G.N. Wright and 'Alexander',
           <u>Leben und Feldzuge des Herzogs von Wellington.</u>
           Trans. F. Bauer, 6 vols., Oldenburg & Leipzig,
           1842.
      A German edition of Maxwell's 1839-41 <u>Life</u>,
containing extra material drawn from other British sources,
both primary and secondary.

362.       <u>Memoir of the Duke of Wellington, Reprinted,</u>
           <u>by Permission, from the Times, September 15 and</u>
           <u>16, 1852.</u>  London, 1852.
           [Reprinted the same year]
      A judicious and balanced review of Wellington's life,
this work forms the basis of most of the popular lives of
Wellington produced shortly after his death.

363.    "Memorials of Wellington." <u>Dublin University Magazine</u>, 42 (July-December 1853): 1-21.
Surveys and comments on a wide range of published works relating to the Duke, and attempts to correct various misconceptions.

364.    "Military Portraits [Portraits Militaires Esquisses, Historiques et Strategique - par Ed. de la Barre Dupareq]" <u>Colburn's United Service Magazine</u>, (1852, Part III): 509-26.
A translation of an article on Wellington, which is then criticised for not doing the Duke justice.

365.    Montgomery, Viscount, Elizabeth Longford, J. Biggs-Davison, V. Percival and R. Innes-Smith, <u>Wellington. A Summary of the career of the 1st Duke of Wellington and an account of Apsley House and its contents.</u> Derby, 1970.
A glossy pamphlet, well illustrated, and an attempt to restore, or even enhance, the Duke's reputation with the general reader.

366.    Morris, William O'Connor, <u>Wellington: Soldier and Statesman, and the revival of the military power of England.</u> New York & London, 1904.
A 'standard' life, relying on the printed Despatches and placing most emphasis on a critical survey of the Duke's active military service.

367.    Morris, William O'Connor, "Wellington." <u>Fortnightly Review</u>, 67 (old series 73) (1900): 200-13.
Reviews favourably Sir Herbert Maxwell's life of the Duke. Takes issue on certain details in Maxwell's assessment, but generally praises Wellington as both a soldier and as a statesman.

368.    N[apier], W.F.P., "The Despatches of Field Marshal the Duke of Wellington, K.G. Lieutenant Colonel Gurwood Volumes I-IX." <u>Westminster Review</u>, 28 (October 1837-January 1838): 367-436.
Long review, mainly devoted to attacking the Duke's political views and, while admiring the Duke as a soldier, reminds readers of his limitations. A violent piece, disavowed by the <u>Review</u>'s editor.

369.    'An Old Soldier', <u>Life, Military and Civil of the Duke of Wellington, digested from the materials of W.H. Maxwell, and in part re-written by an old soldier, with some account of his public funeral.</u> London, 1852.
Based closely on Maxwell's <u>Life</u> of 1839-41, omitting most quotations from primary sources. Rewritings comprise an additional chapter on Wellington's civil life, as well as chapters on anecdotes about, and aphorisms of, the Duke, with full details of his funeral.

370.        Petrie, Sir Charles Alexander, Wellington. A
        Reassessment. London, 1956.
        A balanced and thoughtful account of Wellington's
career - in particular his military career, placing more
emphasis on the assistance the Duke received from Spanish
guerillas than is usually allowed.

371.        Redway, George W., Wellington and Waterloo.
        London & Edinburgh, 1912.
        A popular survey, dealing briefly with Wellington's
career before and after Waterloo, as well as the battle
itself.

372.        Roberts, Earl, The Rise of Wellington. London,
        1895.
        A clear, narrative survey of Wellington's active
military service, including some comments on the Duke's
performance as a peace-time Commander-in-Chief, written by
an eminent soldier. Reissued as a cheap paperback at the
time of the Boer War, in 1902, and again in 1915.

373.        Smith, George Barnett, Heroes of the Nineteenth
        Century. 3 vols., London, 1899-1901.
        A sketch of the Duke's life, with a little said about
his political career in volume 2. Wellington is placed
alongside Garibaldi and Generals Grant and Gordon.

374.        Smith, Goldwin, "Wellington." Atlantic Monthly
        87 (January-June 1901): 771-81.
        A review of Wellington's character, generally well-
informed, but sharing many contemporary misconceptions about
him.

375.        Stanwell, Charles, A sermon preached in the
        Chapel of Wellington College, on May 1, 1866,
        being the commemoration of Arthur, Duke of
        Wellington. Cambridge, 1866.
        Exhorts the scholars to emulate the Duke in his
character, following the call of duty with courage, bravery,
and decency.

376.        Stocqueler, Joachim Hayward, The Life of Field
        Marshal the Duke of Wellington. 2 vols., London,
        1852.
        The earliest full life of Wellington, giving ample
space to the civil as well as the military aspects of his
career. Firmly based on documentary sources. A reasonably
non-partisan account.

377.        Timbs, John, Wellingtoniana: Anecdotes, Maxims,
        and Characteristics of the Duke of Wellington.
        A brief and popular collection of anecdotes, drawn
from the Duke's despatches and other more or less reliable
sources, commenting on the Duke's early life, military
career, 'in Cabinet', 'at home', and recounting a series

of 'characteristic anecdotes'. Typical of its type.
Reprinted in German in 1853.

378.     Tucker, John Montmorency, The Life of the Duke
of Wellington; compiled from Despatches and other
authentic sources and original documents. London,
[1880].
A detailed and reasonably impartial study, primarily
of the Duke's active military career, with numerous
extended quotations from other printed sources. Some
extraneous detail admitted. Illustrated throughout with
engravings.

379.     Waite, Rosamond, The Life of the Duke of
Wellington. New ed., London, 1884.
A 'standard' life, mostly military, and derived from
secondary sources, especially Gleig and Brialmont, and
W.H. Maxwell.

380.     Ward, James, The Life of His Grace the Duke of
Wellington. London, [1852].
A brief narrative account of Wellington's career, by
an admirer, devoting much space to the battle of Waterloo
and the Duke's role in the execution of Marshal Ney.

381.     Ward, S.G.P., Wellington. London, 1963.
A balanced survey of Wellington's life by a military
historian, devoting reasonable space to the Duke's later
career, as well as to his military achievements.

382.     "Wellington's career." Blackwood's Edinburgh
Magazine, 87 (January-June 1860): 397-417,
591-610.
Detailed review of Brialmont and Gleig's Life of the
Duke. A balanced comment, not throwing a veil over the
Duke's mistakes or the weaknesses of his character.

383.     "Wellington's career." Christian Observer
(1861): 134-59.
A review of a work by Captain E.B. Hamley. Very
favourable to Wellington as God's chosen instrument, but
disapproving of his morals and his connection with Peel.
An high Tory view.

384.     Wheeler, Harold F.B., The Story of Wellington.
London, 1912.
Deals primarily with Wellington's military career,
relying on the Despatches and various secondary sources.
Illustrated with stirring paintings of battle. Very typical
of its period.

385.     Williams, William Freke and T. Gaspey, The Life
and Times of the late Duke of Wellington,
comprising the Campaigns and Battlefields of
Wellington and his Comrades, the Political Life of

the Duke and his contemporaries and a detailed
account of England's battles by sea and land.
4 vols., London, [1853-56].
A lengthy study, published in twenty-four numbered
parts.  Volumes 1 and 2, by Williams, comprise a
chronological account of Wellington's active service, with
some background material; volume 3, by Gaspey, is a
'political' life, but closes effectively in 1830; volume 4,
not attributed, is a chronological account of Britain's
battles in the Revolutionary and Napoleonic wars.

386.        Wilson, John Marius, A Memoir of Field Marshal
        the Duke of Wellington; with interspersed notices
        of his principal associates in Council and
        Companions and Opponents in Arms.  2 vols., London,
        Edinburgh & Dublin, [1853-4].
Originally issued in eight parts.  Volume 1 of this
work takes the Duke's life down to the battle of Fuentes
d'Onoro.  Despite its claims to the contrary, this book,
like others  published at this time, tends to lose its way
in extraneous detail.  Nevertheless, it does give some
consideration to the Duke's political career, down to his
last years.

387.        Wright, George Nuneham, Rev., Life and Campaigns
        of Arthur, Duke of Wellington. 4 vols., London,
        [1841].
Volumes 1 to 3 deal with Wellington's life down to
Waterloo; volume 4 covers the years from 1815 to 1835.  A
narrative account, one of several based on the first series
of Wellington's published Despatches.  A friendly survey,
including much background material on the Peninsular war
and British politics.

388.        Yonge, Charles Duke, The Life of Field Marshal
        Arthur, Duke of Wellington.  2 vols., London, 1860.
An 'official' life of the first Duke, approved by his
eldest son, by an academic historian.  Volume 1 of this
edition deals with the Duke's active military career, volume
2 with his political life.  Displays a judicious use of
primary sources, and contains good, clear maps of
Wellington's battlefields.

389.        Yonge, Charles Duke, The Life of Arthur, Duke
        of Wellington.  London, 1891.
A one volume version of Yonge's 1860 Life, using some
new information, but distinguished from the first edition
primarily by a reduction in the space devoted to the Duke's
civil life.

# Part Four
# Military Career
# 1769-1818
## Section A
## General

390.     Bankes, George Nugent, ed., The Autobiography
         of Sergeant William Lawrence. A hero of the
         Peninsula and Waterloo campaigns. London, 1886.
      A view from the ranks, including comment and gossip
about Wellington's conduct of the war.

391.     Bird, Major General Sir W.D., "Wellington's
         Tactical Preferences?" Army Quarterly, 36
         (April-July 1938): 228-41.
      Concludes, after a description of the Duke's most
important engagements, that Wellington had no tactical
preferences.

392.     [Blakiston, J.], Twelve Years Military
         Adventures in Three Quarters of the Globe ...
         2 vols., London, 1829.
      Dedicated to Wellington. Volume one covers the years
to 1806: the author fought under Wellesley at the battle of
Argaum; in volume two he joined the army in the Peninsula,
taking part in the battles of Vitoria and Toulouse. Passes
comments on Wellington's character and conduct, but did not
know him personally.

393.     Bryant, Sir Arthur, The Great Duke or The
         Invincible General. London, 1971.
      A study of Wellington's military career down to 1815.
Based on printed primary material. Notable for the very
strong partiality of the author for its subject.

394.     Campaigns of Field Marshal the Duke of
         Wellington. Paris, 1817.
      A large format work, comprising twenty-four
engravings of battles and incidents in Wellington's career,
with an accompanying text, in English and French, by a
French royalist.

395.     Chandler, David G., Dictionary of the
         Napoleonic Wars. London, 1979.

Includes separate entries of Wellington, his brothers
Richard and Henry, and his subordinates and descriptions of
his Peninsular war battles and Waterloo.

396.        Chandler, David G., "Introduction: Regular and
            Irregular Warfare." The International History
            Review, XI (1989): 2-12.
An introduction to an edition of the Review devoted
to the Duke as wartime commander, including some
reflections on his generalship.

397.        Clarke, Francis L., The Life of the Most Noble
            Arthur, Marquis and Earl of Wellington [etc.]
            London, 1812.
Detailed and accurate survey of Wellington's life to
date, coupled with some details about India and aspects of
the Peninsular war, with which he was not involved. A full
survey for this early date, illustrated with engravings and
maps.

398.        Clinton, H.R., The War in the Peninsula, and
            Wellington's Campaigns in France and Belgium.
            London, 1878.
A chronological survey of the Peninsular War and
Waterloo, derived from secondary sources. A clear account,
prepared for both 'military students' and the general
reader.

399.        "A Comparison between the Duke of Wellington
            and some Commanders of Ancient and Modern Times."
            United Service Journal, 15 (1836): 347-54.
Argues that the measurement of a general's skill
depends on that of his opponents: by this, Wellington was a
better general than Caesar, Pompey, Hannibal and Napoleon.

400.        Culling, Francis, ed., Letters and Journals of
            Field-Marshal Sir William Maynard Gomm, G.C.B.
            London, 1881.
Includes some assessments of Wellington's conduct of
operations in the Peninsula from 1809 and at Waterloo.

401.        Davies, Godfrey, Wellington and his army.
            Oxford, 1954.
Written from printed sources, and to defend
Wellington from charges laid against him. Includes
chapters on Wellington's personality, his generalship, and
his relations with offiers and men.

402.        "Despatches of the Duke of Wellington." The
            Monthly Review, 4th series, 1 (1839): 579-88.
A review of Gurwood's original edition of the
Despatches, using the Duke's actions after Waterloo as
evidence of his greatness and humanity.

403.        "The Despatches of Field Marshal the Duke of

Wellington ... by Lt. Col. Gurwood." The
Edinburgh Review, 68 (October 1838-January 1839):
1-46; 69 (April-July 1839): 297-348.
Detailed reviews: the first article deals with the
Indian despatches, the second with the remainder.  Includes
praise for the editor, and, rather surprisingly, for the
Duke himself, as a soldier and for his great character.

404.        "The Duke of Wellington." The Leisure Hour, 1
            (1852): 713-8.
A review of the Duke's military career, occasioned by
his death.

405.        Elliott, George, The Life of the Most Noble
            Arthur, Duke of Wellington, from the period of his
            First Achievements in India down to his Invasion
            of France, and the Peace of Paris in 1814 ...
            London, 1815.
A full life of Wellington down to the beginning of
1815, based on public sources.  Encompasses the Duke's
campaigns and much background material.  Very partial to
the hero of the story.  Includes, as an appendix, reprints
of some of the most important of Wellington's despatches.

406.        Elliott, George, The Life of the Most Noble
            Arthur, Duke of Wellington ...   2nd ed., London,
            1816.
Exactly the same as the first edition, save for two
new chapters on the Waterloo campaign and new documents in
the appendix.  German and Italian versions of Wellington's
life are based on this edition.

407.        "Extracts from the Despatches and General Orders
            of Field Marshal the Duke of Wellington." Colburn's
            United Service Magazine, 31 (1844): 273-85; 32
            (1844): 429-39; 601-8.
Arranged by subject, retaining chronological order.
The first two parts deal with cavalry charges, the last,
charges by infantry.

408.        Fitchett, W.H., The Great Duke.  2 vols.
            London, 1911.
A survey of Wellington's military life only, based on
Napier and printed primary sources.  A great admirer of
Wellington as a soldier.

409.        Fitchett, W.H., "A Great Soldier on his Battles."
            Cornhill Magazine, new series, 39 (July-December
            1915): 44-56; 188-97.
Discusses Wellington's thoughts on military history,
describes some of his conversations with contemporaries
and reviews the 'Waterloo despatch', rather as a literary
production.

410.        "General Orders of the Duke of Wellington from
            1809-1815." United Service Journal, 8 (1832):

289-96.
A review of Gurwood's edition, used to display Wellington's greatness as a soldier and his care for his men.

411.      Glover, Michael, Wellington as Military Commander. London, 1968.
A narrative account of Wellington's active military service, based on printed sources. Includes some analytical chapters on the arms of the service.

412.      Griffith, Paddy, ed., Wellington, Commander: The Iron Duke's Generalship. Chichester, [1985].
A collection of essays on various aspects of Wellington's generalship. Well illustrated.

413.      Griffith, Paddy, "Wellington - Commander." in Paddy Griffith, ed., Wellington, Commander. pp. 13-53.
An introductory survey of Wellington's character and generalship.

414.      Head, Charles O., The Art of Generalship. Four Exponents and One Example. Aldershot, 1929.
Includes a brief review of Wellington's military career, along with those of Napoleon, Wolseley and Sir Henry Wilson, as 'exponents', and the battle of Salamanca as an 'example', to comment on generalship in the light of the First World War.

415.      Head, Lieutenant Colonel Charles O., "Our Neglect of Wellington." Journal of the Royal Artillery Institution, 62 (1935/6): 450-60.
A survey of Wellington's qualities as a general, using the battles of Salamanca and Waterloo as examples.

416.      Headlam, General Sir John, "The Duke and the Regiment." Journal of the Royal Artillery Institution, 71 (1944) : 1-11.
A survey of the Duke's relations with the Royal Artillery, revealing his often over-hasty judgements on their actions.

417.      "Heroes Ancient and Modern No. II.  Scipio Africanus the elder, and Arthur, Duke of Wellington." Dublin University Magazine 40 (July-December 1852): 407-27.
Primarily a eulogy of the Duke's unprecedented military career and greatness.

418.      Hughes, Quentin, "Wellington and Fortifications." Fort, 15 (1987): 61-90.
A careful survey of Wellington's views on the design of, attacks on and defence of, fortifications, from the Lines of Torres Vedras, through Peninsular war sieges, to

the Netherlands barrier fortresses.

419.        Ingram, Edward, ed., "Wellington at War.", The
           International History Review, XI (1989): 2-118.
     A special number, reprinting some military papers
from the Southampton University Congress on Wellington of
July 1987. See also Gash, Norman, ed., Wellington Essays.

420.        Jackson, Basil and C. Rochford Scott, The
           Military Life of Field Marshal the Duke of
           Wellington. 2 vols., London, 1840.
     Unadorned narrative account, based mainly on Gurwood's
Despatches. Written by two soldiers, admirers of the Duke
both as a soldier and a politician. Volume 1 deals with
the period to 1809. Volume 2 takes the story to Waterloo.

421.        Keegan, John, "Wellington: the anti-hero." in
           Keegan, John, The Mask of Command, London, 1987
           pages 92-163.
     A careful survey of Wellington's generalship, based
on printed primary sources and recent work.

422.        The Life and Exploits of his Grace the Duke of
           Wellington, embracing, at one view, the whole
           Military Career of this Illustrious Warrior,
           including a complete History of the Peninsular
           War, with all the spirit-stirring Incidents and
           Anecdotes of that Memorable Contest. London,
           [1840].
     A popular life of Wellington down to 1815, written
for a mass audience and enlivened by illustrations in the
text. Relates the whole history of the Peninsular War, not
just the Duke's part in it.

423.        "The Life of the most noble Arthur, Duke of
           Wellington ... by George Elliott." The Quarterly
           Review, 13 (April-July 1815): 215-75.
     A favourable review of the work, with some interesting
comments on the Duke's career and character, written before
the battle of Waterloo.

424.        Macfarlane, Charles, Life of the Duke of
           Wellington. London, [1877],
     A revised version of the 1853 edition. Deals solely
with Wellington's active military career. This is a
popular life, written for a mass audience, and reprinted in
1896 for 'Routledge's World Library'.

425.        Malmesbury, Earl of, ed., A Series of Letters
           of the First Earl of Malmesbury, his family and
           friends from 1745 to 1820. 2 vols., London, 1870.
     Volume 2 contains a series of informative letters from
George Bowles, a Guards officer in the Peninsula, at
Waterloo and with the army of occupation in France,
together with other letters about the Duke by some of his

acquaintances.

426.        "Maxwell's Life of Wellington." <u>Dublin
            University Magazine</u>, 19 (January-June 1842): 461-
            75; 626-44; 744-62; 20 (July-December 1842): 75-87.
A review which amounts to a biography of Wellington in
itself.  Praises Maxwell, but reserves its highest praise
for the Duke himself.  Covers the whole of Wellington's
military career.

427.        Maxwell, W.H., <u>The Victories of the British
            Armies, with Anecdotes Illustrative of modern
            warfare.</u>  2 vols., London, 1839.
A narrative of the exploits of the British army from
the battle of Seringapatam to that of Waterloo.  Reissued
in one volume in 1868 and 1885, entitled <u>The Victories of
Wellington and the British Armies.</u>

428.        <u>Memoir of Field Marshal the Duke of Wellington,
            during his Campaigns in Holland, India, Denmark,
            Portugal, Spain, France and the Low Countries.</u>
            London, [1850].
Chronological account, with some extraneous details,
of Wellington's campaigns and battles.  A privately printed
work, illustrated with engravings.

429.        O'Doherty, Morgan [pseud.], "On the military
            errors of the Duke of Wellington: To Lieutenant
            Felix Shufflebottom, Royal African Corps, etc.,
            etc." <u>Blackwood's Edinburgh Magazine</u>, 6 (October
            1819-March 1820): 291-96.
A light-hearted survey of some minor military errors
of the Duke.

430.        "Official and other despatches of Field Marshal
            the Duke of Wellington." <u>The Quarterly Review</u>, 79
            (December 1846-March 1847): 449-63.
Uses the despatches to show how imperfect the
organisation of the army was, and to call for its improve-
ment.

431.        Pemberton, A.L., "The Iron Duke v. Corporal
            John." <u>Journal of the United Service Institution of
            India</u>, 63 (1933): 95-108.
More a study of the development of Wellington's
character than a comparison of his talents with those of
Marlborough.

432.        'A Peninsular and Waterloo Officer', <u>The
            military achievements of the Duke of Wellington,
            contrasted with those of Alexander, Pyrrhus,
            Hannibal, Caesar, Marlborough, Napoleon and other
            celebrated Commanders.</u>  London, 1854.
An absurdly partisan attempt to prove Wellington's
greatness at the expense of Great Captains of the past, and
to educate young officers.

433.      Proudhon, P-J., <u>Commentaires sur les Mémoires de</u>
<u>Fouché suivis du parallèle entre Napoléon et</u>
<u>Wellington.</u> edited by C. Rochel. 3rd ed., Paris,
1900.
Includes a brief resume of Wellington's career in the
war against France, and a general but very favourable
assessment of his achievements.

434.      Robinson, Major-General C.W., <u>Wellington's</u>
<u>Campaigns. Peninsula-Waterloo.</u> 3 vols., London,
1905-6.
A study of the Duke's strategy, based on lectures
given at the Royal Military Academy, Sandhurst, and designed
for young officers.

435.      Saint-Nexant de Gangemon, A.C. de, <u>Le Duc de</u>
<u>Wellington devant l'histoire.</u> Paris, 1853.
A brief survey of Wellington's major battles in Spain
and Waterloo, proving the Duke to have been a poor general
who made many serious mistakes.

436.      Sheppard, Captain E.W., "The First Duke of
Wellington." <u>Army Quarterly</u>, 15 (January 1928):
358-71.
Notes for army officers studying the Duke's active
military career. Displays great admiration for Wellington
as a general, but dislikes him as a man.

437.      Silva Lisboa, José da, <u>Memoria da vida publica</u>
<u>do Lord Wellington.</u> 2 vols., Rio de Janeiro, 1815.
The earliest non-English life of Wellington. The
second half of volume two comprises documents relating to
the Peninsular war.

438.      Smith, William, <u>British heroism exemplified in</u>
<u>the character of His Grace Arthur, Duke and</u>
<u>Marquis of Wellington, and the Brave Officers</u>
<u>serving under his command in Holland, the East</u>
<u>Indies, Portugal, Spain and France.</u> Sunderland,
1815.
A poetic account of Wellington's triumphs - among
other matters - completed before the Battle of Waterloo.

439.      Soane, George, <u>Life of the Duke of Wellington.</u>
<u>Compiled from his Grace's Despatches, and other</u>
<u>authentic records and original documents.</u> 2 vols.,
London, 1839-40.
A plain narrative account, one of several written at
this time based on Gurwood's <u>Despatches</u>. This is a cheap,
'pocket', edition, concentrating on Wellington's role in
the Peninsular war. Volume 1 takes the story to 1811;
volume 2 to Waterloo.

440.      <u>A summary of the Life of Arthur, Duke of</u>
<u>Wellington from the period of his first achieve-</u>

ments in India, to his Invasion of France, and the
Decisive Battle of Waterloo, June 18, 1815.   Taken
from the Quarterly Review.  Dublin, 1816.
A careful survey of Wellington's life, written in a
clear and straightforward style.  Although in general
strongly partisan to the Duke; it does try to present a
balanced survey.

441.         Terraine, John, "Wellington as a Coalition
             General." in Paddy Griffiths, ed., Wellington,
             Commander, pp. 71-88.
A survey of Wellington's relations with his allies in
India, the Peninsula and the Waterloo campaign.

442.         Tomkinson, William, The Diary of a Cavalry
             Officer in the Peninsular and Waterloo Campaigns,
             1809-1815.  Edited by James Tomkinson.  London, 1894.
The author was attached to Sir Stapleton Cotton's
staff, but was nevertheless, close to Wellington at several
critical moments during the campaigns.

443.         Wagner, G.H.A., ed., Arthur, Herzog von
             Wellington.  Sein Leben als Feldherr und Staatsmann
             Nach englischen Quellen, verzuglich nach Elliott
             und Clarke bearbeitet und bis zum Sept. 1816
             fortgesetzt.  Leipzig & Altenburg, 1817.
Based on the second edition of George Elliott's Life
of ... Wellington of 1816 and Francis Clarke's Life of 1812.

444.         "The War in Spain and the battle of Waterloo."
             The Quarterly Review, 13 (April-July 1815): 448-526.
Long review of several works, very much on the Duke's
side, although the reviewer believes he was not harsh
enough on the French in 1814.

445.         Wellesley, Muriel A., The Man Wellington.
             Through the Eyes of those who knew him.  London,
             1937.
Covers only Wellington's military career down to 1818.
Quotes extensively from printed primary sources, but this is
a scholarly biography, not a compilation of extracts.

446.         "The Wellington Despatches."  The Monthly Review,
             4th series, 2 (1841): 144-58.
A review of Gurwood's abridgement of the Duke's
despatches, used as the basis for an examination of his
straightforward and noble character, albeit with
reservations about his attitude to the press.

447.         "Wellington's Despatches and General Orders."
             British and Foreign Review, 10 (1840): 127-222.
Comments at length and very favourably on the Duke's
character and conduct, as revealed in the first three
volumes of Gurwood's Despatches and the two volumes of
General Orders.

# Section B
# Early Life and Career
# 1769-1796

448.      Barrington, Sir Jonah, Personal Sketches of
          his Own Times. Volume 1. London, 1827.
     A view of Wellington in his early days as an Irish
M.P. Valuable background information on Ireland at the end
of the eighteenth century.

449.      Murray, John, The Lost Escutcheon; or a Page
          restored to the Memoirs of Dublin. Dublin, 1850.
     Murray's original attempt to fix exactly the place
and date of Wellington's birth, which he does by careful
research in local newspapers.

450.      Murray, John, Wellington; the place and day of
          his birth ascertained and demonstrated. 2nd ed.,
          Dublin, 1852.
     Another version of Murray's pamphlet, The Lost
Escutcheon, with some additional information.

451.      Murray, John, The Birthplace of Wellington
          ascertained; or a page restored to the Archives of
          Dublin. 2nd ed., revised, Dublin, 1852.
     Primarily verbal alterations to the second edition of
The Lost Escutcheon, with a small amount of additional
evidence.

452.      Thomas, R.N.W., "Wellington in the Low
          Countries, 1794-5." The International History
          Review, XI (1989): 14-30.
     A careful study of Wellington's first campaign, based
on memoirs and some unpublished sources.

# Section C
# India
# 1796-1805

453.          Archer, Mildred, "Wellington and South India."
Appollo: the Magazine of the Arts, (July 1975):
30-35.
A brief description of the campaign against Mysore,
and the Duke's purchase of a series of portraits of actors
in the drama.

454.          Beatson, Lieutenant-Colonel Alexander, A View
of the Origin and Conduct of the War with Tippoo
Sultan; comprising a Narrative of the Army under
the Command of Lt. General George Harris ...
London, 1800.
Includes a factual account of Wellington's role in
the defeat of Tipu Sultan of Mysore.

455.          Bennell, A.S., "Wellesley's Settlement of
Mysore, 1799." Royal Asiatic Society Journal,
(1952): 124-32.
Discusses the arrangements made by Marquess Wellesley
after the defeat of Tipu, with comments and suggestions by
Wellington.

456.          Bennell, A.S., "Factors in the Marquis
Wellesley's failure against Holkar, 1804."
Bulletin of the School of Oriental and African
Studies, 28 (1965): 553-81.
Discussion of the diplomacy behind, as well as the
operations of, the war, recounting Wellington's role, as
well as his elder brother's actions.

457.          Bird, W.D., "The Assaye Campaign." Journal of
the United Services Institution of India, 41
(1912): 101-24.
A study of the campaign leading to Wellington's first
great military success: a straightforward, rather detailed,
narrative.

458.          Bryant, Arthur, The Years of Endurance, 1793-
1802. London, 1942.

Dramatically written general survey, with some mention of Wellington's Indian campaigns.  First of three volumes.

459.     Burton, R.G., "Wellesley's campaign in the Deccan." Journal of the United Service Institution of India, 29 (1900): 363-84.
Careful study of the Mahratta war and the battle of Assaye.  A straightforward narrative, attempting to show the "lessons" of the conflict.

460.     Burton, R.G., "The fall of Tipu Sultan." Journal of the United Service Institution of India, 34 (1905): 536-54.
"Scientific" study of the war leading to the assault on Seringapatam and the death of Tipu.

461.     Burton, R.G., "Wellesley and the Conquest of Mysore." Journal of the United Service Institution of India, 36 (1907): 311-21.
Gives details of Wellington's early operations in the campaign against Mysore.

462.     Cooper, Randolph G.S., "Wellington and the Mahrattas in 1803." The International History Review, XI (1989): 31-8.
A brief study of Wellington's campaign of 1803, giving much attention to his opponents' weaknesses.

463.     "The Despatches of the Duke of Wellington edited by Colonel Gurwood. Volume 1." The Quarterly Review, 51 (March-June 1834): 399-426.
A review which points out how Wellington's great career was foreshadowed in his days in India.  Stresses that the Duke did not depend on his brother, and, in fact, that he could do no wrong.

464.     "The Despatches of the Duke of Wellington ... by Lieut. Col. Gurwood Vols. II and III." The Quarterly Review, 58 (February-April 1837): 82-107.
A review of volumes 2 and 3 of the Indian despatches with much revealed about Wellington's character and conduct for the reviewer to praise.

465.     "Despatches of the Duke of Wellington. No. 1. Campaigns in India." Blackwood's Edinburgh Magazine, 41 (January-June 1837): 1-20; 200-17; 445-62; 706-14; 42 (July-December 1837): 661-72; 43 (January-June 1838): 408-20.
A series of articles summarising Wellington's despatches, and using them as proof of his greatness.

466.     "The Duke of Wellington." The Edinburgh Review, 110 (July-October 1859): 191-222.
A review of several works on the Duke and the Supplementary Despatches on India, which defends him

against all criticisms, from whatever source.

467.         "The Final Campaign against Tippu." The Journal
         of the United Service Institution of India, 41
         (1912): 251-60.
     A further study of the preparations for, and the
conduct of, the campaign against Tipu, and the lessons to
be drawn from it.

468.         Forrest, Sir G.W., Sepoy Generals. Wellington to
         Roberts. Edinburgh & London, 1901.
     A careful survey of Wellington's career in India,
based on Wellington's printed Despatches, supplemented by
other printed primary source material.

469.         Laager, Fridolin, Ueber Arthur's, des ersten
         Herzogs von Wellington Thatigkeit in Indien.
         Zurich, 1872.
     A Swiss university research thesis, based primarily on
Gurwood's Despatches, covering the Duke's active military
service in India.

470.         Maurice, Major General F.D., "Assaye and
         Wellington: An Anniversary Study." Cornhill
         Magazine, new series, 1 (July-December 1896):
         291-304.
     A rather disorganised attempt to describe Wellington
as a soldier and a man: Maurice has a high opinion of the
former, but a less high opinion of the latter.

471.         The military history of the Duke of Wellington
         in India. London, 1852.
     An interesting review of military operations in India,
marred somewhat by being too strongly in favour of the Duke.

472.         Monson, Lord and George Leveson Gower, eds.,
         Memoirs of George Elers, Captain in the 12th
         Regiment of Foot. London, 1903.
     Includes useful material on Wellington in his days in
India, by a former comrade.

473.         Pearse, N.E.L., "The Mahratta War of 1803-4."
         Journal of the United Service Institution of India,
         58 (1928): 780-93.
     A straightforward survey of the campaign, including
very useful plans of the major engagements.

474.         Phillips, C.H., The Young Wellington in India.
         London, 1973.
     A public lecture, comprising a critical appraisal of
Wellington and his brothers' careers in India in the
context of Wellington's personal development and the growth
and nature of British power there.

475.         Roberts, P.E., India under Wellesley. London,

1929.
A scholarly account of Marquess Wellesley's term as Governor-General of India. Includes many quotations from printed primary sources, including Wellington's Indian despatches.

476.          Rush, H.M., "Wellesley's Mahratta campaign of 1803, in the neighbourhood of Ahmednagar and Aurangabad." Journal of the United Service Institution of India, 60 (1930): 317-30.
A survey of the campaign and of the battle of Assaye, indicating how the battle fitted the pattern laid down in official "Field Service Regulations" and the "lesssons" to be learned from it.

477.          Seth, Ś.D., "Wellesley's Indian Campaigns." Journal of the United Service Institution of India, 86 (1956): 190-8.
A survey of the Duke's Indian campaigns from an Indian viewpoint, emphasising more than usual the qualities of his opponents, but doing justice to his own talents.

478.          Spencer, Alfred, ed., Memoirs of William Hickey (1749-1809). 4 vols., London, 1913.
Volume 4 includes two interesting anecdotes of Wellington's time in India.

479.          Weller, J., Wellington in India. London, 1972.
A straightforward chronological survey of Wellington's political and military career in India. Based on printed primary and secondary sources.

# Section D
# Ireland and Denmark
# 1805-1808

480.　　　　"Civil Correspondence and Memoranda of the Duke
　　　of Wellington. Ireland." The Edinburgh Review, 110
　　　(January-April 1860): 394-421.
　　Review of Supplementary Despatches relating to Ireland,
which prove, as the reviewer is careful to point out, that
Wellington was not always perfectly straightforward in his
political dealings.

481.　　　　"Civil Correspondence and Memoranda of Field
　　　Marshal Arthur, Duke of Wellington." Dublin Review,
　　　48 (May-August 1860): 497-526.
　　A precis and review of Wellington's Irish correspondence between 1807 and 1809. Generally favourable, but
disapproves of the Duke's attitude towards Ireland as
revealed in his papers.

482.　　　　Inglis, Brian, "Sir Arthur Wellesley and the
　　　Irish Press, 1807-1809." Hermathena, 83 (1954):
　　　17-29.
　　Discusses Wellington's handling of the Irish press by
means of subsidies and by giving access to confidential
information.

483.　　　　Warner, Oliver, "Wellington meets Nelson."
　　　History Today, 18 (1968): 125-28.
　　A brief account, based on Croker's version of
Wellington's recollections.

484.　　　　"The Wellington Papers." Dublin University
　　　Magazine, 57 (January-June 1861): 435-45.
　　A review of the volumes of the Supplementary Despatches
dealing with Ireland, which vigorously defends Wellington's
conduct as Irish Secretary.

# Section E
# The Peninsular War
# 1808-1814

485.       Aitchison, John, An Ensign in the Peninsular
     war. Letters of John Aitchison. Edited by
     W.F.K. Thompson. London, 1981.
     Interesting letters, including much comment on events
and on Wellington: a good view of the Duke by an
intelligent and not uncritical junior officer.

486.       Atkinson, C.T., "The Peninsular War." The
     Quarterly Review, 219 (July-October 1913): 1-25.
A review of several works on the Peninsular war, with
comments on the Duke's skill as a general. Takes the story
down to 1811.

487.       Atkinson, C.T., "The Peninsular War." The
     Quarterly Review, 257 (July-October 1931): 355-74.
     An account of the Peninsular war after 1812 combined
with a review of several works, British and French, on the
subject and Wellington's role in it.

488.       Atkinson, C.T., ed., "A Peninsular Brigadier.
     Letters of Major-General Sir F.P. Robinson, K.C.B.
     dealing with the campaign of 1813." Journal of
     the Society for Army Historical Research, 34
     (1956): 153-70.
Several letters describing Wellington's actions in
the campaign, written by a close associate of the Duke.

489.       Beatson, F.C., With Wellington in the Pyrenees.
     Being an account of the operations between the
     Allied army and the French troops from July 25 to
     August 2, 1813. London, 1914.
     A general narrative of the campaign, illustrated with
modern photographs and plans.

490.       Beatson, F.C., Wellington. The Crossing of the
     Gaves and the Battle of Orthez. London, 1925.
     An illustrated account of Wellington's campaign in
January and February 1814.

491.        Beatson, F.C., <u>Wellington.  The Bidassoa and
            Nivelle</u>.  London, 1931.
    Covers Wellington's campaign in the period from
October to November 1814.  Illustrated.

492.        Bird, Major-General Sir W.D., "Examples of
            Wellington's Strategy."  <u>Army Quarterly</u>, 16
            (April 1928): 102-14.
    Takes as the example the Peninsular campaigns of
1809-10, and critically examines the Duke's actions.

493.        Bird, Major-General Sir W.D., "Some of
            Wellington's Strategic Problems."  <u>Army Quarterly</u>,
            17, 18 (January, April 1929): 296-309; 43-59.
    A close study of the campaign in the Peninsula in
1812, intended to show how a great general organised his
campaign.

494.        Bird, Major-General Sir W.D., "Examples of
            Wellington's Strategy: The Vitoria Campaign,
            1813."  <u>Army Quarterly</u>, 19 (October 1929-January
            1930): 34-44; 270-81.
    A careful narrative account of the campaign,
together with some analysis of events.

495.        Blanco, Richard L., <u>Wellington's Surgeon
            General: Sir James McGrigor</u>.  Durham, N.C., 1974.
    Comments on Wellington's medical services in the
Peninsula, based heavily on McGrigor's autobiography.

496.        Bonnal, E., <u>Wellington.  Général en Chef</u>. 2
            vols., Paris, 1912.
    Not simply a narrative of Wellington's campaigns in
Portugal: it places them fully in the context of the war
against Napoleon, and includes material relating to the
actions of the Duke's opponents.

497.        Brett-James, Anthony, "Wellington in his war-
            time letters."  <u>History Today</u>, 9 (1959): 552-59.
    A survey of the Duke's character as revealed by his
despatches.  Generally, although not completely, favourable.

498.        Bryant, Arthur, <u>Years of Victory, 1802-1812</u>.
            London, 1944.
    Includes a vivid account of the Peninsula war;
influenced by events of the day.  Second volume of a
trilogy.

499.        Bryant, Arthur, <u>The Age of Elegance, 1812-1822</u>.
            London, 1950.
    Third volume of a 'Napoleonic wars' trilogy:
concentrates on Wellington's military duties: his post-
Waterloo career is hardly mentioned.

500.        Burne, A.H., "The Enigma of Toulouse: A Study
            in Psychology."  <u>Army Quarterly</u>, 13 (January 1927):

274-90.
Lays great stress on the human and morale factors in
warfare, and uses Wellington's campaign against Soult in
1813-14 as an example of this.

501.          Burne, Alfred H., "Why Wellington won - some
              lessons from the Peninsular Campaign." Journal of
              the Royal United Service Institution, 94
              (February-November 1949): 584-90.
A study of part of the campaign of 1813, stressing
the Duke's boldness and his correct assessment of risks.

502.          Butler, L.W.G., Wellington's operations in the
              Peninsula, 1808-14.  2 vols., London, 1904.
A detailed and "scientific" narrative of the war,
concentrating on the minutae of military manoeuvres and
providing little background information.  Apparently based
on Napier and Wellington's printed despatches.

503.          Cassels, S.A.C., ed., Peninsular Portrait
              1811-1814: The Letters of Captain William Bragge,
              Third (King's Own) Dragoons.  London, 1963.
Interesting letters, giving some description of
Wellington, as well as ideas of his future course of action.

504.          Chambers, George Lawson, Wellington's Battle-
              fields Illustrated. Bussaco.  London, 1910.
A detailed study of the battle; illustrated with many
modern photographs and plans.  Reprints Fra Silvestre's
diary.  No further volumes in this series were published.

505.          Choumara, T., Considérations militaires sur la
              Mémoires de Maréchal Suchet et sur la bataille de
              Toulouse.  Deuxieme edition, augmentée de la
              correspondance entre un ingénieur militaire
              francais et le duc de Wellington sur cette
              Bataille.  2 vols., Paris, 1840.
A revisionist work.  Volume two deals with the
British side at the battle of Toulouse.  It includes
extracts, in French translation, of Wellington's printed
despatches relating to that battle and comments on them.

506.          [Costello, Edward], The Adventures of a Soldier
              .... London, 1841.
Graphic account of life in the Peninsular army, with
some anecdotes of the Duke of Wellington.

507.          Cowell, J.S., Leaves from the Diary of an
              officer in the Guards.  London, 1854.
Anecdotes of the Duke from Portugal in 1810 and 1811,
drawn mostly from the Despatches and Napier's Peninsular
War.

508.          [Donaldson, Joseph], Recollections of the
              Eventful Life of a Soldier by the late Joseph
              Donaldson, Sergeant in the 94th Scots Brigade.

New ed., London & Glasgow, 1856.
A view of Wellington from the ranks, during and after
the Peninsular war. Donaldson believed the Duke of York a
better Commander-in-Chief.

509.          Edwards, Edward, "Some unpublished Letters of
          Sir Thomas Picton." West Wales Historical Records,
          12, 13 (1927-8): 133-62; 1-32.
Useful eyewitness accounts of engagments in the
Peninsular war and information of Picton's relationship with
Wellington.

510.          Esdaile, Charles, The Duke of Wellington and
          the Command of the Spanish Army, 1812-14.
          London, 1989.
A study of Wellington's appointment and term of duty
as Commander-in-Chief of the Spanish army, based on
unpublished material in the Wellington papers.

511.          Esdaile, Charles, "Wellington and the Military
          Eclipse of Spain, 1808-14." The International
          History Review, XI (1989): 55-67.
An attempt to explain why the Spanish did less than
Wellington to drive the French from the Peninsula.

512.          Esdaile, Charles, "Wellington and the Spanish
          Army", in Norman Gash, ed., Wellington Essays,
          (forthcoming).

513.          Fitzclarence, F., An Account of the British
          campaign of 1809 under Sir Arthur Wellesley, in
          Spain and Portugal. London, undated.
A good account of the campaign by a veteran of it.
Includes many comments on Wellington.

514.          Glover, Michael, Wellington's Peninsula
          Victories. Busaco, Salamanca, Vitoria, Nivelle.
          London, 1963.
A straightforward narrative of the campaigns
preceding the battles described, based on printed sources.

515.          Glover, Michael, Britannia Sickens. Sir Arthur
          Wellesley and the Convention of Cintra. London,
          Actually a narrative account of the campaign of 1808
in Portugal, based on printed sources, as well as the
Convention and the Enquiry which followed it.

516.          Glover, Michael, The Peninsular War, 1807-1814.
          Newton Abbot, 1974.
A relatively brief account of the war, based in large
part on Wellington's printed despatches.

517.          Glover, Michael, Wellington's Army in the
          Peninsula, 1808-1814. Newton Abbot and London,
          1977.
A good description of the organisation of the British

army in the Peninsula, with a chapter on Wellington and his command of it.

518.       Glover, Michael, A Very Slippery Fellow: The
           Life of Sir Robert Wilson, 1777-1849.  Oxford,
           1978.
An interesting biography of an incredible character, with material on the Duke in 1809 and in political life (including the Queen Caroline affair), after 1815.

519.       Glover, M., "Letters from Headquarters."
           Journal of the Society for Army Historical
           Research, 43 (1965): 92-104.
Publishes letters from a Staff Officer to his family, with frequent references to Wellington, especially as regards the social life at Headquarters.

520.       Glover, Michael, "Wellington as an attacking
           general - the Peninsular War." in Paddy Griffths,
           ed., Wellington, Commander, pp. 55-69.
A brief survey of the Duke's tactics, with special attention given to the crossing of the Douro and the battle of Vitoria.

521.       Glover, Richard, Peninsular Preparation: The
           Reform of the British Army, 1795-1809.  Cambridge,
           1963.
A scholarly survey, giving Wellington's views on army administration, and the essential background to the achievements of his army during the Peninsular war.

522.       Granville, Castalia, Countess, ed., Letters of
           Lord Granville Leveson Gower (First Lord Granville)
           Private Correspondence, 1781-1821.  2 vols.,
           London, 1916.
Volume 2 contains much correspondence on Wellington at the time of the Peninsular war.  Granville was in contact with many officers of the army.

523.       Grattan, William, Adventures with the
           Connaught Rangers.  2 vols., London, 1847.
A first hand account of the war, including comments, not first hand, but not always friendly toward Wellington, his conduct of operations and his attitude toward the army.

524.       Griffith, Paddy, "The Myth of the Thin Red
           Line." in Paddy Griffith, ed., Wellington,
           Commander, pp. 141-55.
A discussion of Wellington's tactics, with particular reference to the Peninsular War.

525.       Hennell, George, A Gentleman Volunteer: The Letters
           of George Hennell from the Peninsular War, 1812-1813.
           Edited by Michael Glover.  London, 1979.

Includes comments on Wellington's conduct and opinions, some based on first-hand, others on second-hand, information.

526.     "History of the War in the Peninsula." The Christian Remembrancer, 25 (January-June 1853): 1-28.
Uses Napier's Peninsular War as a basis for an eulogy on the Duke, and especially of his conduct in 1810.

527.     Horward, Donald D., The Battle of Busaco: Massena vs Wellington. Tallahasee, 1965.
Scholarly survey, based on primary sources, of the campaign of 1810, the battle and Wellington's role in these events.

528.     Horward, Donald D., "Wellington and the Defence of Portugal." The International History Review, XI (1989): 39-54.
A study, based on Gurwood's Despatches, of Wellington's campaigns in Portugal, and of his relations with the British and Portuguese governments.

529.     Horward, Donald D., "Wellington as Strategist, 1808-14.", in Norman Gash, ed., Wellington Essays. (forthcoming).

530.     Howson, Lieutenant Colonel J.M., "The Administration of Wellington's Army in the Peninsula, 1809-1814." The Army Quarterly, 90 (July 1965): 168-72.
A brief survey, primarily of how the Duke's army was supplied, and his contribution to its administration.

531.     Jackson, Lady, ed., The Diaries and Letters of Sir George Jackson, K.C.H., from the Peace of Amiens to the Battle of Talavera. Volume 2, London, 1872.
Makes interesting comments on Wellington's campaign in Denmark in 1807 and on the situation in Iberia in 1808-9.

532.     Jones, John T., Account of the War in Spain and Portugal and in the South of France from 1808 to 1814 inclusive. London, 1818.
An impartial account of the war, and Wellington's role in it, by an eminent Engineer officer attached to the army.

533.     Jones, John T., Journals of Sieges carried on by the army under the Duke of Wellington in Spain, between the Years 1811 and 1814. 2 vols., London, 1827.
Comments on Wellington's conduct of sieges by an eminent Engineer officer attached to the army.

534.     Kincaid, J., Random shots from a Rifleman. London, 1835.

Lively, anecdotal account, with many stories of Wellington at war.

535.     Larpent, Sir George, ed., The Private Journals of F.S. Larpent, Esq., Judge Advocate General of the British Forces in the Peninsula, attached to the Headquarters of Lord Wellington in the Peninsular War, from 1812 to its close. 3 vols., London, 1853.
Many comments on Wellington by the head of his judiciary. A sympathetic observer of Wellington's troubles.

536.     Lawford, J. and P. Young, Wellington's Masterpiece. The Battle and Campaign of Salamanca. London, 1973.
Essentially a narrative study of the campaign, beginning in January 1811. Includes biographies of the opposing generals and orders of battle, as well as a detailed account of the engagement. Based on printed sources.

537.     Lendy, Auguste Frederic, Campaigns of Napoleon 1812-1814, Campaigns of Wellington, 1812-1814. [London, 1861].
A brief survey, describing Napoleon's campaigns in chronological order, then Wellington's. Drawn up purely for professional purposes - for army officers reading for the Staff Examinations in 1862.

538.     Leslie, John H., ed., The Dickson Manuscripts, being diaries, letters, maps, account books, with various other papers, of the Late Major General Sir Alexander Dickson, K.C., G.C.B., Royal Artillery. Series C, 2 vols., London, 1905-12.
Reproduces a very detailed diary, and some letters, dating from 1809 to 1813. Dickson was a senior artillery officer with Wellington's army, and has much to say about the Duke.

539.     Londonderry, Charles William Vane, Marquess of, Narrative of the Peninsular War from 1808 to 1813. 2nd edition, London, 1828.
An account of the war, by an officer apparently well informed about Wellington's aims and opinions.

540.     Londonderry, Charles William Vane, Marquess of, Narrative of the War in Germany and France in 1813 and 1814. 2nd edition, London, 1830.
Includes a record of a conversation between Wellington and Londonderry at Vienna in 1815, giving the Duke's views on the forthcoming campaign in the Low Countries.

541.     Longford, Fifth Earl of, ed., Pakenham Letters, 1800 to 1815. Privately printed, 1914.
Interesting comments on Wellington and the war in the

Peninsula by the Duke's brothers-in-law, Edward, William, and Hercules Pakenham.

542.         "Lord Wellington in Spain." Blackwood's
             Edinburgh Magazine, 72 (January-June 1853): 580-97.
      A general survey of the Duke's great character and
military achievements, using a brief French biography and
Larpent's Journal as the basis of the assessment.

543.         Lowry Cole, Maud and Stephen Gwynn, eds.,
             Memoirs of Sir Lowry Cole. London, 1934.
      Comments on the Duke in 1813 and 1814 by one of his
divisional commanders, but includes very little else
relating to Wellington.

544.         Ludovici, Anthony M., ed. and trans., On the
             Road with Wellington: The Diary of a War
             Commissary in the Peninsula Campaign by August
             Ludolf Friedrich Schaumann ... London, 1924.
      Schaumann was in the Peninsula from 1808 to 1814, and
comments frequently on Wellington's orders and conduct of
operations.

545.         [McGrigor, Sir James], The Autobiography and
             Services of Sir James McGrigor, Bart. Late
             Director-General of the Army Medical Department...
             London, 1861.
      Deals with the period of the Peninsular War, providing
some anecdotes of Wellington.

546.         McGuffie, T.H., ed., Peninsular Cavalry General
             (1811-13): The Correspondence of Lieutenant-
             General Robert Ballard Long. London, 1951.
      Letters from a cavalry general, not usually with
Wellington's army, but well-informed about him.

547.         Maguire, T.M., The British Army under Wellington
             1811-1813. A summary. London, 1906.
      A brief survey of Wellington's campaigns, 1811-1813,
written to instruct junior officers and the general reader.
Very "scientific".

548.         Marindin, A.H., The Salamanca Campaign. London,
             1906.
      A detailed account of the campaign and battle of
Salamanca, with numerous maps and plans, designed to enable
the "military student" to "deduce lessons" for the future.

549.         Memoir of the early Campaigns of the Duke of
             Wellington, in Portugal and Spain. By an officer
             Employed in his army. London, 1820.
      This book, which includes some personal reminiscences,
is a short work on the Peninsular War, from Wellington's
arrival in Portugal down to the battle of Fuentes d'Onoro.
Published in Italy in the same year.

550.        "Military Operations in Spain." The Edinburgh
            Review, 15 (October 1809-January 1810): 197-236.
     A strong attack on the government's conduct of the
war, with scathing comments on the Talavera campaign and
Wellington's conduct.

551.        Moore Smith, G.C., The Autobiography of
            Lieutenant-General Sir Harry Smith, Bart., G.C.B.,
            2 vols., London, 1901.
     Volume 1 covers the years of the Peninsular war and
Waterloo and includes some anecdotes of Wellington and
comments on his conduct.

552.        Napier, W.F.P., History of the war in the
            Peninsula and in the south of France from A.D.
            1807 to 1814.  6 volumes, London, 1828-40.
     The classic account of the British army's campaign,
marked by strong personal bias.  Napier gives due credit to
Wellington's efforts, but is less fulsome in his praise
than many other commentators.

553.        "Napoleon and the Peninsular War." Temple Bar,
            44 (May-August 1875): 390-408.
     Despite the title has much to say on Wellington's
conduct of operations, as well as comments on Napoleon's
views of events.

554.        [Neale, Adam], Letters from Portugal and Spain;
            Comprising an Account of the Operations of the
            Armies under their Excellencies Sir Arthur
            Wellesley and Sir John Moore; from the landing of
            the troops in Mondego Bay to the Battle of Corunna.
            London, 1809.
     Includes a general account of the campaigns with one
letter, dated 'Lisbon, 6th October 1808', giving a favourable and prophetic description of Wellington's character
and an account of his military service.

555.        O'Byrne, Robert, The Victories of the British
            Army in the Peninsula and the South of France from
            1808 to 1814.  London, 1889.
     An epitome of Napier's Peninsular War and Gurwood's
edition of the Despatches, based more heavily on the former
and, as the title says, dealing only with British
"victories".

556.        Oman, C.W.C., Wellington's Army 1809-1814.
            London, 1912.
     An excellent thematic study, including a discussion of
sources used and their value and limitations, a character
sketch of Wellington and the Duke's use of, and relationship
with, his officers and men.

557.        Oman, Sir Charles, A History of the Peninsular
            War.  7 vols., London, 1910-20.
     A scholarly and reasonably objective account of the

war and Wellington's role in it, from an English viewpoint.

558.         The Peninsular War.  Some observations on the
             General Orders of Field Marshal the Duke of
             Wellington, in Portugal, Spain and France, from
             1809 to 1814.  London, 1834.
     An expanded review of Gurwood's edition of the Duke's
General Orders, commenting on them and in general terms on
the life of an army on active service.

559.         Percival, Colonel Sir Harold, "Lost Armies:
             Private Interests Versus Public Service." Army
             Quarterly, 22 (April-July 1931): 96-106.
     A study of the 1809 Talavera campaign, discussing the
Duke's attitude to his Spanish allies and other reasons for
the campaign's failure.

560.         "The Private Journals of F.S. Larpent." North
             British Review, 19 (May-August 1853): 243-54.
     Review of Larpent's Journal, which praises its
accuracy as regards Wellington's character and actions.

561.         "A Reminiscence of the Duke of Wellington at
             Orthes." Tinsley's Magazine, 6 (February-July
             1870): 475-9.
     Reminiscences of the landlady of an hotel in Orthes
where Wellington spent the night.  Of doubtful veracity.

562.         Robinson, H.B., Memoirs of Lieutenant-General
             Sir Thomas Picton, G.C.B....  2 vols., 2nd ed.,
             London, 1836.
     A defence of Picton, including some account of
Wellington's relations with him.

563.         de Santo Silvestre, Jose, Wellington at Busaco:
             The Monk's Diary.  Being an account by Fra Jose
             de S. Silvestre of the Battle of Busaco, September
             1810.  Introduced & translated by M.L. de
             Havilland.  London, 1911.
     An eyewitness account of events leading up to, and
following, the battle, by a monk whose convent served for a
time as Wellington's headquarters.

564.         Schneer, Richard M., "Arthur Wellesley and the
             Cintra Convention: A New Look at an Old Puzzle."
             Journal of British Studies, 19, 2 (Spring 1980):
             93-119.
     A detailed look at the Convention stressing
Wellington's role in its formulation and showing the steps
taken by the British government to preserve his reputation
because they needed his military skill.

565.         Severn, John, "The Wellesleys and Iberian
             Diplomacy." in Norman Gash, ed., Wellington Essays.
             (forthcoming).

566.         Sherer, Moyle, <u>Military Memoirs of the Duke of</u>
        <u>Wellington.</u> 2 vols., London, 1830.
        Volume 1 covers Wellington's military career down to
the Talavera campaign.  Volume 2 takes the story to the end
of the Peninsular war.  A carefully written survey relying
heavily on histories of the Peninsular War that had already
been published.

567.         "Supplementary Despatches, Correspondence and
        Memoranda of Field Marshal Arthur, Duke of
        Wellington, Vols. VI, VII, VIII." <u>The Edinburgh</u>
        <u>Review</u>, 116 (July-October 1862): 47-71.
        A review of the volumes covering the Peninsular War,
by an author who praises the Duke for his conduct,
especially when faced with unhelpful governments at home.

568.         "Supplementary Despatches of the Duke of
        Wellington, volumes 6,7,8." <u>The Quarterly Review</u>,
        122 (January-April 1867): 507-41.
        A review of events in the Peninsula from 1809,
indicating how the <u>Supplementary Despatches</u> do much to
restore the reputation of Lord Liverpool's government.

569.         Teffeteller, Gordon L., "Wellington and Sir
        Rowland Hill." <u>The International History Review</u>,
        XI (1989): 68-75.
        An assessment of Hill's career in the Peninsula and
his relations with Wellington.

570.         Thorn, Captain, G.W., "The Salamanca Campaign,
        1812: An illustration of modern ideas." <u>Army</u>
        <u>Quarterly</u>, 29 (October 1934-January 1935): 117-24.
        Interesting account of the battle, concentrating on
the mobility of both armies, and what use the generals
would have made of modern technology.

571.         Vickness, Samuel E., "Lord Wellington and the
        Francisco de Mello affair." <u>Journal of the Society</u>
        <u>for Army Historical Research</u>, 53 (1975):22-5.
        Quotes in full a letter from Wellington, respecting
the refusal of de Mello to serve under Marshal Beresford,
indicating the Duke's views on duty and discipline.

572.         Ward, S.G.P., <u>Wellington's Headquarters: A</u>
        <u>Study of the Administrative Problems in the</u>
        <u>Peninsula, 1809-1814</u>. Oxford, 1957.
        A scholarly review of the work of the Quarter-Master
General and Commissary General's departments.  Based on
primary sources, and including much material on Wellington's
view, relations with his staff and intelligence.

573.         Ward, S.G.P., "Brenier's Escape from Almeida,
        1811." <u>Journal of the Society for Army Historical</u>
        <u>Research</u>, 35 (1957): 23-35.
        A discussion of Wellington's failure to prevent
Brenier's escape, placing the blame on General Erskine.

574.        Warre, Rev. Edmund, <u>Letters from the Peninsula</u>
        <u>1808-1812 by Lieutenant-General Sir William Warre,</u>
        <u>C.B., K.T.S.</u>  London, 1909.
    Letters by an officer attached to Wellington's staff,
covering all the major events.

575.        Weller, J., <u>Wellington in the Peninsula, 1808-</u>
        <u>1814</u>.  London, <u>1962</u>.
    A detailed, "technical" study of the war, concen-
trating on Wellington's role in it, and his battlefield
strategy and tactics.  Based on Fortescue's <u>British Army</u>,
Napier's <u>Peninsular War</u> and some printed primary sources.

576.        Weller, Jac, "Wellington's use of guerillas."
        <u>Royal United Service Institution Journal</u>, 108
        (1963): 153-8.
    A brief but interesting survey of a neglected aspect
of Wellington's generalship.

577.        Weller, Jac, "Wellington's Peninsular War
        Logistics." <u>Journal of the Society for Army</u>
        <u>Research</u>, 42 (1964): 197-202.
    Brief survey of Wellington's logistical arrangements
and the factors bearing upon them.

578.        "Wellington in Cadiz; or the Conqueror and the
        Cortes - An Episode in the life of the Great
        Captain." <u>Blackwood's Edinburgh Magazine</u>, 26
        (July-December 1829): 918-34.
    An account of the 1809 campaign, very favourable to
Wellington and to those Spaniards who supported him.

# Section F
# Waterloo and the Army
# of Occupation 1815-1818

579.         "The Battle of Waterloo." Fraser's Magazine,30
        (July-December 1844): 17-31.
    Review of Siborne's Battle of Waterloo, defending
Wellington against charges that he was surprised before the
battle.

580.         "The Battle of Waterloo." Leisure Hour, 39
        (1890): 531-41.
    A straightforward and "popular" account of the battle.

581.         Bird, Major-General Sir W.D., "The Waterloo
        Campaign: Wellington's Point of View." Army
        Quarterly, 15 (January 1928): 303-14.
    A straightforward description of the campaign of 1815
leading up to the battle of Waterloo.

582.         Brett-James, Anthony, ed., The Hundred Days:
        Napoleon's last campaign from eye-witness accounts.
        London, 1964.
    A compilation, from printed sources, of the campaign,
including the many famous incidents in which the Duke was
involved.

583.         Chalfont, Lord, ed., Waterloo, Battle of Three
        Armies: Anglo-Dutch by William Seymour; French
        by Jacques Champagne; Prussian by E. Kaulbach.
        London, 1979.
    Detailed, if somewhat anecdotal, accounts of the
battle from different national perspectives, and based on
printed primary and secondary sources.

584.         Chandler, David G., The Campaigns of Napoleon.
        London, 1967.
    Straightforward account of the Hundred Days, written
from Napoleon's point of view.

585.         Chesney, Lieutenant Colonel Charles C., Waterloo
        Lectures: A Study of the Campaign of 1815.  2nd

edition, London, 1869.
A series of lectures expanded into a very scholarly
and impartial analysis of events.

586.          Cotton, E., A Voice from Waterloo.  A History of
           the Battle fought on the 18th June 1815.  Rev.
           ed., London, 1849.
Includes copies of the Waterloo despatch, and other
orders and letters by Wellington relating to the battle.

587.          Creasy, E.S., The Fifteen Decisive Battles of
           the World, from Marathon to Waterloo.  London,
           1851.
A scholarly description of the battle of Waterloo,
reflecting the prevailing dislike of war in British middle
class circles.
588.          Creasy, E.S., The Battle of Waterloo.  London,
           1852.
An enlarged account of the battle, based on the
author's Fifteen Decisive Battles of the World.  Includes
extra comments on Wellington's character.

589.          [D'Arblay, Fanny], Diary and Letters of Madame
           D'Arblay.  Vol. 7, London, 1846.
Includes an account of the battle of Waterloo from an
unusual perspective, also details of secret negotiations
between Wellington and Napoleon.

590.          [Egerton, Lord Francis], "Marshal Marmont,
           Wellington and the fall of Napoleon." The Quarterly
           Review, 76 (June-September 1845): 204-47.
Review of a book by Marshal Marmont and Siborne's
War in France and Belgium.  Strongly critical of both, and
defends Wellington from the "slights" of both authors.
This review may have been personally inspired by the Duke.

591.          Escott, T.H.S., "Wellington and Blucher."
           London Quarterly Review, 125 (January-April 1916):
           211-26.
Comments on Wellington's and Blucher's characters and
actions.  Somewhat inaccurate.

592.          Fleischan, T., Le Quartier général de Wellington
           à Waterloo.  Charleroi, 1956.
A brief survey of Wellington and the battle of
Waterloo, combined with descriptions of life for the local
inhabitants at the time and the present state of the
building which housed the Duke's Quarter Master General's
office.

593.          Forbes, Archibald, "A Myth of Waterloo." The
           Century, new series, 33 (November 1897-April 1898):
           464-7.
Conclusively explodes the myth that Wellington and
Blucher met at Wavre on 17 June 1815.

594.       Fraser, Sir William Augustus, Words on
        Wellington. The Duke, Waterloo, the Ball.  London,
        1889.
   A collection of unconnected anecdotes relating to
Wellington, some from the author's personal knowledge;
some from those who knew Wellington; and some apparently
unsubstantiated.

595.       Galesloot, L., Le Duc de Wellington a Bruxelles.
        Ghent, 1884.
   Essentially a reproduction of primary source material,
edited and linked together by the author, concentrating on
the 1815 campaign, but also including material from 1814 and
from some of the Duke's later visits.

596.       Head, Lieutenant-Colonel C.O., "The Waterloo
        Campaign." Journal of the Royal Artillery
        Institution, 65 (April 1938-January 1939): 510-27.
   A straightforward account of the campaign, praising
Wellington's role in it, and comparing his character and
later life with those of Napoleon.

597.       Hooper, George, Waterloo: The Downfall of the
        First Napoleon: A History of the Campaign of 1815.
        London, 1862.
   Good account of the campaign, despite a political
bias, based on printed sources available at the time of
writing.

598.       Houssaye, Henri, 1815: Waterloo.  Edited by A.
        Evan Smith; translated by Arthur Mann. London,
        1900.
   A reasonably impartial survey of the battle from the
French side.  Uses Wellington's despatches and other printed
primary sources to make informed assessments of the Duke's
actions.

599.       Howarth, David, "Waterloo: Wellington's Eye for
        the Ground." in Paddy Griffith, ed., Wellington,
        Commander, pp. 91-107.
   A good survey of the terrain of the battlefield, with
some description of the fighting.

600.       Jackson, B., Notes and Reminiscences of a Staff
        Officer chiefly relating to the Waterloo campaign
        ... Edited by R.C. Seaton.  London, 1903.
   First hand account of Wellington at Waterloo by an
officer of his staff.  Not uncritical.

601.       James, W.H., The Campaign of 1815 chiefly in
        Flanders.  Edinburgh and London, 1908.
   A well-written account of the campaign, using some
printed primary sources.  Rather anti-Prussian.

602.       Keegan, John, "Under Fire: Wellington at
        Waterloo." in Paddy Griffith, ed., Wellington,

Commander, pp. 109-24.
A study of Wellington's character and actions while
in battle, and, in particular, of his ability to animate
his men.

603.        Kelly, Christopher, A full and circumstantial
            account of the memorable battle of Waterloo ...
            and biographies and sketches of the most
            distinguished Waterloo heroes. London, 1828.
A bombastic and pro-English account of the battle.
Includes a copy of the Waterloo despatch and a biography of
Wellington.

604.        Kennedy, Sir James Shaw, Notes on the Battle of
            Waterloo ...  London, 1865.
Detailed account of the battle, with assessments of
the Duke's conduct of it.  An important work for the study
of the battle.

605.        Kraehe, Enno E., "Wellington and the Recon-
            struction of the Allied Armies during the Hundred
            Days." The International History Review, XI (1989):
            84-97.
Interesting survey of the Duke's efforts to collect
together forces to oppose the restored Napoleon, highlighting many of the logistical and political difficulties
he faced.

606.        Lamartine du Prat, M.L.A., Wellington and
            Waterloo.  London, 1852.
A specially reprinted extract from the author's
History of the Restoration of Monarchy in France, this
elegant study of 15-18 June 1815 tells more about Napoleon
losing the battle, than Wellington winning it.

607.        "The Life of Blucher and the Campaign of
            Waterloo." The Quarterly Review, 72 (May-September
            1843): 291-98.
A brief account of how Wellington may have been
"surprised", but he was non "out-manoeuvred" or "out-
generalled", at Waterloo.

608.        Macirone, F., Interesting Facts relating to the
            Fall and Death of Joachim Murat, king of Naples;
            the Capitulation of Paris in 1815; and the Second
            Restoration of the Bourbons.  London, 1817.
Includes an account of the author's dubious role in
arranging an armistice in 1815, amid a great deal of self-
justificatory material.  Went through three editions in
1817.

609.        Mansel, Philip, "Wellington and the French
            Restoration." The International History Review,
            XI (1989): 76-83.
A careful study, based on archival sources, of the
Duke's relations with the restored Bourbons, and of the

Royalists' gratitude to him.

610.        Maurice, Colonel J.F., "Waterloo: I: Apropos of
           the Panorama." United Service Magazine, new series,
           1 (April-September 1890): 61-81.
    A general survey of the campaign, setting the scene
for some detailed studies on aspects of the battle.

611.        Maurice, Colonel J.F., "Waterloo: II: The
           Origin of the Legends." United Service Magazine,
           new series, 1 (April-September 1890): 137-52.
    Discusses "legends" of the battle, including the
Duchess of Richmond's ball and the reasons for Wellington's
hesitancy before 18 June.

612.        Maurice, Colonel J.F., "Waterloo: III: Charges
           against Wellington." United Service Magazine,
           new series, 1 (April-September 1890): 257-63.
    Defends the Duke against the charge that he lied about
his position to the Prussians, to get them to support him.

613.        Maurice, Colonel J.F., "Waterloo: IV:
           Historical Difficulties: The Three Staffs."
           United Service Magazine, new series, 1 (April-
           September 1890): 533-50.
    Examines relations between Wellington's and Blucher's
Staffs, and whether Wellington "rode to Wavre" on the
night before Waterloo.

614.        Maurice, Colonel J.F., "Did the Duke ride to
           Wavre?" United Service Magazine, new series, 2
           (October 1890-March 1891): 330-9.
    Concludes tentatively that the Duke may have made the
ride, but calls for more research on the subject.

615.        Mercer, Cavalie, Journal of the Waterloo
           Campaign. 2 vols., London and Edinburgh, 1870.
    Justly famous memoirs of the campaign, including a
first hand account of some of Wellington's action, during
and after the battle, not all of which are favourably
interpreted.

616.        Mills, Dudley, "The Duke of Wellington and the
           Peace negotiations at Ghent in 1814." Canadian
           Historical Review, 2 (1921): 19-32.
    Considers Wellington's views as instrumental in
Britain's decision to end the war with the United States,
without territorial annexations.

617.        Moore Smith, G.C., The Life of John Colborne,
           Field Marshal Lord Seaton from his letters,
           records of his conversations and other sources.
           London, 1903.
    Comments, not uncritically, on Wellington's oper-
ations in the Peninsula and in the Waterloo campaign, and on

Seaton's relations with the Duke in later life.

618.        Morris, William O'Connor, The Campaign of 1815:
            Ligny: Quatre Bras: Waterloo. London & New York,
            1900.
     A straightforward and reasonably unbiased study of
the campaign, not uncritical of Wellington.

619.        Morris, William O'Connor, "Disputed Passages of
            the Campaign of 1815." English Historical Review
            10 (1895): 55-85.
     A judicious survey of the campaign, critical in some
ways of both Wellington and Napoleon.

620.        Mudford, William, An Historical Account of the
            Campaign in the Netherlands, in 1815, under His
            Grace the Duke of Wellington and Marshal Prince
            Blucher. London, 1817.
     A lavishly produced work, reproducing Wellington's
Waterloo despatch and various official papers by the Duke
and others.

621.        Muffling, Baron, Passages from my Life together
            with Memoirs of the Campaigns of 1813 and 1814.
            Edited by Colonel Philip Yorke. London, 1853.
     A good account of Wellington's relations with the
Prussians before and after Waterloo, including the battle
and Wellington's thoughts on tactics, by the Prussian
liaison officer.

622.        Murphy, Lieutenant Colonel C.C.R., "The
            Waterloo Ball." Army Quarterly, 50 (April 1945):
            88-96.
     A rather lightweight description of the Duchess of
Richmond's famous ball.

623.        Naylor, John, Waterloo. London, 1960.
     Uses some memoirs and secondary accounts to make a
rather critical assessment of the Duke's conduct of the
battle.

624.        Picton, Lieutenant G.W., The Battle of Waterloo,
            or a General History of the Events Connected with
            that important era ... London, [1816].
     Includes eye witness accounts of the battle as well as
Wellington's official despatch.

625.        "Popular Errors respecting the Battle of
            Waterloo." United Service Journal, 21 (1839):
            198-201.
     Defends Wellington from charges that he was surprised,
that he chose a poor site for the battle and that he was
"saved" by the Prussians.

626.        Redding, Cyrus, Fifty Years' Recollections,

literary and personal, with observations on men
and things. 3 vols., London, 1858.
Contains in volume 2 interesting anecdotes concerning
Wellington when Commander-in-Chief in Paris.

627.      Ropes, John Codman, The Campaign of Waterloo:
          A Military History. 3rd edition, New York, 1903.
A careful study of 15-18 June 1815, including some
reproduced documents. Written by an admirer of Napoleon,
and rather from his point of view, but makes not unfavourable mention of the Duke.

628.      Ropes, John Codman, "The Campaign of Waterloo."
          Scribner's Magazine, 3 (January-June 1888):
          259-76, 387-407.
A not unsuccessful attempt at an impartial account of
the campaign: is generally accurate, given the information
available to the author.

629.      Rouse, W.H.D., ed., Waterloo: Being Selections
          from Wellington's Despatches, along with A Voice
          from Waterloo By Sergeant-Major Edward Cotton.
          London, 1913.
A small, cloth-backed text, with extracts from
Wellington's printed despatches, covering the period from
12 March to 23 June 1815, including the 'Waterloo Despatch',
with a participant's account of the battle.

630.      Saunders, Edith, The Hundred Days. London,
          1964.
Straightforward account based on printed sources.
Makes some reference to controversies surrounding the
Duke's actions before, during and after the battle.

631.      Sheppard, Major E.W., "The Waterloo Campaign
          after 150 years." The Army Quarterly, 90 (July
          1965): 218-30.
A brief and rather superficial account, not free from
factual error.

632.      Siborne, H.T., ed., Waterloo Letters. A
          Selection from original and hitherto unpublished
          Letters bearing on the operations of the 16th,
          17th and 18th June 1815, by officers who served in
          the campaign. London, 1891.
A collection of most interesting letters from
numerous officers present at Waterloo in various capacities,
mostly dating from twenty years after the battle, often
containing comments and anecdotes connected with Wellington.

633.      Siborne, William, The Waterloo Campaign. 1815.
          4th edition, Birmingham, 1894.
A very detailed account of the campaign, reproducing
many official documents, by a great admirer of the Duke.

634.      A Sketch of the Battle of Waterloo, to which

are added official despatches of Field Marshal the Duke of Wellington; Field Marshal Prince Blucher, and Reflexions on the Battles of Ligny and Waterloo by General Muffling. Brussels, 1833. A brief general survey of the battle, including a copy of the "Waterloo Despatch".

635.      Tilney, Chrystal, "'A Compleat Trial of Principle': Southey, Wellington and The Quarterly Review." The National Library of Wales Journal, 20 (1977-8): 377-86.
Recounts Southey's suspicions that the Duke ordered alterations favourable to himself to be made in Southey's account of the battle of Waterloo.

636.      Vere, Thomas D., "Wellington and the Army of Occupation in France, 1815-18." The International History Review, XI (1989): 98-108.
Based on archival sources, this article deals with the administration of the British troops in France.

637.      Vivian, Hon. Claud, Richard Hussey Vivian, First Baron Vivian: A Memoir. London, 1897.
Includes a good account of Wellington at Waterloo, written within a few days of the battle, by an experienced officer. Some other mention of the Duke.

638.      W., C. de, Histoire de la campaigne de l'armée anglaise, hanovrienne, des Pay-bas et de Bronswick sous les ordres du duc de Wellington et l'armée prussienne sous les ordres du Prince Blucher de Wahlstadt. 1815. Stuttgart and Tubingen, 1817.
A careful survey of the campaign by a Prussian officer, including maps and orders of battle, and Wellington's Waterloo despatch in French translation.

639.      Weller, J., Wellington at Waterloo. London, 1967.
A detailed study of the campaign and battle, based on secondary and some primary sources. Basically a chronological account, some space is devoted to a thematic analysis of the action.

640.      Whithead, Lieutenant Colonel J.G.O., "Wellington at Waterloo." Army Quarterly, 91 (October 1965): 42-6.
Defends Wellington against charges of neglecting his allies and "forgetting" the detachment of troops at Hal.

# Part Five
# Political Life
# 1819-1852
## Section A
## General

641.    Anglesey, 7th Marquess of, One Leg: The Life and
        Letters of Henry William Paget, First Marquess of
        Anglesey K.G., 1768-1854. London, 1961.
    Reflects the hero's association with Wellington from
Waterloo, while Anglesey was Lord Lieutenant of Ireland and
Master General of the Ordnance, and their friendship in
later years.

642.    Birrell, Augustine, "Notes of conversations with
        the Duke of Wellington." The Nineteenth Century: A
        Monthly Review, 25 (January-June 1889): 224-27.
    A review of Stanhope's conversations with the Duke,
which deals in general terms with Wellington's character.

643.    Blanco, Richard L., "Reform and Wellington's
        Post-Waterloo Army, 1815-1854." Military Affairs,
        25 (1965): 123-31.
    Brief review of the problems of the army between 1815
and 1854, blaming Wellington, among other factors, for the
failure to achieve any significant military reforms.

644.    Bowring, Sir John, Autobiographical
        Recollections. London, 1877.
    Contains a brief appraisal of Wellington as a
politician by a Radical opponent.

645.    Broglie, duc de, Memoirs of the Prince de
        Talleyrand. Translated by Raphael Ledas de
        Beaufort; introduced by Whitelaw Hall Reid. 5 vols.
        London, 1891-2.
    Volume 2 has some information on the Peninsular
campaign, and part of volume 3 on that of Waterloo. The
remainder of volume 3, and volumes 4 and 5, deal with the
years from 1830 to 1832. Includes comments on Wellington,
and material written by the Duke relating to Talleyrand and
other political matters.

646.    Broughton, Lord [J.C. Hobhouse], Recollections
        of a long life. edited by Lady Dorchester.

6 vols., London, 1909.
A collection of specially written memoirs and extracts
from Broughton's diaries.  Broughton had some contact,
both personal and political, with the Duke from 1818 until
1852, although Wellington features in all volumes.
Especially useful for the Duke's relations with the Whig
Ministry of 1830-4.

647.        Buchan, Susan, <u>The Sword of State: Wellington</u>
            <u>After Waterloo.</u>  London, 1928.
An early attempt to deal with this part of Wellington's
life.  It is nicely written and brings characters and
incidents to life well.  More at home in the personal than
in the political and official aspects of the Duke's later
career.

648.        "Despatches, Correspondence and Memoranda of
            Field Marshal the Duke of Wellington." <u>The Edinburgh</u>
            <u>Review</u>, 141 (January-April 1875): 301-30.
Praises the second Duke for publishing these
supplementary despatches which reveal the first Duke,
despite some faults, to have been a truly great man.

649.        "Despatches, Correspondence and Memoranda of
            Field Marshal Arthur, Duke of Wellington, volumes 1
            to 4." <u>The Quarterly Review</u>, 133 (July-October 1872):
            293-342.
An appreciative review of Wellington's career as a
politician: very favourable to the Duke.

650.        Dinwiddy, J.R., "The early nineteenth-century
            campaign against flogging in the army." <u>English</u>
            <u>Historical Review</u>, 97 (1982): 308-31.
Outlines the campaign and fully describes Wellington's
attitude and opposition to it.

651.        "The Duke of Wellington." <u>Littell's Living Age</u>,
            VI (July-September 1845): 95-100.
Brief comments on Wellington's <u>Despatches</u> and on his
exemplary character as a politician.

652.        "English Premiers XIV: Canning and Wellington."
            <u>The Month</u>, VII (July-December 1867): 397-413.
A brief survey of the Duke's career down to his
premiership, with some mention of his relations with
Canning.  Written from a liberal Catholic viewpoint.

653.        Finlayson, Geoffrey, "Wellington, the Constitution,
            and the Condition of England Question." in Norman
            Gash, ed., <u>Wellington Essays.</u> (forthcoming).

654.        Foster, Russ, "Wellington and Local Government."
            in Norman Gash, ed., <u>Wellington Essays.</u> (forthcoming).

655.        Gash, Norman, ed., <u>Wellington Essays.</u> Manchester,

1989.
A collection of essays on various aspects of the
Duke's long career, to be published in 1989.  Based on
papers presented to the Wellington Congress at Southampton
University in 1987.

656.        Holland, Henry Richard Vassall, Third Lord,
            Further Memoirs of the Whig Party 1807-1831, with
            some miscellaneous reminiscences.  Edited by Lord
            Stavordale. London, 1905.
Includes a long description of Wellington's
personality and politics, as well as some comments on his
operations in the Peninsula, by a political opponent.

657.        Hylton, Lord, ed., The Paget Brothers, 1790-
            1840. London, 1918.
Includes letters on Wellington's political and
private life after Waterloo, and a memorandum by the first
Marquess of Anglesey on the Duke in politics in 1835.

658.        Ingram, Edward, "Wellington and India." in
            Norman Gash, ed., Wellington Essays. (forthcoming).

659.        Le Strange, Guy, ed. and trans., Correspondence
            of Princess Lieven and Earl Grey. 3 vols.,
            London, 1890.
Volumes 1 and 2 contain some reflections on the Duke,
between 1827 and 1834.  Princess Lieven, in these letters
at least, was well-inclined to Wellington.

660.        Leveson Gower, Hon. F., Letters of Harriet
            Countess Granville, 1810-1845.  2 vols., London,
            1894.
Letters on private and public matters, by a witness
friendly to the Duke personally, but not to his politics,
mostly for the period from 1817 to 1834.

661.        Metternich, Richard, Prince, ed., Memoirs of
            Prince Metternich.  Private papers arranged by
            M.A. Klinkowstrom; translated by Mrs. Alexander
            Napier.  5 vols., London, 1880-2.
Volume 3 mentions Wellington at the Congresses of
Aachen and Verona; volume 4 has more comments on the Duke
and British foreign policy in the mid-1820s, and volume 5
has material on the Duke's policy over Belgium (1830) and
as foreign secretary (1834-5).

662.        Partridge, Michael S., Military Planning for
            the Defense of the United Kingdom, 1814-1870.
            Westport, 1989.
Includes a full assessment of Wellington's
contribution to the debate about Britain's "national
defences" between 1819 and 1852.

663.        [Raikes, Thomas], A Portion of the Journal

kept by Thomas Raikes, Esq., from 1831 to 1847.
4 vols., London, 1856.
Comments and reflections on the Duke in public and
private life. Raikes was often abroad, but the Duke saw him
annually between 1831 and 1844.

664.          Robinson, Lionel G., ed., Letters of Dorothea,
          Princess Lieven during her residence in London,
          1812-1834. London, 1902.
Comments on the Duke as a political figure in British
and European affairs.

665.          Romilly, S.H., ed., Letters to "Ivy" from the
          First Earl of Dudley. London, 1905.
Includes letters on the Duke's career from 1808 until
1832. Dudley was a Canningite who resigned from the Duke's
Ministry in 1828.

666.          Sack, James, "Wellington and Tory Press
          Opposition." in Norman Gash, ed., Wellington Essays.
          (forthcoming).

667.          Stewart, Robert, The Foundation of the
          Conservative Party 1830-1867. London and New York,
          1978.
Discusses the Duke's role in the development of the
Tory Party, especially during his time as Prime Minister,
but also during the period of his leadership of the House
of Lords.

668.          Stirling, A.M.W., comp., The Letter-Bag of Lady
          Elizabeth Spencer-Stanhope, compiled from the
          Cannon Hall Papers, 1806-1873. 2 vols., London,
          1913.
Both volumes include some correspondence about
Wellington, and some personal and political anecdotes
concerning him.

669.          Thompson, Neville, Wellington After Waterloo.
          London, 1986.
A well researched book concentrating on the Duke's
active career as a politician.

670.          Thompson, Neville, "The Uses of Adversity." in
          Norman Gash, ed., Wellington Essays. (forthcoming)

671.          Turberville, A.S., The House of Lords in the
          Age of Reform, 1784-1837. London, 1958.
A general survey, shedding some not unfavourable light
on Wellington's career as a politician.

672.          Twiss, Horace, The Public and Private Life of
          Lord Chancellor Eldon, with Selections from his
          Correspondence. vol. 3, London, 1844.
Gives some coverage to Wellington's political career
in the late 1820s and early 1830s.

673.        Wellesley, M., <u>Wellington in Civil Life.</u>
        London, 1939.
    A detailed survey of Wellington's later life,
closely based on a wide range of printed primary sources.

# Section B
# Early Political Career
# 1819-1827

674.       Aspinall, Arthur, ed., <u>The Diary of Henry</u>
           <u>Hobhouse</u>. London, 1947.
     A journal of political events, covering the years
between 1820 and 1827, written by an Under Secretary at
the Home Office, well-informed about Wellington's role in
public life.

675.       Brock, W.R., <u>Lord Liverpool and Liberal Toryism.</u>
           Cambridge, 1941.
     An interesting view of the Duke's declining position
in the Liverpool Cabinet due to the emergence of Canning.

676.       Colchester, Charles, Lord, ed., <u>Diary and</u>
           <u>Correspondence of Charles Abbot, Lord Colchester.</u>
           <u>Speaker of the House of Commons 1802-1817.</u>
           3 vols., London, 1861.
     Volume 2 includes some mention of Wellington during
the closing stages of the Peninsular War. Volume 3 deals
with political events in the 1820s, and during the Duke's
Ministry of 1828-30.

677.       "Despatches, Correspondence and Memoranda of
           Field Marshal Arthur, Duke of Wellington, edited
           by his son ... vols. I & II." <u>The Edinburgh</u>
           <u>Review</u>, 128 (July-October 1868): 124-57.
     Reviews Wellington's conduct as a European statesman
between 1819 and 1825, and praises him for his many noble
qualities: for example, his perception, diligence, self-
reliance and strength of will.

678.       "The Duke of Wellington's Despatches ... January
           1819 to December 1825." <u>Dublin Review</u>, new series,
           10 (January-June 1868): 291-310.
     Identifies several major issues from the Duke's career
in these years, and discusses them in some detail.

679.       Gash, Norman, <u>Mr. Secretary Peel: The Life of</u>
           <u>Sir Robert Peel to 1830.</u> London, 1961.
     The first of two volumes. Scholarly and based on

primary sources.  Much mention of Wellington's relations
with Peel, especially after 1818.

680.        Green, J.E.S., "Wellington, Boislecomte, and the
            Congress of Verona (1822)." Transactions of the
            Royal Historical Society, 4th series, 1 (1918):
            59-76.
    Argues, from evidence in Boislecomte's diary, that the
Duke "betrayed" Canning at the Congress, deliberately
ignoring his instructions.

681.        Green, J.E.S., "Wellington and the Congress of
            Verona, 1822." English Historical Review, 35
            (1920): 200-11.
    Argues that the Duke fell completely under
Metternich's influence and substituted an "Austrian" for a
"British" foreign policy.

682.        Lackland, H.M., "Wellington at Verona." English
            Historical Review, 35 (1920): 574-80.
    Defends the Duke against charges of incapacity and
disloyalty to Canning at the Congress, and argues he did
his best.

683.        Nelson, C., "The Duke of Wellington and the
            barrier fortresses after Waterloo." Journal of
            the Society for Army Historical Research, 42
            (1964): 36-43.
    A straightforward review of the Duke's thoughts
regarding the forts erected as a barrier between France and
the Kingdom of the Netherlands, between 1815 and 1830.

684.        Paston, George, ed., Little Memoirs of the
            Nineteenth Century. London, 1902.
    Includes a memoir by Prince Puckler-Muskau describing
Wellington's poor performance as a speaker in the House of
Lords in 1827.

685.        Peers, Douglas M., "The Duke of Wellington and
            British India during the Liverpool administration,
            1819-1827." Journal of Imperial and Commonwealth
            History, XVII (1988): 5-25.
    A fully documented survey of the Duke's contribution
to Britain's Indian policy, especially relating to defence
matters.

686.        Quennell, Peter and Dilys Powell, eds., The
            Private Letters of Princess Lieven to Prince
            Metternich, 1820-1826.  London, 1937.
    Interesting comments on Wellington as a socialite, and
on his political activities.

687.        "The Rejected Corn Law." Blackwood's Edinburgh
            Magazine, 22 (July-December 1827): 240-49.
    Justifies Wellington's conduct in the debate leading

to the rejection of Canning's attempt to amend the Corn
Laws, and praises the Duke and those Peers who voted with
him.

688.          Temperley, Harold, ed., <u>The Unpublished Diary</u>
          <u>and Political Sketches of Princess Lieven,</u>
          <u>together with some of her letters.</u>  London, 1925.
     Comments on Wellington in the 1820s, mainly of a
political nature.

689.          Temperley, H.W.V., "Canning, Wellington and
          George the Fourth." <u>English Historical Review</u>,
          38 (1923): 206-25.
     A study of the crisis in relations between Wellington
and Canning over the Spanish American question in 1823 and
Canning's emergence as the King's leading foreign policy
adviser.

690.          "The Wellington Despatches, volumes 1 & 2."
          <u>Colburn's United Service Magazine</u>, (1867-Part II):
          81-90; (1867-Part III): 553-63.
     A review of the first two volumes of the <u>Civil</u>
<u>Correspondence</u>, relating it to current events, especially
on policy toward Russia.

# Section C
# Prime Minister
# 1828-1830

691.       Baldick, Robert, <u>The Duel: A History of</u>
         <u>Duelling.</u> London, 1965.
Includes a straightforward account of Wellington's
duel with Lord Winchelsea and its consequences.

692.       Beales, A.C.F., "Wellington and Louis Philippe,
         1830." <u>History</u>, 18 (April 1933-March 1934): 352-6.
Examines Wellington's decision to recognise Louis
Philippe's regime, and concludes the Duke acted wisely but
against his own inclinations in agreeing to the move.

693.       Bennet, Scott, "Catholic Emancipation, the
         'Quarterly Review' and 'Britain's Constitutional
         Revolution'." <u>Victorian Studies</u>, 12 (1968-9):
         283-304.
A survey showing how and why the Duke was able to
ignore the hostility of the Tory press and secure the
passage of Catholic Emancipation.

694.       'Calm Observer', "The Court and the Cabinet."
         <u>Blackwood's Edinburgh Magazine</u>, 26 (July-December
         <u>1829</u>): 696-710.
Argues that the Duke has been converted to a pro-
Catholic and "liberal" policy by machinations at George IV's
Court.

695.       Clark, John, "The Duke of Wellington" in
         Herbert van Thal, ed., <u>The Prime Ministers: Volume</u>
         <u>the First: Sir Robert Walpole to Sir Robert Peel.</u>
         London, 1974: 321-36.
A brief account of Wellington's premiership, concentrating on Catholic Emancipation and reform, and commenting
on his strengths and weaknesses as Prime Minister.

696.       Davis, R.W., "The Tories, the Whigs and Catholic
         Emancipation, 1827-1829." <u>English Historical</u>
         <u>Review</u>, 97 (1982): 89-98.
Argues that Wellington's old-fashioned views of the
constitution delayed a settlement of the question in 1828-9

and allowed opposition to it to grow up within the Tory
party.

697.          "The Death of Mr. Huskisson and the approaching
          Parliament." Fraser's Magazine, 2 (October 1830):
          251-65.
     Argues that Wellington's government has not lost a
great deal by Huskisson's death, and should survive the
forthcoming meeting of Parliament.

698.          "Despatches, Correspondence and Memoranda of
          Field Marshal Arthur, Duke of Wellington ..." The
          Edinburgh Review,   145 (January-April 1877):
          534-63.
     A review drawing parallels between the Eastern
Question in 1877 and in 1829 and some conclusions, favouring
non-intervention.

699.          "A Dissolution of Parliament." Blackwood's
          Edinburgh Magazine, 29 (July-December 1829):
          251-9.
     An attack on Wellington's government and the supposedly
liberal principles on which it acts.

700.          "The Downfall of the Wellington Administration."
          Fraser's Magazine, 2 (December 1830): 592-603.
     A strong attack on the Wellington Ministry, the
incapacity of its ministers and the style of the Duke's
leadership.

701.          Flick, Carlos, "The Fall of Wellington's
          Government." Journal of Modern History, 37 (1965):
          62-71.
     A survey of the factor's behind the Duke's fall,
crediting it to the new-found unity of the opposition in
Parliament, growing popular discontent and Wellington's own
failure to appreciate the gravity of the situation.

702.          Gash, Norman, "English Reform and French
          Revolution in the General Election of 1830." in
          Pares, R. and A.J.P. Taylor, eds., Essays Presented
          to Sir Lewis Namier. London, 1956.
     A careful study assessing the reasons for the fall of
Wellington's government in 1830, concluding that events in
France were not responsible.

703.          Gash, Norman, "Wellington as Prime Minister."
          in Norman Gash, ed., Wellington Essays. (forth-
          coming).

704.          Gwyn, Dennis, "Wellington's surrender to the
          Catholics." Fortnightly Review, new series, 124
          (July-December 1928): 389-99.
     Generally accurate survey of the Catholic Emancipation
crisis of 1829, concluding the Duke surrendered for
humanitarian and practical reasons.

705.        "History of the Whig Ministry from 1830 to the
            Passing of the Reform Bill." British Quarterly
            Review, 15 (February-May 1852): 390-425.
     Hostile review of this work by J.A. Roebuck, M.P.,
including much comment on Wellington's Ministry, and the
circumstances surrounding its downfall.

706.        Law, Edward, Lord Ellenborough, A Political
            Diary 1828-1830. Edited by Lord Colchester.
            2 vols., London, 1881.
     A detailed diary covering the years when Ellenborough
was Lord Privy Seal in Wellington's Ministry. Includes
accounts of Cabinet discussions, and Wellington's opinions.

707.        McGee, Michael C., "The Fall of Wellington: A
            Case Study of the relationship between theory,
            practice and rhetoric in History." The Quarterly
            Journal of Speech, 63 (1977): 28-42.
     Concludes that Wellington fell from power because of
popular disillusion with his reputation as a leader.

708.        Machin, G.I.T., "The Duke of Wellington and
            Catholic Emancipation." Journal of Ecclesiastical
            History, 14 (1963): 190-208.
     Argues that Wellington had long regarded Catholic
emancipation as an empirical, political, question, and that
he was prepared to pass it, hoping to keep his party
together.

709.        Machin, G.I.T., "Canning, Wellington and the
            Catholic question, 1827-1829." English Historical
            Review, 99 (1984): 94-100.
     Sees the Duke's attitude to Catholic Emancipation and
the Constitution as justifiable and different from Cannings.
Disagrees with R.W. Davis.

710.        Manning, Helen Taft, "Colonial Crises before
            the Cabinet, 1829-1835." Bulletin of the Institute
            of Historical Research, 30 (1957): 41-61.
     Includes a discussion of the formulation of colonial
policy in Wellington's Cabinet in 1829-30, and the Duke's
eventual mastery of Huskisson.

711.        Noyce, Karen, "Wellington and Catholic
            Emancipation." in Norman Gash, ed., Wellington
            Essays. (forthcoming).

712.        Oman, Sir Charles, "The Duke of Wellington", in
            F.J.C. Hearnshaw, ed., The Political Principles of
            some notable Prime Ministers of the Nineteenth
            Century. London, 1926, pp. 15-42.
     An analysis of Wellington's time as Prime Minister,
concluding that he was unlucky, but also that his
personality rather unfitted him for high political office.

713.         Paget, Sir Augustus B., ed., <u>The Paget Papers.</u>
<u>Diplomatic and other correspondence of the Right</u>
<u>Hon. Sir Arthur Paget, G.C.B., 1794-1807.</u>
Volume 2, London, 1896.
Includes an appendix containing letters from Lord
Anglesey when Lord Lieutenant of Ireland and relating to his
quarrel with Wellington in 1829.

714.         "'Political Fragments', 'Church Reform' and
reasons for a Revision of our Fiscal Code." The
<u>Quarterly Review</u>, 42 (January-March 1830): 228-77.
Not so much a review as a call to Wellington's government to take action about the economy and Parliamentary
Reform - by restricting the franchise.

715.         "The Prospects of the Ministry." <u>Fraser's</u>
<u>Magazine</u>, 2 (August 1830-January 1831): 190-9.
A sympathetic portrait of the state of Wellington's
government, showing why, and how widely, it was disliked.
Hopes the Duke will resign before being beaten.

716.         "Public Affairs." <u>Blackwood's Edinburgh</u>
<u>Magazine</u>, 26 (July-December 1829): 711-16.
Strong attack on the Duke (and on Peel) for running an
Irish, military, government.

717.         'R', "Wellington and Emancipation." <u>New Monthly</u>
<u>Magazine and Literary Journal</u>, 25 (January-June
1829): 201-10; 300-10.
Strongly favourable to the Duke because of his passing
Catholic Emancipation, and expressing general approval of
his character and administration.  Attacks the ultra-Tories.

718.         "Reply to a pamphlet entitled 'What has the
Duke of Wellington gained by the Dissolution?'
1830." <u>Westminster Review</u>, 14 (January-April 1831):
232-45.
Begins by ridiculing the "achievements" of the Duke's
administration, and goes on to call for democracy, to stave
off revolution.

719.         "Review of the Last Session of Parliament."
<u>Blackwood's Edinburgh Magazine</u>, 26 (July-December
1829): 224-37.
Very bitter attack on Wellington for his "betrayal" of
conservative principles and for granting Catholic Emancipation.

720.         "Speech of Sir Robert Peel, Bart., June 26th
1846." <u>Eclectic Review</u>, 22 (July-December 1847):
1-19.
Includes interesting comments on the fall of
Wellington's ministry in 1830 and his "predilection for
despotism."

721.         Stuart, Charles, "British Prime Ministers, XIV:
        The Duke of Wellington." <u>History Today</u>, 2 (1952):
        624-31.
    A survey of the whole of Wellington's political career,
mainly between 1819 and 1830, defending the Duke and
challenging his popular reputation as an incompetent
politician.

722.         "Thoughts on the Wellington Administration."
        <u>Fraser's Magazine</u>, 1 (February-July 1830): 729-37.
    A very anti-Wellington survey, both personally and
politically.  Written from a High Tory viewpoint.

# Section D
# Later Political Career
# 1831-1852

723.        "On the China and the Opium Question." Black-
            wood's Edinburgh Magazine, 47 (January-June 1840):
            847-53.
            Cites Wellington's speech in a Lords' debate on
British relations with China, defending the government's
conduct, and goes on to approve the Duke's character and
achievements in more general terms.

724.        Clark, G.K., Peel and the Conservative Party:
            A Study in Party Politics.  London, 1929.
            A political biography of Peel, including material on
the Duke's career as a politician, his relationship with
Peel and his role in Conversative Party politics.

725.        "Contemporary Orators. No. V.  The Duke of
            Wellington." Fraser's Magazine, 32 (July-December
            1845): 688-91.
            An interesting view of the Duke as an orator, and of
his influence over the House of Lords.

726.        "Despatches, Correspondence and Memoranda of
            Field Marshal Arthur, Duke of Wellington ...
            volumes 5 to 7." The Quarterly Review, 146 (July-
            October 1878): 69-100.
            A survey of the last twenty-two years of Wellington's
political career, with some comments on his saving the
aristocratic "interest".

727.        "Dissolution of the Short Parliament." New
            Monthly Magazine and Literary Journal, 31 (January-
            June 1831): 477-84.
            Describes Wellington's outright opposition to the
reform bill, but prefers his open opposition to the
"moderate" Tories who claim to support a measure of reform.

728.        "English Premiers XV: Wellington and Grey."
            The Month, VII (July-December 1867): 503-17.
            The first half of this article deals effectively with
the Duke's public career from 1830 until his death.

729.        Esher, Viscount, ed., The Girlhood of Queen
            Victoria.  A Selection from her Majesty's diaries
            between the years 1832 and 1840.  2 vols., London,
            1912.
    Both volumes include some comments on the Duke and his
actions; volume two covers the famous "Bedchamber Crisis" of
1839.

730.        "Fall of the Melbourne Ministry." Blackwood's
            Edinburgh Magazine, 37 (January-June 1835): 30-48.
    An ultra-Tory account, praising the Duke for his
courage in forming the caretaker ministry in November 1834.

731.        Gash, Norman, Sir Robert Peel: The Life of Sir
            Robert Peel after 1830.  London, 1972.
    The concluding volume, covering Peel's relations with
the Duke from the fall of Wellington's Ministry in 1830 to
Peel's death in 1850.  Includes details of Wellington's role
in Peel's Ministries, and covers specific issues such as
corn law repeal and national defences.

732.        Hertz, Bertha Kereson, "Disraeli and the Duke."
            Cornhill Magazine, 1083/4 (Spring/Summer 1975):
            219-38.
    Fully describes Disraeli's various and varied attempts
to get close to the Duke, and the Duke's lukewarm response,
as well as Wellington's place in Disraeli's writing.

733.        "History of the Indian administration of Lord
            Ellenborough in his correspondence with the Duke
            of Wellington ... edited by Lord Colchester." The
            Edinburgh Review, 141 (January-April 1875): 31-52.
    A review which generally praises the Duke's attitude
to Indian policy and also reveals some of his other
attitudes, for example, to the press.

734.        Kent, Peter, "The Militant Trinity: the role of
            Wellington, Burgoyne and Palmerston in fortifi-
            cation policy, 1830-1860." Fort, 4 (1986): 39-46.
    A brief review of some of Wellington's assessments of
the national defences.

735.        McN[aghton], Captain, "Some remarks ... on the
            question of Corporal Punishment." East Indian
            United Service Journal, 9 (November 1836): 146-76.
    Includes quotations from Wellington on the use of
corporal punishment in the army.

736.        Mather, F.C., "Wellington and British Politics
            after 1832." in Norman  Gash, ed., Wellington
            Essays.  (forthcoming).

737.        'N., C.' "Shall we have a Conservative govern-
            ment?" Blackwood's Edinburgh Magazine, 37 (January
            -June 1835): 431-44.
    Defence of Peel's Ministry and of Wellington, both on

account of his political record and for his personal
qualities. Very High Tory.

738.            Partridge, Michael, "Wellington and the Defence
                of the Realm, 1819-1852." in Norman Gash, ed.,
                Wellington Essays. (forthcoming).

739.            "The Prospects of the Session." Blackwood's
                Edinburgh Magazine, 41 (January-June 1837):
                301-11.
        An attack on Melbourne's ministry, combined with an
eulogy of Wellington, Lyndhurst and Peel, especially the
Duke.

740.            Strachan, H.F.A., Wellington's Legacy: The
                Reform of the British Army, 1830-54. Manchester,
                1984.
        Scholarly survey of the reform of the British army,
based on primary sources, and detailing Wellington's involvement in the process of change.

741.            Turberville, A.S., "The House of Lords and the
                Reform Act of 1832." Leeds Philosophical and
                Literary Society: Proceedings, Literary and
                Historical Section 6 (1944-7): 61-92.
        A scholarly survey of Wellington's, and other Tory
Peers', attitudes to the Reform Act and other legislation
Of the 1830s.

742.            "Political Retrospect 1830-1841." Westminster
                Review, 37 (January-April 1842): 394-427.
        An attack on the Whigs, explaining why the Tories
were back in power, but including some comments on
Wellington's conduct in 1830.

743.            "Wellington and Reform." Blackwood's Edinburgh
                Magazine, 128 (July-December 1880): 105-23.
        Defends Wellington's opposition to the 1832 Reform
Act. Argues that the Duke's position was both logical and
sensible: he could have postponed the measure, and introduced a better one in "calmer" times.

744.            "Whig practices and Whig professions."
                Blackwood's Edinburgh Magazine, 43 (January-June
                1838): 791-804.
        Contrasts the evident failings of the Melbourne
Ministry with the brave struggles of the Duke and his
colleagues to support the constitution.

# Part Six
# Private Life

745.      Airlie, Mabell, Countess of, <u>Lady Palmerston</u>
          <u>and her times.</u>  2 vols., London, 1922.
     Recounts stories of the Duke's life, mostly from the
1820s, when Lady Palmerston was a close friend of
Wellington.

746.      Avery, Charles, "Neo-Classical portraits by
          Pistrucci and Rauch." <u>Appollo: The Magazine of the</u>
          <u>Arts</u>, (July 1975): 36-43.
     Describes busts of the Duke and others, and includes
letters to the Duke about their purchase.

747.      B., E.V., "The Duke." <u>Cornhill Magazine</u>, new
          series, 25 (1908): 326-44.
     Personal recollections of the Duke at Walmer Castle in
old age, as well as some of his last letters, and a
description of his funeral.

748.      Bagot, Mrs. Charles, <u>Links with the Past.</u>
          London, 1901.
     Includes anecdotes, recalled from memory, about the
Duke's later life.

749.      Barrington, Daines, <u>Miscellanies</u>. London, 1781.
     Includes a sketch of Wellington's father, the first
Earl of Mornington, as an infant musical prodigy.

750.      Bell, G.H., ed., <u>The Hamwood Papers of the</u>
          <u>Ladies of Llangollen and Caroline Hamilton.</u>
          London, 1930.
     Includes some material on the Duke's grandmother and
other members of his family, by two friends of the
Wellesley family.

751.      Butler, Iris, <u>The Eldest Brother.  The Marquess</u>
          <u>Wellesley, the Duke of Wellington's Eldest</u>
          <u>Brother.</u>  London, 1973.
     Includes material on the Duke's relationship with his
eldest brother, from their early days, in India and the

Peninsula, down to the Marquess Wellesley's death in 1842.

752.       Cecil, Algernon, "Lady Shelley and her
           Acquaintance." The Quarterly Review, 219 (July-
           October 1913): 464-82.
     Discusses Lady Shelley's friendship with Wellington
from 1815 to the Duke's death.

753.       Chancellor, E. Beresford, "Apsley House." The
           Contemporary Review, 148 (July-December 1935):
           72-8.
     An idiosyncratic and rather inaccurate description and
brief history of the property.

754.       Crombie, Theodore, "The Legacy of Vitoria:
           Spanish Paintings at Apsley House." Appollo: The
           Magazine of the Arts, (September 1973): 210-15.
     Describes the acquisition of these pictures by the
Duke, as well as the individual pieces (including Goya's
equestrian portrait).

755.       Curzon of Kedleston, Marquess, The History of
           Walmer Castle and its Lords Warden.  London, 1927.
     Interesting view of Wellington's public and private
life as Lord Warden of the Cinque Ports, based on primary
sources.

756.       Elvin, Charles R.S., The History of Walmer and
           Walmer Castle.  Private printing, Canterbury, 1894.
     Gives details of Wellington's tenure as Lord Warden
of the Cinque Ports.

757.       Edgecumbe, Richard, ed., The Diary of Frances,
           Lady Shelley.  2 vols., London, 1912.
     A record kept by an intimate friend of the Duke, from
their first meeting in 1814, and includes comments on a
wide variety of social and political events.

758.     - Fitchett, W.H., "A Curious Chapter in
           Wellington's Life." Cornhill Magazine, new series,
           40 (January-June 1916): 48-58.
     Comments on the Duke's extensive correspondence with
Miss Jenkins, stressing the Duke's patience, courtesy and
humility in matters of religion.

759.       Ford, Brinsley, "The Pictures at Stratfield
           Saye." Appollo: The Magazine of the Arts, (July
           1975): 19-29.
     Describes pictures presented to, or bought by, the
Duke, as well as portraits of him in the house.

760.       Gifford, Margaret Jeune, ed., Pages from the
           Diary of an Oxford Lady, 1843-1862.  Oxford, 1932.
     Includes some interesting passages on Wellington's
life as Chancellor of the University.

761.        Gleig, George Robert, <u>Reminiscences of the</u>
            <u>First Duke of Wellington, with sketches of some</u>
            <u>of his Guests and Contemporaries.</u>  Edited by Mary
            E. Gleig. London, 1904.
        Recollections of the Duke's personal and political
life, written in extreme old age, but not uncritically,
although it tells us perhaps rather more about Gleig than
Wellington.

762.        Glover, Michael, "An excellent young man: the
            Rev. Samuel Briscall 1788-1848." <u>History Today</u>,
            18 (1968): 578-84.
        The life of one of the Duke's Peninsular war
chaplains, and his relationship with Wellington during the
war and after.

763.        Hannay, Prudence, "Wellington and Lady Shelley."
            <u>History Today</u>, 25 (1975): 98-109.
        Straightforward account of the Duke's relationship
with Lady Shelley, based primarily on her journals.

764.        Harding, John, "The Building and Decoration of
            Apsley House." <u>Appollo: The Magazine of the Arts.</u>
            (September 1973): 170-79.
        A brief history and lavishly-illustrated description
of the Duke's London residence.

765.        Hare, Augustus J.C., <u>The Life and Letters of</u>
            <u>Maria Edgeworth.</u>  2 vols., London, 1894.
        Comments on Wellington and his marriage, by a friend
of the Duchess.

766.        Herrmann, F., "The Duke of Wellington as a
            Field Marshal of Prussia and Austria." <u>Journal of</u>
            <u>the Society for Army Historical Research</u>, 47
            (1969): 89-95.
        Primarily a description of Wellington's Austrian Field
Marshal's uniform, which survives, and a list of his offices
in the two armies.

767.        Hudleston, F.J., <u>Warriors in Undress.</u>  London,
            1925.
        Pages 15 to 29 contain a critical view of Wellington's
private life and character.

768.        Hudson, Derek, "The Duke of Wellington's Miss
            J." in Derek Hudson, <u>The Forgotten King and other</u>
            <u>essays.</u>  London, 1960, pp. 136-43.
        A study of the Duke's relationship with Miss Jenkins:
concludes that he was a lonely old man who needed her
friendship.

769.        Kurtz, Harold, "Madame de Stael and the Duke of
            Wellington." <u>History Today</u>, 13 (1963): 735-46.
        Includes many quotations from letters between the
Duke and his friend, on political and social matters, at the

time of the allied occupation of France.

770.         Lees-Milne, James, "Stratfield Saye House."
        Appollo: The Magazine of the Arts, (July 1975):
        8-18.
    A brief history and description of the house,
indicating the Duke's alterations to it.

771.         [Lennox, Lord William Pitt], Three Years with
        the Duke, or Wellington in Private Life, by an
        ex-Aid-de-Camp. London, 1853.
    Memoirs covering the period from Wellington's
despatch to France as Ambassador late in 1814 down to July
1815, taking in the Congress of Vienna, Waterloo, and some
comments on the Duke's private character.

772.         Lennox, Lord William Pitt, Fifty Years'
        Biographical Reminiscences.  Volume 1, London,
        1863.
    Memories of the Duke in France between 1814 and 1818,
by former A.D.C.

773.         Linstrum, Derek, "The Waterloo Palace."
        Architectural Review, 155 (April 1974): 217-23.
    Concerns Benjamin Wyatt's plans for the conversion of
Wellington's house at Stratfield Saye into a "palace", and
explains why they did not come to fruition.

774.         Longford, Elizabeth, "The Duke of Wellington's
        Books." History Today, 17 (1967): 22-8.
    A brief sketch, pointing out that the Duke was not as
unconcerned with books and scholarship as he suggested, and
as many of his biographers believed.

775.         Longford, Elizabeth, "The Duke of Wellington's
        Search for a Palace." Horizon: A Magazine of the
        Arts, XI (Spring 1969): 106-13.
    A well-researched account of Wellington's relations
with his architects, as well as a review of his projected
house purchases.

776.         Martineau, John, The Life of Henry Pelham,
        Fifth Duke of Newcastle. London, 1908.
    Includes some anecdotes of Wellington's private life
in the 1820s to 1840s, and a letter from him on Chelsea
Pensioners.

777.         Memoir of Charles Gordon Lennox, Fifth Duke of
        Richmond, K.G., P.C. London, 1862.
    A biography of the Duke of Richmond, including
information on his relations with Wellington as a young
staff officer in the Peninsula and later as a political
opponent.

778.         Mitchell, J., "Apsley House, Piccadilly, the
        Town Residence of His Grace the Duke of Wellington."

The Quarterly Review, 92 (December 1852-March 1853)
: 446-86.
A full description of the house and its contents - just
opened to the public by the second Duke - as well as
anecdotes and very favourable character sketch of the late
Duke.

779.          [Mozley, Anne, ed.], Letters of the Rev. J.B.
              Mozley, D.D., late Canon of Christ Church, and
              Regius Professor of Divinity in the University
              of Oxford.  London, 1885.
Includes details of Wellington's election as Chancellor
of the University of Oxford, and his installation and other
matters connected with the Duke's work as Chancellor.

780.          Oman, Charles, "The Plate at the Wellington
              Museum." Appollo: The Magazine of the Arts,
              (September 1973): 197-205.
Describes Wellington's acquisition of plate, throughout
his career.

781.          Ouverleau-Lagasse, F.A., Le Duc de Wellington.
              Fût-il creé Duc de Brunoy par Louis XVIII?
              1920.
Discusses question of whether or not Wellington was
created a French Duke.

782.          Raymond, John, ed., Reminiscences and
              Recollections of Captain Gronow, being anecdotes
              of the Camp, Court, Clubs and Society, 1810-1860.
              London, 1964.
Lively reminiscences of English society in the early
nineteenth century, with several Wellington anecdotes.  The
author, however, was not personally acquainted with the
Duke.

783.          Russell, George W.E., "Miss Jenkins and the
              Duke." Cornhill Magazine, new series, 40 (January-
              June 1916): 641-8.
Very similar to Dr. Fitchett's article on this subject,
arguing that the Duke's relationship with Miss Jenkins was
less spiritual than Fitchett said.  (Volume 41, p. 384
contains a brief reply by Fitchett).

784.          Sharpe, W., ed., Recollections by Samuel Rogers.
              London, 1859.
Includes some different anecdotes about Spain and
Waterloo, as well as other, more familiar, stories of
Wellington's life.

785.          Smailles, Helen, "Thomas Campbell and the
              'camera lucida': the Buccleuch Statue of the 1st
              Duke of Wellington." The Burlington Magazine,
              129 (1987): 709-14.
Adds some detail on the Duke's relations with various
artists.

786.　　　　Smith, C.H.C. and H.V.T. Percival, The
　　　　Wellington Museum, Apsley House.  A Guide.  London,
　　　　1952 and later editions.
A descriptive guide to Wellington's collections of
objets d'arts, prefaced by a biographical sketch and
including a description of Apsley House.  The 1964 edition
includes a newly-opened display of caricatures.  Illustrated.

787.　　　　Sutton, Denys, "The Great Duke and the Arts."
　　　　Appollo: The Magazine of the Arts.  (September,
　　　　1973): 161-9.
A description of the Duke's tastes and his attitude to
art, with a description of some of his paintings, intro-
ducing a series of articles on the subject, and on various
paintings and objets d'arts at Apsley House.

788.　　　　Sutton, Denys, "The Fruits of Victory." Appollo:
　　　　The Magazine of the Arts. (July 1975): 2-7.
Discusses Wellington's association with Stratfield
Saye, and introduces a special issue of the Journal devoted
to this subject.

789.　　　　Thornton, James, Your Most Obedient Servant:
　　　　Cook to the Duke of Wellington.  Introduced by
　　　　Elizabeth Longford.  Exeter, 1985.
Based on a questionnaire sent by Lord Frederick
Fitzclarence to Wellington's former cook, and provides
valuable views of Wellington's domestic arrangements during
the Peninsular and Waterloo campaigns.

790.　　　　Tollemache, Hon. Lionel A., Old and Odd
　　　　Memories.  London, 1908.
Includes some uncommon, but not necessarily accurate,
anecdotes concerning the Duke.

791.　　　　Truman, Charles, "Emperor, King and Duke - The
　　　　Sevres Egyptian service acquired for the nation."
　　　　The Connoisseur, 202 (1979): 148-55.
A full description of the Duke's "Egyptian" dinner
service, originally made for the Empress Josephine.

792.　　　　Tussaud, John Theodore, The Romance of Madame
　　　　Tussauds.  London, 1920.
Describes how the Duke was modelled and his many
visits to Madame Tussaud's, including the Chamber of
Horrors.

793.　　　　Tylden, G., "The First Duke of Wellington as a
　　　　Horseman." Journal of the Society for Army
　　　　Historical Research, 43 (1965): 67-72.
Comments on the Duke's horsemanship during the Penin-
sular War and after.

794.　　　　Watson, F.J.B., "The Great Duke's Taste for
　　　　French Furniture." Appollo: The Magazine of the

<u>Arts.</u>   (July 1975): 44-9.
Includes a description of some pieces purchased by the Duke at Stratfield Saye.

795.        Weigall, Lady Rose, ed., <u>The Correspondence of Priscilla, Countess of Westmorland.</u>  London, 1909.
Includes letters about the Duke from 1812 until his death, covering many aspects of his political, social and private life.

796.        Weigall, Rachel, <u>Lady Rose Weigall: A Memoir.</u> London, 1923.
Includes interesting recollections of the Duke dating from Lady Rose's childhood in the 1830s.

797.        [Wilson, Harriette], <u>Memoirs of Harriette Wilson, written by herself.</u>  London, [1823].
The infamous memoirs, giving a different view of the Duke to that usually published.  Of doubtful veracity.

798.        Wilson, Joan, <u>A Soldier's Wife. Wellington's Marriage.</u>  London, 1987.
A biography of the Duchess of Wellington, and the story of the Duke's marriage down to 1815, based mainly on primary sources preserved at Stratfield Saye.

799.        Wyndham, Hon. Mrs. Hugh, ed., <u>Correspondence of Sarah Spencer, Lady Lyttleton.</u>  London, 1912.
Includes stories of embarassments arising from Wellington's deafness, by a Lady-in-Waiting at Queen Victoria's Court.

# Part Seven
# Iconography
## Section A
## Descriptions

800.       The Builder
    Issues of 12 July 1845, 23 May, 1 August, 17 and 21
October, 14 November and 26 December 1846, 10 and 22 April,
5 June and 17 July 1847, 24 December 1881 and 1 April 1882
have articles on the Wellington Arch and Statue, deprecating
the scheme.

801.       The Constitution Hill Archway and the Duke of
           Wellington's Statue. London, 1882.
    A publication occasioned by the death of Decimus
Burton, reproducing extracts from The Builder from 1845 to
1847, remonstrating against the placing of the large
equestrian statue of Wellington on Burton's arch, and
approving of its proposed removal.

802.       "The Duke of Wellington's Statue." The Art-
           Union: A Monthly Journal of the fine Arts, 4,
           (1842): 106; 8 (1846); 19, 169, 216, 240, 264, 284,
           313; 9 (1847): 110, 262, 300.
    Notes reflecting the controversy surrounding the
placing of Wyatt's huge equestrian statue of the Duke at
Hyde Park Corner.

803.       Foster, R.E., "Mr. Punch and the Duke." History
           Today, 34 (May 1984): 36-42.
    An overview of how the Duke was portrayed in the pages
of Punch, from its foundation in 1842 to Wellington's death.

804.       H., V.I., The Iron Duke or the Wellington
           Monument Removal. London, 1882.
    A brief satirical pamphlet, comprising in part a
conversation between the Duke's statue and the Arch at Hyde
Park Corner.

805.       Henry, C. Bowdler, "The Iron Duke's Dentures."
           British Dental Journal, 125 (July-December 1968):
           354-6.
    A brief, technical, survey of an unusual relic of the
Duke's life. Illustrated.

806.       The Illustrated London News.
Issues of 11 July, 15 August and 3 October 1846
contain engravings of the construction of Wyatt's huge
equestrian statue of the Duke, and also on 3 October a full
page engraving showing the statue in place on Burton's arch
at Hyde Park Corner.  Unlike the architect of the Arch, and
many others, The Illustrated London News approved of the
statue and its placement.

807.       Memorial of the Military Achievements of his
           Grace the Duke of Wellington. [?1837].
Copy of a resolution for the construction of a
memorial to Wellington, with a list of the contributors and
the sums contributed.

808.       Miller, A.E. Haswell, and N.P. Dawnay, Military
           Drawings and Paintings in the Collection of Her
           Majesty the Queen.  2 vols., London, 1966-70.
Includes descriptions of several paintings of
Wellington, including watercolours by Dennis and Richard
Dighton (1819) and views of the Duke's lying-in-state and
funeral by Louis Haghe.

809.       Paine, J., "Links with the Iron Duke." United
           Empire: The Royal Colonial Institute Journal.
           19 (new ser.), (1928): 138-43.
A list of places named after, or associated with,
Wellington, including statuary and other monuments.

810.       Percival, Victor, The Duke of Wellington. A
           Pictorial Survey of his Life (1769-1852).
           London, 1969.
Includes reproductions, not only of portraits of the
Duke, but also of his comrades and colleagues, of places
connected with his career and artefacts associated with
him, giving details and current locations.

811.       Percival, Victor, "Momentoes of the Iron Duke."
           Appollo: The Magazine of the Arts.  (September,
           1973): 216-19.
A description of Wellington's swords, dressing-case,
orders, medals, marshals batons and captured standards.

812.       Physick, John, The Duke of Wellington in
           Caricature.  London, 1965.
A collection of reproductions of forty-four political
caricatures dating from Wellington's Premiership.  Each is
reproduced full page in black and white, with an
explanatory description on the facing page.

813.       Reflections in Rhyme, on the Wellington
           Memorial and the Column of Napoleon. London, 1839.
An attack on, amongst other things, the style of the
Wellington statue, which the author feels should not be an
equestrian figure, and on its proposed position at Hyde Park
Corner.

814.      A series of Drawings of the Orders of Knight-
          hood, together with the Batons and Medals,
          conferred upon His Grace the Duke of Wellington.
          London, 1852.
     A lavish edition of colour plates of all the Duke's
order and decorations, with a brief history of them, and
the occasion of their being conferred on him.

815.      Stadler, J.C., The Wars of Wellington.  London,
          undated.
     Engravings by J. Duplessi Bartoux of paintings by
Stadler, with a brief description of the battles.

816.      de Tivoli, V., Description of the model of a
          monument to be erected to the Duke of Wellington in
          St. Paul's Cathedral; marked with the motto: "'Tis
          not my profit that doth lead mine honour.  Mine
          honour it."  (Shakespeare, Anthony and Cleopatra).
          Florence, 1857.
     An entry for the competition to build the Wellington
monument, detailing the style of the work and an estimate of
its cost.

817.      Victories of the Duke of Wellington from
          Drawings by R. Westall, R.A.  London, 1819.
     A series of coloured engravings coupled with explan-
atory text, of the battles of Vimiero, Talavera, Busaco,
Salamanca, Vittoria, "the Pyrenees", Saint Sebastian,
Toulouse and Waterloo, and the capture of Oporto, Badajoz,
and Madrid.  Engravings by T. Fielding.

818.      Walker, Richard, Regency Portraits.  2 vols.,
          London, 1985.
     Volume 1, pages 525-42 describes and lists the current
whereabouts (if known) of portraits, busts and statues of
the Duke, including those now lost.  Supplements Wellesley
and Steegman's now rather out of date work.  Volume 2,
plates 1314-46, reproduces thirty-two of the surviving
portraits of the Duke, from youth to old age.

819.      Wellesley, Lord Gerald, and John Steegman,
          Iconography of the Duke of Wellington.  London,
          1935.
     A full catalogue of portraits of the Duke, including
some whose present whereabouts were not known, arranged by
artist.  Includes extracts from the Memoirs of B.R. Haydon,
and reproductions of important pieces.  Effectively updated
by Walker [818], but still the most complete survey of
"Wellington Iconography".

# Section B
# Portraits

For a complete survey of "Wellington Iconography" the reader is referred to the works of Walker (818) and Wellesley and Steegman (819).  The following list includes paintings in collections known to be open to the public, and one or two important works in private collections. In most cases only one location is given.  Many of the following works were later copied or engraved, and some survive in several slightly different versions.

820.        Austissier, Louis-Marie.
                Miniature. Oil. Head and Shoulders. Uniform.
                1816
                (Apsley House, London)

821.        Bauzil, Juan.
                Watercolour. Full length. Civilian dress.
                1812-16.
                (National Portrait Gallery, London).

                Miniature. Oil. Head and Shoulders.
                (Stratfield Saye, Hampshire)

822.        Beechey, Sir William
                Oil. Full Length. 1814.
                (Hecksher Museum, New York)

823.        Chantrey, Sir Francis
                Fourteen pencil drawings, drawn with the aid
                of a camera lucida, in preparation for later
                busts. 1822-39.
                (National Portrait Gallery, London)

824.        Cooper, Abraham
                Oil. Equestrian. 1837.
                (Stratfield Saye, Hampshire)

825.        Copley, John Singleton
                Oil. Equestrian. Unfinished.

(Museum of Fine Art, Boston)

826.        Dawe, George.
                Oil. Full Length. 1818.
                (Goodwood, West Sussex).

                Oil. Half Length. Uniform. 1818.
                (Stratfield Saye; National Army Museum,
                London).

827.        D'Orsay, Alfred
                Oil. Full Length. Evening Dress. 1845.
                (Copy at Stratfield Saye; original at King's
                College London, on loan from the National
                Portrait Gallery).

828.        Evans, William (or Richard)
                Oil. Half Length. Uniform. 1829.
                (Eton College, Berkshire; Copy in the Henry
                E. Huntington Library, San Marino,
                California).

829.        Gerard, Francois
                Oil. Full Length. Uniform. 1814.
                (Original at the British Embassy, Paris;
                copy at the Hermitage Museum, Leningrad)

830.        Goya, Francisco
                Chalk Sketch. Head and Shoulders. 1812.
                (British Library, London)

                Oil. Half Length. 1812.
                (National Gallery, London)

                Oil. Equestrian. 1812.
                (Apsley House)

831.        Haydon, Benjamin Robert
                Oil. "Wellington musing on the Field of
                Waterloo". c. 1840.
                (Walker Art Gallery, Liverpool).

832.        Hayter, Sir George
                Oil.  "The Trial of Queen Caroline". 1820
                (National Portrait Gallery)

833.        Heaphy, Thomas
                Watercolour. Miniature. Head and Shoulders.
                1813.
                (National Portrait Gallery)

                Watercolour. Full Length. 1813.
                (National Portrait Gallery).

834.        Home, Robert
            Oil. Half Length. As Major General. 1806.
            (National Portrait Gallery)

835.        Hoppner, T.
            Oil. Half Length. As Lieutenant Colonel.
            c. 1795.
            (Stratfield Saye)

836.        Isabey, Jean-Baptiste
            Oil. Head and Shoulders. 1818.
            (Apsley House)

837.        Jackson, John
            Oil. Head and Shoulders. 1827.
            (National Portrait Gallery)

838.        Lawrence, Sir Thomas
            Oil. Full Length. Uniform. 1814.
            (Windsor Castle, Berkshire)

            Oil. Half Length. Uniform. 1814
            (Apsley House)

            Oil. Full Length. Civilian Dress. 1824-5.
            (Wellington College, Berkshire)

839.        Leslie, Charles Robert
            Oil. Full Length. Evening dress. With
            Marchioness of Douro. 1848.
            (Stratfield Saye)

            Oil. Full Length. Evening dress. With bust
            of Napoleon. 1848.
            (Stratfield Saye)

840.        Lilley, John
            Oil. Full Length. As Lord Warden of the
            Cinque Ports. Undated.
            (Town Hall, Dover, Kent)

841.        Lucas, John
            Oil. Full Length. As Lord Lieutenant of
            Hampshire. 1839.
            (Town Hall, Winchester, Hampshire)

            Oil. Full Length. As Chancellor of the
            University of Oxford. 1841.
            (Examination Schools, University of Oxford)

            Oil. Full Length. Field Marshal's uniform.
            1842.
            (Plas Newydd, Anglesey)

            Oil. Half Length. In Austrian Field Marshal's
            uniform. 1849.

(Pamatnik Osnobozeni Museum, Prague)

842.     Morton, Andrew
         Oil. Full Length. c. 1835.
         (Apsley House)

843.     Paget, Clarence
         Watercolour. With Lord Anglesey and his
         family. c. 1840.
         (Plas Newydd)

844.     Pellegrini, Domenico
         Oil. Half Length. Portuguese Uniform. 1809.
         (National Museum, Lisbon)

845.     Phillips, Thomas
         Oil. Half Length. Uniform. 1814.
         (Stratfield Saye)

846.     Pieneman, J.W.
         Oil. "The Battle of Waterloo". 1821.
         (Rijksmuseum, Amsterdam)

847.     Salter, William
         Oil. "The Waterloo Banquet". 1836.
         (Apsley House)

         Oil. Full Length. Field Marshal's Uniform.
         Undated.
         (National Portrait Gallery)

848.     Simpson, John
         Oil. Full Length. Civilian dress. 1835-7.
         (Apsley House)

849.     Smith, W.A.
         Oil. Full Length. 1852.
         (Cheltenham Art Gallery, Gloucestershire)

850.     Stroehling,
         Oil. Full Length. Uniform. 1815.
         (National Army Museum, London)

851.     Thorburn, Robert
         Oil. Miniature. With grandchildren. The last
         painting dating from Wellington's lifetime,
         executed for Miss Burdett-Coutts. 1852.
         (Stratfield Saye)

852.     Unknown artist.
         Silhouette. Head. 1780
         (Stratfield Saye)

853.     Ward, James
         Sketches. Head and Shoulders. 1829.

(National Portrait Gallery)

854.      Wilkie, David
          Oil. Full Length. Civilian dress. 1832-4.
          (Hatfield House, Hertfordshire)

855.      Winterhalter, Francis Xavier
          Oil. Civilian dress. With Sir Robert Peel.
          1845.

          Oil. "The First of May". With Prince Arthur.
          1851.
          (Royal Collection, Windsor Castle)

# Section C
# Caricatures

856.    "The Master of the Ordnance exercising his
        hobby".  1819.
    Wellington sits astride a cannon and "rides" it past
a group of young ladies.

857.    "The Tory Band.  Concerting an overture to the
        Serio, Ludicro, Tragico, Comico, Whimisculo,
        Burletta, called the Resignations." John Doyle.
        1827.
    Wellington with a "band" made up of people who
resigned when Canning became Prime Minister.

858.    "Achilles in the Sulks after his Retreat, or
        The Great Captain on the Stool of Repentance!!"
        7 May 1827.
    Wellington sits sulking in Apsley House after his
resignation from Canning's Ministry and as Commander-in-
Chief.

859.    "Raising Bread on Amendment". 1827.
    Wellington raises a loaf of bread out of reach of the
starving poor - a comment on his attitude to the Corn Laws.

860.    "A Wellington Boot or the Head of the Army."
        "Paul Pry". October 1827.
    Wellington's head emerges from a huge boot.

861.    "The Prime-Ear of Great Britain. A new species
        of Ass, presented by his M -  to the Zoological
        Society." "Paul Pry". c. January 1828.
    Wellington as the front legs and head of an ass, with
very large ears.

862.    "The Prime Lobster."  "Paul Pry". January 1828.
    Wellington's head and cloak on a huge lobster.
"Lobster" was a slang  word for soldier.

863.    "The Mut¢-ability of affairs!!! Undertaker-in-
        Chief & Cabinet maker to His M - y." "Paul Pry".

c. January 1828.
Wellington as an undertaker's mute.

864.        "Political Conveyancer." "Paul Pry". c.
            January 1828.
    Wellington speaks to George IV and Lady Conyngham -
actually it is Peel, standing behind him and using a
speaking trumpet who does the talking.

865.        "A Commanding View of the Wellington Hill!!!."
            "Paul Pry". February 1828.
    Lord Hill's head pokes out of a hill in Horse Guards
Parade. Wellington stands in the background.

866.        "A Draught of the Old Well. Ah help, in this
            extreme need - if water-gods are deities indeed -
            vide Dryden." "Paul Pry". August 1828.
    Wellington walks off, clutching his stomach, saying
"It's no mistake ..." - the words he used to Huskisson when
the latter tried to withdraw his resignation.

867.        "The Saveall or Economy." "Paul Pry". 1828.
    Wellington trying to extinguish a candle on top of
an inverted ducal coronet.

868.        "The Promenade - or a sketch for Windsor. Plate
            1st." "Paul Pry". December 1828.
    Wellington makes a low bow to a very large George IV
and a very small Queen of Portugal.

869.        "Going to Downing Street - a Sketch." "Paul Pry".
            [?1828].
    Wellington myopically reads a letter on horseback.

870.        "The Triumph of Mars. An Allegory." "HB" [John
            Doyle]. 1828.
    Wellington in military uniform astride a huge pudding
pulled by cherubs.

871.        "The Presentation of Dollalolla accompanied by
            the mighty thumb." "Paul Pry" [1828].
    Wellington stands beside George IV receiving a huge
Duchess of St. Albans and a very small Duke.

872.        "John Bull asking a few questions of orator
            Mum. Shall I vouchsafe your worship a word or two,
            Shakespeare." "Paul Pry". [c. February 1829].
    Wellington, as undertaker's mute, asked about the
Roman Catholic problem, merely replies "Mmm".

873.        "Leaving the Lords through the assembled
            Commons." March 1829.
    Wellington rides over a mob of Protestants.

874.        "Portrait of a Noble Duke." 1829.
    Wellington's head, made up of military artefacts.

875.        "The Field of Battersea." "Paul Pry" 1829.
        Wellington, as a lobster, fires a pistol at Lord
Winchelsea.

876.        "Burking Poor Old Mrs Constitution. Aged 141."
            "Paul Pry". April 1829.
        Wellington and Peel stifle a lady: the "Doctor", a
Priest, waits at the door.

877.        "Terrors of Emancipation.  A Bugabo for Old
            Women and Children."  "Argus" [Charles Williams]
            1829.
        Wellington and Peel see old women (Eldon, etc.) run
away from a bundle of straw with a face marked "Inquisition"
on it.

878.        "The Noblest Roman of them all." "Paul Pry".
            April [1829].
        Wellington  as a statue on top of a column: Peel flies
by as a bird.

879.        "The Man Wot Drives the Sovereign." "Paul Pry".
            April 1829.
        Wellington as a mail coachman.

880.        "A Quartette in Character." "Paul Pry". May
            1829.
        Wellington as a coachman, with George IV, Marchioness
Conyngham as the guard, and Peel - as a ratcatcher.

881.        "O'h What a Falling Off was There - fully
            accoutred the Hero lay." "Paul Pry". May 1829.
        Wellington, at a parade, falls off his horse, into a
cow pat.

882.        "Parish Characters in Ten Plates ... Plate II:
            Caleb Quotem the Parish Factotum." "Paul Pry".
            12 June 1829.
        Wellington in civilian dress, with a whip: the man
who does everything.

883.        "Take Care of Your Pockets - A Hint for the
            Orthodox." "Paul Pry". 2 June 1829.
        Wellington as a down and out soldier, and Peel as a
ratcatcher, pick the pocket of Church of England bishop.

884.        "To be Sold with all his Trappings that
            splendid Charger "Arthur" who served in the
            Peninsular & other Campaigns - who must be rode
            with a Curb as he is not used to restraint & will
            kick at it - he comes from notorious stock & is
            throughbred - will not be warranted sound - must
            be taken with all his faults - & must be sold."
            "Paul Pry". 22 June 1829.
        Wellington as a horse.

885.        "Weeding by the Head Gardener." [June 1829].
Wellington hoes money from around the Church of
England and is warned by George IV not to injure it.

886.        "Good Humour." W. Heath. 22 September 1829.
Wellington looks in shop window at caricatures of
himself.

887.        "Take up Your Bed - and Walk!!!" William Heath.
            [1829].
Wellington walks with a bed on his head: this is a
suggestion that he should resign.

888.        "Household Servants - in Six Plates - No. 3. Mrs.
            Double U. the Housekeeper." William Heath. 10
            October 1829.
Wellington as a housekeeper, tries to make cuts and
keep things in order.

889.        "The Omni-buss." William Heath. 15 October 1829.
            Wellington drives a coach downhill into a "sinking
fund".

890.        "Theatrical Characters - in Ten Plates - No. 5 -
            Stagemanager and Prompter." William Heath. 30
            October 1829.
Wellington with a list of performers, including
Huskisson and others.

891.        "Sketches of the Kennel - No. 2. A portrait of
            that Excellent Old Dog Waterloo." William Heath.
            16 November [1829].
One of a set. Wellington as a dog.

892.        "The Lords of Misrule!!!" William Heath. 15
            February 1830.
Wellington as a jester: with Peel's head on his staff.

893.        "Retrenchment - Dock Yards." William Heath.
            [c. March 1830].
Wellington, in military uniform, steals "chips" from
poor worker's family.

894.        "The Sign Manual!!!" William Heath. May 1830.
            Wellington at a table signs a letter - as the "Dean of
Windsor".

895.        "The Jolly Waterman and his Fare!!!" William
            Heath. 11 June 1830.
Waterman King William IV tried to bring Queen Adelaide
ashore in a boat which Wellington fends off.

896.        "The New Landlord's First Orders - open the park
            for the people quick I say - Shakespeare." William
            Heath. July 1830.
William IV orders workmen (Peel and Wellington) to

open Parliament.

897.         "All Among the Hottentots - Capering A Shore."
             William Heath. July 1830.
     William IV as a jolly sailor watches, while
Wellington and the rest of the Cabinet, as Hottentots,
dance.

898.         "Refuge for the Destitute!!!" William Heath.
             August 1830.
     Wellington invites Charles X and his family to
Holyrood House.

899.         "Pleasant Intimation." William Heath. November
             1830.
     Wellington, seated at a table, reads a threatening
letter.

900.         "Thou Can'st Not Add-Minister unto a mind
             diseased." William Heath. November 1830.
     Wellington, dressed in a frock coat, stands alone,
unhappy, having just been beaten.

901.         "Partial Distress, or the Old Cabinet Maker and
             his Man Bob Out of Employment." "A Sharpshooter".
             November 1830.
     Wellington and Peel beg for money.

902.         "The Cobblers Last." William Heath. December
             1830.
     Wellington, as a workman, complains about a procession
to see William IV.

903.         "A Sketch in the Park." HB [John Doyle] c. 1830.
     Wellington walks with Mrs. Arbuthnot.

904.         "A Walk by the Sea Shore." HB [John Doyle] 9
             November 1832.
     Wellington, alone, walks by the guns of Walmer Castle.

905.         "Land Lubbers & Over Laden." William Heath.
             [c. 1830].
     Wellington and his colleagues in an open boat weighed
down by millstones have dropped one labelled "Catholic
Emancipation" over the side, but retain others.  The Duke
declares no further lightening of the boat is required.

906.         "Up and Down, or Political See Saw." HB [John
             Doyle] 18 May 1832.
     Wellington is "down", Lord Grey, supported by John
Bull, is "up": King William IV teeters in the middle.

907.         "The Waterloo Cock Bolting from the Grey Gander."
             [c. 1832].
     Lord Grey pursues the Duke: "I will teach you my bill

is a match for your spurs anyday, my Dunghill."

908.         "Taking an Airing in Hyde Park. Framed, but not
            yet Glazed." 10 June 1833.
      Wellington peers through the broken windows of Apsley
House.

      Wellington also figures in the early volumes of
Punch, which began publication in July 1841.

909.         "A Scene from Romeo and Juliet - as played in
            House of Lords. Nurse, by the D - e of W - n,
            Peter, by L - d B - m."
            Punch's Pencillings, No. LXX, Punch, 4 (January-
            June 1843).
      A comment on Brougham's sycophantic attentions to
the Duke.

910.         "A scene at Greenwich Fair - A Game of Knock 'em
            down."
            Punch's Pencillings, No. LXXV. Punch, 4 (January-
            June 1843).
      The Duke and Peel stand by while Brougham throws
sticks at various targets.

911.         "After the originals in the Queen's Collection."
            Punch's Pencillings, No. LXXVI, Punch, 4
            (January-June 1843).
      Wellington and Peel, in medieval dress, pore over a
ledger, with large amounts of income tax money lying about.

912.         "The Original Industrious Flea." Punch's
            Pencillings, No. LXXVII, Punch, 4 (January-
            June 1843).
      Wellington, in uniform, rides on the back of a flea
(Lord Brougham).

913.         "Genuine Agitation (Ghost of Caesar - D - e of
            W - n; Brutus - Mr. D. O'C - n - 1)." Punch's
            Pencillings, No. LXXIX, Punch, 4 (January-June
            1843).
      A scene from Shakespeare's Julius Caesar. Wellington
addresses Daniel O'Connell.

914.         "Triumphal Entry into London of the King of
            Hanover." Punch's Pencillings, No. LXXXII, Punch,
            4 (January-June 1843).
      Peel and Wellington, dressed as Beefeaters, smuggle
the King of Hanover (the very unpopular Duke of Cumberland)
into London, hidden in a barrel.

915.         "King Arthur's Court." Punch, 5 (July-December
            1843).
      Wellington as a king sits on his throne surrounded by
courtiers - Peel, Brougham and others.

916.        "A scene in Westminster Circus." Punch, 5
        (July-December 1843).
    Wellington as the ringmaster, Brougham as a clown,
offering to do anything for the Duke.

917.        "Crusoe and his man Friday." Punch, 5 (July-
        December 1843).
    Wellington as Robinson Crusoe, Brougham as Man Friday.

918.        "Extraordinary Feat of the Driver of the Indian
        Mail." Punch, 6 (January-June 1844).
    Wellington and Peel drive the coach of state.

919.        "Remarkable resemblance between the two
        greatest characters of the Present Day." Punch, 7
        (July-December 1844).
    The "two characters" are Wellington and Mr. Punch, and
the "resemblance" lies in their noses.

920.        "Peel's Cheap Bread Shop." Punch, 10 (January-
        June 1846).
    Wellington stands outside the shop as a sandwich
board man.  This cartoon refers to Peel's determination to
repeal the Corn Laws.

921.        "The Greedy Boy." Punch, 10 (January-June 1846).
    Wellington as the boy, who refuses to let "Master
Hardinge" (General Sir Henry Hardinge) and "Master Gough"
(General Sir Hugh Gough) share any of his honorary offices.

922.        "Awful apparition to a gentleman while shaving
        in the Edgware Road. 29 September 1846." Punch,
        11 (July-December 1846).
    A man, shaving in an upstairs room, drops his razor
in horror as an enormous image of the Duke's head - the top
of Benjamin Wyatt's statue - suddenly appears by his
window.

923.        "The Lords out of work." Punch, 13 (July-
        December 1847).
    Wellington and Brougham represented as labourers
looking for work.

924.        "Wellington stirring up the British Lion."
        Punch, 14 (January-June 1848).
    Wellington pokes a sleeping and untroubled lion with a
quill pen, in an effort to awaken it to danger, in this case,
of French invasion.

925.        "John Bull between Peace and War." Punch, 14
        (January-June 1848).
    "John Bull" is pulled in opposite directions by the
Duke ("war") and Richard Cobden ("peace").

926.        "A Bright Idea - the Peace recruiting sergeant
        trying to enlist the Duke." Punch, 17 (July-

December 1849).
A recruiting sergeant for the Peace Society, John Bright, attempts to recruit Wellington to the cause.

927.          "Sending for the old doctor." Punch, 20
          (January-June 1851).
Prince Albert sends for Wellington to ask his advice about Russell's resignation and the formation of a new government.

928.          "The Rivals, or, a military position." Punch,
          22 (January-June 1852).
Wellington, in uniform, points out details on a map to Britannia, warning again of possible invasion, whilst a Peace Society representative stands in the background.

929.          "The Poor old Koh-i-Noor again!" Punch, 23
          (July-December 1852).
Wellington "helps" the Diamond, dressed as an Eastern potentate, to the cutter's wheel.

930.          "Wellington. September XIV. MDCCCLII." Punch,
          23 (July-December 1852).
A portrait of Wellington with a sorrowing British lion. This is not intended as a caricature, and is not an especially good likeness of the Duke.

# Section D
# Portrait Statues,
# Busts, and Miscellanea

The principles of selection for this section are identical to those applied to Portraits.

931.        Adams, George Gammon
            Death Mask, Plaster Cast, 1852.
            (National Portrait Gallery, London. Many
            copies).

            Bust. Marble. 1852.
            (Apsley House).

932.        Amatucci, Carlo
            Wax Relief. Profile. c. 1812.
            (Apsley House and Stratfield Saye, Hampshire)

933.        Boehm, J.E.
            Equestrian statue. Bronze. 1888.
            (Opposite Apsley House).

934.        Campbell, Thomas
            Bust. Marble. 1827.
            (Stratfield Saye).

935.        Chantrey, Francis
            Equestrian statue. Bronze. 1844.
            (Outside the Royal Exchange, London).

            Bust. Marble. 1814.
            (Ashmolean Museum, Oxford).

            Bust. 1823.
            (Apsley House).

936.        Francis, T.
            Bust. Marble. 1852.
            (National Portrait Gallery).

937.        Geefs, G.
            Bust.

(Waterloo Church, Belgium).

938.    Marochetti, Baron
        Equestrian statue. 1844.
        (Glasgow).

        Bust. Marble. 1841.
        (Bethnal Green Museum, London).

939.    Milnes, Thomas
        Full length statue. Stone. 1841.
        (Royal Arsenal, Woolwich).

940.    Nollekens, Joseph
        Bust. Marble. 1809, 1812.
        (Copies at Apsley House and Stratfield Saye).

941.    Pistrucci, Benedetto
        Bust. Heroic Size. Marble. 1832.
        (Stratfield Saye)

942.    Steell, John Robert
        Equestrian statue. 1852.
        (Edinburgh).

        Bust. Marble. 1846.
        (Apsley House. Many copies)

943.    Wyatt, Matthew Cotes
        Equestrian statue. 1846.
        (Formerly at Hyde Park Corner, now at
        Aldershot).

944.    Monument. Recumbent effigy and equestrian
        statue.
        Designed by Alfred Stevens. 1878. Statue
        completed by J. Tweed. 1912.
        (St. Paul's Cathedral, London)

945.    Monument. Baron Marochetti. 1863.
        (Stratfield Saye).

946.    Monument
        (Aberystwyth, Dyfed).

947.    "Achilles".
        Statue by Sir Richard Westmacott. 1822.
        (Hyde Park Corner, London).

948.    Obelisk. 1817.
        (Wellington, Somerset).

949.    Obelisk. 1827.
        (Wynyard Park, Cleveland)

950.            Tower.
               (Woodford, Northamptonshire)

     Numerous mementoes of the Duke's career survive among
the collections at Apsley House, Stratfield Saye, and
Walmer Castle.

     Wellington has given his name to several towns,
several warships, numerous public houses, a public school,
a Royal Air Force bomber aircraft, an article of footwear
("Wellington boots") and a tree (Wellingtonia).

# Part Eight
# Death and Funeral
## Section A
## Descriptions

951.        Authorized and Official Guide to the Grand
            Funeral Procession of the late Field Marshal Arthur
            Duke of Wellington, K.G. to be solemnized in St.
            Paul's Cathedral, on Thursday, the 18th November,
            1852. London, [1852].
A complete list of the order of the procession
escorting the Duke's coffin to St. Paul's, including the
route of the cortege.

952.        "The Funeral Ceremonial of the Duke of
            Wellington." Colburn's United Service Magazine,
            (1852 - Part III): 589-621.
A full description of the Duke's funeral with some
anecdotes relating to his character and career.

953.        Greenhalgh, Michael, "The Funeral of the Duke of
            Wellington." Appollo: The Magazine of the Arts,
            (September 1973): 200-10.
An illustrated description, and comments on the
significance of the Duke's funeral, seeing it as a sign to
the world that Britain had not renounced military prowess.

954.        The Illustrated London News, 21, Issues of 18
            September (with supplement); 25 September (with
            supplement); 2, 9, 16, 23, 30 October, 13
            November (with supplement), 20 November (with
            supplement), 27 November (with supplement), 4 and
            11 December 1852.
The Illustrated London News devoted considerable space
to Wellington's death and funeral. The issue for 18
September 1852 presented a brief obituary notice, but this
was complemented by a supplement entirely devoted to the
Duke's career. The supplement covered all aspects of this,
and included engravings of momentous events and of
Wellington himself, as an army officer and statesman
(including one of the Duke as a Roman Emperor).

The issue of 25 September announced and approved of
the government's decision to have a public funeral for

for Wellington, and reproduces an engraving of his mother.
A supplement was again devoted to Wellington, principally
to his political career, and consisted of a judicious
appreciation of his qualities as a politician.   The
supplement also included engravings of Walmer Castle,
reports from other (including French) newspapers, and a song
"Mourn for the Mighty Dead", by Charles Mackay and H.R.
Bishop.

On 2 October The Illustrated London News provided its
readers with further anecdotes of the Duke, pictures of
Stratfield Saye and comments on the reasons behind the delay
in the funeral.

The issue of 9 October included more pictures of
Stratfield Saye and comments about Wellington's horse,
Copenhagen.

The issue of 16 October dealt with the question of
Wellington's birth place and reproduced an engraving of the
ruins of his "ancestral home", Dangan Castle.

On 23 October an engraving of a bust of the Duke was
reproduced, together with an account of his last official
visit to Dover.

The issues of 30 October and 6 November contained
comments on the preparations for the funeral.   Further
details of this were reported on 13 November, when a
supplement was produced, discussing the Duke as an orator,
a diplomatist and socialite.

On 20 November much space was given to the Duke's
funeral, with engravings of the lying-in-state and the
funeral procession. The supplement of this date reproduced
further drawings of the funeral and articles on this
subject, on the Duke's career as Lord Warden of the Cinque
Ports and Leader of the House of Lords and on his private
life.

On 27 November comment was passed on the conduct of the
crowd at the funeral and various pictures of scenes from
the Duke's professional life were reproduced.   The supplement dealt with the funeral and included pictures of the
procession at various points en route.

On 4 December a picture of the funeral procession
entering St. Paul's Cathedral was reproduced.

Finally on 11 December 1852 an article appeared on
the Duke as administrator of the army and various tributes
to him were reproduced, as was Dr. Cummin's lecture on the
Duke at Exeter Hall.   Further pictures of the funeral were
reproduced, including a very large pull-out picture of the
scene in St. Paul's Cathedral at the time of the Duke's
interment.

955.        Smith, Charles Eastlake, <u>Journals and Corres-</u>
            <u>pondence of Lady Eastlake.</u> Vol. 1, London, 1895.
       Includes a detailed description of Wellington's
funeral.

956.        Wellington, Seventh Duke of, "The Great Duke's
            funeral." <u>History Today</u>, 2 (1952):778-84.
       A brief account of Wellington's lying-in-state and
funeral, with some comments on his family's reaction to
these events.

# Section B
# Sermons

957.    Wellington's death, on 14 September 1852, and
        his funeral, nine weeks later, on 18 November,
    occasioned a great outburst of national feeling and
led to preaching and eventual publication of many sermons.

    Most of the printed sermons throw little light on
Wellington's career or personality, but they give a good
indication of how the Duke's place in history was viewed by
his contemporaries.

    Most sermons were preached on the Sundays following
the Duke's death and burial, usually by clergymen of the
Church of England.  Most of them, too, were published "by
request", or privately printed, in London.

    For the majority of preachers, the really telling
point was the evidence of the Duke's - and hence everyone
else's - mortality.  Wellington's death inspired sermons on
this theme by Revs. A. Morton Brown, Wellington and Victory;
or Christians More than Conquerors; J.A. Emerton, The Might
and Majesty of Death: Two Sermons...; W.B. Holland, A
Sermon Preached in the Parish Church of Walmer on September
19th 1852 (Deal); G.M. D'Arcy Irvine, A Sermon Preached in
the Parish Church of St. Saviour, Bath, September 26, 1852
... (Bath); John Monson, The Mighty Fallen! A Tribute to
the Memory of Arthur, Duke of Wellington...; Augustus
Frederick Pettigrew, A Sermon Preached September 26th 1852,
on the Occasion of the Demise of Field Marshal His Grace the
Duke of Wellington ...; and Joseph Sortain The Last
Conqueror. A Sermon Occasioned by the Death of the Duke of
Wellington ...

    When Wellington was buried, more sermons on this theme
were preached: Thomas Jackson, "One Star Differing from
Another Star in Glory." Being a Discourse on the Occasion of
the Funeral of the Duke of Wellington; John Jefferson, The
Funeral of Wellington, Its Lesson for this World and the
Next ...; Henry William Maddock, A Sermon Preached on Sunday
Morning, Nov. 21, 1852, being the Sunday After the Funeral

of the Duke of Wellington ... (Oxford); James William
Martwell, Doctrinal and Practical Reflections on the Funeral
of Arthur, Duke of Wellington ...; Evan Nepean, A Sermon
Preached in Grosvenor Chapel, South Audley Street on Sunday
November 21st, 1852 on the Occasion of the Funeral of the
Late Duke of Wellington ... and John Scott, The Vanity of
All Earthly Greatness. A Sermon preached before the Mayor
and Corporation of Hull (Hull).

Many of the sermons used Wellington's death or burial
as the starting point for general reflections on the
transcience of human existence and contain only passing
references to the Duke. This can be seen in Alfred Gatty,
Death the Leveller. A Sermon ... and George Albert Rogers'
Victory Beyond the Grave! A Sermon Occasioned by the Funeral
of the Duke of Wellington. The same theme was carried
further by G. Currey, Christian Comfort amidst National
Mourning ... while Alexander Fletchet, Sermons on the Death
and Funeral of the Captain of Salvation; preached on the
Occasion of the Death and Funeral of the Late Duke of
Wellington managed to preach two sermons on these lines.

Many preachers stressed the lessons to be learnt from
the Duke's illustrious career. This theme dominated the
sermons preached after his burial, although some were
preached on this subject immediately following his death.
The latter included, Henry Batchelor, Wellington the Warrior
A Model for the Battle for Life; J.H. Bowhay, A Pulpit
Tribute to the Memory of His Grace the Duke of Wellington..;
Thomas Hugo, The Voice of the Dead. A Sermon Preached upon
the Occasion of the Death of the Duke of Wellington ...;
John G. Manley, A Pulpit Estimate of Wellington...; C.
Marriott, Singleness of Purpose the Secret of Success. A
Sermon preached ... Upon occasion of the Death of the Duke
of Wellington ... (Oxford); Charles Roger, The Death of
Wellington, A Discourse (Perth); and Henry Sulivan, "A
Great Man Fallen". A Sermon preached ... the Sunday after
the Death of the Duke of Wellington.

Sermons preached on this theme after Wellington's
funeral included James S.M. Anderson, Every Man the Bearer
of his Own Burden. A Sermon Preached ... the Sunday after
the Funeral of the Duke of Wellington; Charles Boutell,
The Hero and His Example; A Sermon preached ... on the
evening of Thursday, Nov. 18th, 1852 ...; G.W. Conder,
Duty and Destiny, or the Ruling Ideas of Wellington and
Napoleon ...; John Hayden, Wellington: His Character and
Actions ...; Charles J. Heathcote, A Sermon Preached on the
Sunday After the Funeral of the Duke of Wellington ...;
Thomas Robinson, A Sermon Preached ... on occasion of the
Funeral of His Grace the Duke of Wellington; William Sewell,
The Servant of Christ. A Sermon ... with Reference to the
character of the Late Duke of Wellington, and H.M. Wagner,
A Sermon Preached ... after the Funeral of Field Marshal
His Grace the Duke of Wellington.

All of these are favourable reviews of Wellington's life and career, but not everyone believed Wellington's life constituted a good example to follow. Rev. J.O.W. Hawes, The Ministry of Heroes. A Sermon ... on the Occasion of the Funeral of the late Duke of Wellington, and J. de Kewer Williams, "Iron and Clay." A Funeral Sermon for the Duke of Wellington both believed the Duke's career had been great in secular terms, but was not that of a fully committed Christian. J.H. Gurney, The Lost Chief and the Mourning People ... defended Wellington against criticisms of this sort among his congregation.

The only Irish sermon published on Wellington's death was that by Rev. John Booker, A Sermon on the Death of the Duke of Wellington, preached in the Church of Killurin [Wexford], which argued that Wellington's life did constitute a good example to follow. For Rev. J.J. Blunt A Sermon in Memory of the late Duke of Wellington..., the greatest lesson to be learnt from Wellington's life was that it had come to an end.

Two sermons appear as simple eulogies on the Duke of Wellington, namely, W.L. Coughton, Extract from a Sermon preached ... on Sunday November 21st 1852... and John Osmond Dakeyne, Virtutis Fortuna Corres. A Sermon ... on Thursday, November XVIII, MDCCCLII. More preachers combined eulogy on Wellington's career with an awareness of the role of the Almighty in it. Wellington's greatness was the work of God, stated John R. Conor, "A Prince and a Great Man has Fallen" ... the substance of a Sermon ... to the Troops Comprising the Garrison of Liverpool ... (Liverpool); Richard Reade, The Conquerors Rest. A Sermon Preached on the occasion of the Death of the Duke of Wellington ...; C.A.J. Smith, A Sermon on the Death of the Duke of Wellington. "The Lord Gave, and the Lord hath taken Away"... Henry Howarth, On Human Greatness. A Sermon preached ... the Sunday after the Funeral of the Duke of Wellington; and Francis H. Maude, The "Mighty Man of Valour". A Sermon preached ... the Sunday after the Funeral of the late Duke of Wellington. William N. St. Leger, "The World Passeth Away". A Sermon preached ... the Day of the burial of Field Marshal the Duke of Wellington combines an eulogy on Wellington's career with a warning about the transience of human existence.

According to some, Wellington's life and career were proof of the direct intervention of God in the day-to-day life of the world. This is the theme of C.R. Alford, Wellington's Victories. Divine Deliverance...; E. Tottenham, A Great Name the Gift of God... and R.A. Thompson, Christian Realities ... "Sermon XII. God in History". (London, 1853).

A number of preachers took the opportunity to denounce hostile forces in the world: the "enemy" tended to be the Roman Catholic Church and the French. To J. Alton Hatchard,

Romanism Overthrown by Wellington. A Sermon preached ...
on the Death of the Duke of Wellington, the two enemies
were indistinguishable (this sermon went through two
editions); Edward Miller, The Battle-Axe of God ... and
John Sandford , "The Man of Duty"..., agreed with Hatchard,
as did R.A. Gent, A Sermon on the Death of the Duke of
Wellington... and George Croley, A Sermon on the Death of
the Duke of Wellington. George Batt, A Sermon on the
Funeral of the Duke of Wellington believed the main threat,,
which Wellington had successfully countered, was the
Catholic Church. Richard Glover, Esraelon and Waterloo. A
Sermon on the Death of the Duke of Wellington, attacked both
the Peace Society and others who refused to fight for the
defence of England, and also the Roman Catholic Church.

Certain other themes are touched on in some sermons.
Henry N. Barrett, The Victor Vanquished. A Discourse
Occasioned by the Death of the Duke of Wellington, and D.J.
Harrison, Greatness, Godliness, Glory. A Sermon on the Death
of the Duke of Wellington both subjected Wellington's
career to a more critical appraisal. Laurence Ottley, A
Scriptural View of a Soldier's Office and Honors ... a
sermon preached on the day of Wellington's funeral, to
soldiers of the North York Rifle Militia, stressed the
lawfulness of the profession of a soldier, and how
Wellington had helped to raise the status of the British
soldier. John Barnes, Honourable Sepulchre the Christian's
Due ..., and F. Close, National Obsequies sanctioned by Holy
Writ, both attempted to show that the pageantry and cost of
the Duke's funeral was fully justified.

Two preachers, George Armstrong, "The Duke": Some
outlines of his Character in a Discourse on the Occasion of
his Funeral and G.F. Whidborne, England doing Honour to her
Departed Hero (Hanley) are both concerned with the possible
consequences of the Duke's death.

Finally, some sermons touched upon many themes. Much
the best of these is Charles James Blomfield, Bishop of
London, The Mourning of Israel, A Sermon ..., which combines
an eulogy on the Duke, with details of the lessons to be
learned from his life, and strikes a blow against war at
the same time. The sermons by Rev. Charles Overton, The
Burial of Wellington, A Sermon... and Rev. Benjamin Street,
The Deliverer raised up by the Lord. A Sermon ... are, on
the other hand, confused mixtures of eulogy on the Duke,
reflections on human morality and crude attacks on the
French and the Roman Catholic Church. The Rev. Nathaniel
Meeres, A Sermon on the Death of Wellington, relies heavily
upon the tribute to Wellington by Lord John Russell.
Finally, T. Binney, Wellington, is an expanded version of a
sermon preached on Wellington's funeral. It covers the
whole of the Duke's career in a reasonably impartial
fashion.

# Section C
# Funeral Poems

958.　　　　As well as sermons, Wellington's death and
burial inspired numerous tributes in verse.  All
share a common admiration for the Duke and a conscious-
ness of the great loss suffered by the country.  The only
work of real quality is that by the Poet Laureate, Alfred,
Lord Tennyson, Ode on the Death of the Duke of Wellington.

　　　　Some authors, perhaps wisely, preferred to remain
anonymous.  Typical of these is A Dirge for Wellington,
apparently printed in 1852, but no author, publisher or date
of publication is known.  A "Graduate of the University of
Oxford" published his Elegy Supposed to be Written in the
Cathedral on the occasion of the Funeral of Wellington in
1852.  Anonymous poems published in 1853 included a Dirge
on His Grace the Duke of Wellington; The Fourteenth of
September: A Martial Dirge; and "G.W.F.", Lines on the
Death of the Duke of Wellington.

　　　　Other authors were less reticient: Thomas Braithwaite
published an Ode on the Duke of Wellington in 1852, and
other poems published in that year were Sidney Hodges'
Dirge for the Buried Duke; Robert Montgomery's Forty Lines
on Wellington; Henry J. Staples' Elegaic Stanzas suggested
by the Funeral of Arthur, Duke of Wellington, Martin
Tupper's A Dirge for Wellington (one of the better
attempts) and John Yarrow's Monody on the Death of the Duke
of Wellington.  Further poems were published in 1853:
James Reid Browne, Ode on the Death of Field Marshal the
Duke of Wellington; a further work by Robert Montgomery,
The Heroe's Funeral. A Poem, and Rev. William Stone, Elegy
to the Memory of the Immortal Wellington, which has a
suitably religious theme.

　　　　Sebastian Evans was inspired to write no less than
twelve Sonnets on the Death of the Duke of Wellington in
1852, although Francis Higginson was apparently able to
complete only four books of his Wellington; or the Mission
of Napoleon: an Epic Poem in Twelve Books.  This is an epic
poem in the style of Milton, but not of the same quality.

In 1854, an anonymous <u>Poem and a Pamphlet</u> on the Duke's death was published. This comprises a twenty page poem with twenty more pages of explanatory notes.

# Part Nine
# Theses and Dissertations

959.        Beales, A.C.F., "The Foreign Policy of
            Wellington, 1828-1830." M.A. thesis, University
            of London, 1927.
    A survey of Wellington's foreign policy, based on such
material as was available at the time of writing.

960.        Brook, Graham Warden, "British Policy towards
            the Concert of Europe, 1822-1832." Ph.D. thesis,
            University of Cambridge, 1974.
    Includes a survey of Wellington's views and policy,
based on printed sources, since the Duke's unpublished
correspondence was unavailable.

961.        Cowell, Phyllis M., "The attitude of the British
            Government to the Portuguese Rebellion of 1826-
            1834." M.A. thesis, University of London, 1927.
    Includes a survey of Wellington's attitudes and
response to the crisis in Portugal.

962.        Foster, R.E., "Leadership, Politics and Govern-
            ment in the County of Hampshire during the Lord-
            Lieutenancy of the First Duke of Wellington, 1820-
            1852." Ph.D. thesis, University of Southampton,
            1986.
    A review of relations within the governing elite and
the impact of popular feeling on local government.

963.        Jones, Alwen Irvona, "The Influence of
            Wellington on French internal politics, 1815-1818."
            B. Litt. thesis, University of Oxford, 1935.
    Considers the Duke's involvement with French politics
during his time as Commander of the Allied army of
occupation, and his views on his duties there. Based on
foreign office papers and the printed Despatches.

964.        Meyer, J.A., "Wellington's Generalship: A Study
            of his Peninsular Campaigns." Ph.D. thesis,
            University of South Carolina, 1985.

A scholarly study of the Peninsular campaign.

965.        Mullen, R.F., "The House of Lords and the
            Repeal of the Corn Laws." D.Phil. thesis, Univer-
            sity of Oxford, 1974.
    Includes an assessment of Wellington's role in the
maintenance and final repeal of the Corn Laws.

966.        Redgrave, T.M.O., "Wellington's Logistical
            Arrangements in the Peninsular War, 1809-14."
            Ph.D. thesis, University of London, 1984.
    A scholarly study of a neglected aspect of the Duke's
generalship.

967.        Smith, D.C.H., "Wellington, Aberdeen and the
            Miguellist Crisis in Portugal, 1826-1831."
            Masters thesis, University of Kent, 1973.
    A review of British relations with Portugal at this
difficult time and a defence of Wellington's and Aberdeen's
policy of non-interference.  Based mainly on printed sources,
including Wellington's Supplementary Despatches, speeches,
and "Maxims".

968.        Smith, D.C.H., "The Conservative Opposition and
            Foreign Policy, 1830-1834." M.Litt thesis, Univer-
            sity of Cambridge, 1976.
    Includes an assessment of the opinions of the Duke on
questions of foreign policy during the administration of
the second Earl Grey.

969.        Sweeney, J. Morgan, "The House of Lords in
            British Politics, 1830-1841." D.Phil. thesis,
            University of Oxford, 1973.
    A study of the composition and political actions of
the House of Lords, based in part on Wellington's papers,
and giving a full account of his role as Conservative
Leader of the House.

# Index to
# Authors and Subjects

- Despatches, 14-16,
- extracts from, 7, 12, 13,
22, 25, 27, 36.
- reviews of, 151, 177, 322,
354, 407, 446, 447, 463,
465.
- Despathes, Civil, 32,
- extracts from, 11, 36,
- reviews of, 648, 649, 677,
678, 690, 726.
- Despatches, Supplementary,
31.
- extracts from, 7, 26, 36,
37.
- reviews of, 466, 480,
481, 484, 567, 568.
- and foreign policy, 39,
46, 661, 959-961, 967, 968.
- as Foreign Secretary,
38, 60, 266, 737.
- as "French Duke", 781.
- furniture of, 794.
- and general election (1830),
204.
- General Orders, 30.
- extracts from, 17, 24.
- reviews of, 407, 410, 447,
558.
- as a horseman, 793.
- as Irish M.P., 448.
- and local government, 119,
654.
- as Lord Lieutenant of
Hampshire, 962.
- as Lord Warden of the Cinque
Ports, 755, 756.
- and Madame Tussauds, 792.
- as Master General of the
Ordnance, 40, 68, 195, 351,
- mission to St. Petersburg,
(1826), 114.
- obituary, 239, 282, 318,
340, 353.
- official banquet (1814),
196.
- papers of, published, 5-
37, 283-89.
- papers of, unpublished,
1-5.
- plate belonging to, 780,
791.
- portraits of, 818-855.
- as Prime Minister, 32, 47,
56, 59, 60, 69, 102, 109,
119, 165, 173, 211, 212, 214,
225, 227, 231, 238, 240, 241,

247-249, 253-255, 256-260,
262, 280-282, 691-722.
- property of, 4, 775.
- and Punch, 803, 909-930.
- resignation of (1827), 107
282, 313.
- and the Whigs (1830-34),
119, 282, 646, 705, 742,
744.
Wellington, Arthur Richard,
Second Duke of, 31, 32,
Wellington, Catherine,
Duchess of, 798.
Wellington, Gerald, Seventh
Duke of, 33, 34, 147, 193,
819, 956.
Wellington memorial, 69,
141, 807.
Wellington statue (Hyde Park
Corner), 142, 800-802, 804,
806, 813, 843.
Wesley, Garrett, First Earl
of Mornington, 749.
Westmacott, R., 947.
Wheeler, H.F.B., 384.
Whidborne, G.F., 957.
"Whig Commoner", 280.
Whithead, J.G.O., 640.
"Wholesale Grocer", 281.
Wilkie, D., 854.
Williams, C, ("Argus"), 877.
Williams, J. de K., 957.
Williams, W.F., 385.
Willoughby Gordon, J., 61.
Wilson, H., 797.
Wilson, J., 798.
Wilson, J.M., 386.
Wilson, General Sir Robert,
518.
Wilton, Second Earl of, 34.
Wilton, Mary, Countess of,
34.
Winchelsea, Earl of, 691.
Winterhalter, F.X., 855.
Wood, W., 36.
Woolgar, C.M., 5.
Wright, G.N., 361, 387.
Wrottesley, G., 194.
Wyatt, M.C., 943.
Wyndham, Hon. Mrs Hugh, 799.
Wynter, P., 102.

Yarrow, J., 958.
Yonge, C.D., 195, 388, 389.
Young, P., 536.

# Index to
# Periodicals and Newspapers